urban DESIGN

Urban design is a process of establishing a structural order within human settlements; responding to dynamic emergent meanings and functions in a constant state of flux. The planning/design process is complex due to the myriad of ongoing (urban) organizational and structural relationships and contexts. This book reconnects the process with outcomes on the ground, and puts thinking about design back at the heart of what planners do. Mixing accessible theory, practical examples and carefully designed exercises in composition from simple to complex settings, *Urban Design* is an essential textbook for classrooms and design studios across the full spectrum of planning and urban studies fields. Filled with color illustrations and graphics of excellent projects, it gives students tools to enable them to sketch, draw, design and, above all, think.

This new edition remains focused on instructing the student, professional and layperson in the elements and principles of design composition, so that they can diverge from conventional and packaged solutions in pursuit of a meaningful and creative urbanism. This edition builds upon established design principles and encourages the student in creative ways to depart from them as appropriate in dealing with the complexity of culture, space and time dynamics of cities. The book identifies the elements and principles of compositions and explores compositional order and structure as they relate to the meaning and functionality of cities. It discusses new directions and methods, and outlines the importance of both buildings and the open spaces between them.

Ron Kasprisin, architect, urban planner, artist and academic, has over 40 years of professional practice experience, and 27 years of academic experience, now Professor Emeritus in Urban Design and Planning, College of Built Environments, University of Washington, Seattle, Washington. Ron is an accomplished and nationally recognized watercolor painter and teacher. He lives on Whidbey Island northwest of Seattle in Puget Sound, a part of the Salish Sea.

urban DESIGN

THE COMPOSITION OF COMPLEXITY

2nd Edition

Ron Kasprisin

Routledge
Taylor & Francis Group

LONDON AND NEW YORK

Second edition published 2020
by Routledge
2 Park Square, Milton Park, Abingdon, Oxon, OX14 4RN

and by Routledge
52 Vanderbilt Avenue, New York, NY 10017

Routledge is an imprint of the Taylor & Francis Group, an informa business

First edition published by Routledge 2011

British Library Cataloguing-in-Publication Data
A catalogue record for this book is available from the British Library

Library of Congress Cataloging-in-Publication Data
Names: Kasprisin, Ronald J., author.
Title: Urban design : the composition of complexity / Ron Kasprisin.
Description: 2nd Edition. | New York : Routledge, 2019. | Revised edition
    of the author's Urban design, 2011. | Includes index.
Subjects: LCSH: City planning. | Design.
Classification: LCC HT166 (ebook) | LCC HT166 .K359 2019 (print) |
    DDC 307.1/216—dc23
LC record available at https://lccn.loc.gov/2019007257

ISBN: 978-1-138-08563-3 (hbk)
ISBN: 978-1-138-08565-7 (pbk)
ISBN: 978-1-315-11125-4 (ebk)

Typeset in Garamond
by Apex CoVantage, LLC

CONTENTS

v

CONTENTS

FOREWORD AND ACKNOWLEDGMENTS

This revised edition has been an enjoyable experience as it gave me the opportunity to play. In many ways, it is an extension of the *Play in Creative Problem-solving* book (Kasprisin, 2016) using the symbolic object principles of Friedrich Froebel, the founding energy behind "kindergarten". I know that some colleagues wanted to see an emphasis on digital visual technology as well as the crafting methods used in the book. I initially had that in mind but as I engaged the experiments and exercises I realized that the use of the construction paper tools was more suitable for the semi-abstract compositional constructions. Students and professionals can choose their own comfort level regarding methods; and I encourage those who are dedicated computer technologists in their design work to at least explore the methods I used for their ease and ability to be quickly manipulated into various shapes. My studio is now adorned from wall to wall with colorful paper constructs, paper sculptures, leading to my first acknowledgement: my granddaughter who has renamed the main studio room as "grandpa's castle room". Thank you, sweetie!

This is a major revision of the first *Urban Design* effort. I have had a lot of fun doing this work, almost regretting the end of the process. And I hope students will share the same enjoyment as they engage in the suggested exercises on design composition.

It is both humbling and exciting to revisit an older work, assess its value and content, and readdress the educational issues and efforts in the work. Based on valuable critiques from reviewers in the field, practice and academia, and a seasoned personal perspective, the revised book addresses a number of my key aspirations in working with students: first, to increase the knowledge, skills and abilities of students in urban studies to enable them to engage in the design process—beyond rhetoric—making spatial compositions in cities, reflecting the interactions among people and between people and their built and natural environments. Second, to enable planners and other urbanists to utilize urban design as both a generative process and one of testing and evaluation of planning policy. Many professionals will say that urban designers already engage this connection. I argue too many, albeit well intentioned, do not; they understand the connection intellectually and are remiss in engaging the design connection—the generative, testing and assessment process of planning only possible through design. Urban design is more than fancy poster boards and examples of what others have done—it can lead to a creative urbanism.

Human settlements, from hamlet to metropolis, are messy, complex and at times chaotic and always in flux. Working *in the trenches* for over 40 years in the US and Canada exposed me to the complicated and complex nature of human settlements—human behavior, politics, economic forces, capitalism, and the impacts of these forces on the built form. In many instances, the urban design contribution is superficial band-aid applications, small alterations and tinkering to dynamic complex patterns and large-scale drastic interventions—large-scale architecture that is misconstrued as urban design. As I reflected on these experiences, balanced by 25 years of academic engagement with students, I questioned the role of urban design from my perspective: was it purely a design exercise in the domain of a few practitioners? Is it an exercise in regulations through controlling policies? Is it an exercise in branding or capital marketing? Or, is it a detached and isolated academic research process driven exclusively by rhetoric? And again, where does *urban design—the making of built form*—enter all of this?

The urban meaning and functionality of towns and cities are the basis for design—not a need for more regulation and franchisement of urban form. They demand attention and awareness of reality: the sensual nature of cities where people are the life-blood; the sensual actions of people that lie between and throughout the planning quantification data units and alluring cutting-edge technologies of the urban studies fields. Cities are real and filled with stories of achievement and dysfunction. Urban design is a process of translation and interpretation of these stories, the connecting tissue binding the artifacts of the built form together—hopefully with cohesion and harmony.

I have long appreciated the credo of Pablo Neruda in his "Some Thoughts on Impure Poetry", a lesson for designers and planners of all stripes, excerpted from *Pablo Neruda: Residence on Earth* (New Directions Books, 2004). Neruda reflects on the reality of life (and cities) and the imprint of humans on the landscape; impure, stained, worn, sometimes tragic, and always reflecting a "magnetism that should not be scorned" because it is reality—not some clean, neat, spiffy "smart" techno city. He states that this is the poetry that we are seeking and reminds us of the daily realities within our cities—messy, complicated, tragic, complex and creative—not static. This reality is a weaving or painting of culture, space and time/history, forming order from complex relationships—order that is not regimented or rigid but an order of creativity constantly in flux and adapting to our actions.

I am including an encaustic painting by friend and artist Lisa Butters, wherein she weaves and superimposes the complexity of culture, in my perception represented by the abstract patterns, the myriad of temperatures and intensities of color, into a spatial pattern and order, working as a rich and provocative compositional whole.

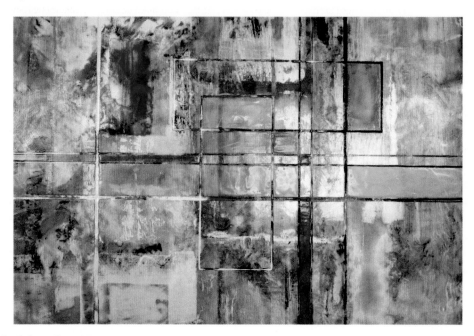

"Nilsdotter", Lisa Butters, 2019

What does this have to do with urban design and us, the designers and planners of cities? Have we and our field of endeavor become detached and separated from the reality and complexity of cities? In our search for effective and workable (smart?) cities, have we glazed over the marks of humans on the landscape and given in to the packaging of design, the repeated franchisement of spatial urban components—no longer spatial metaphors?

As designers, we seek to improve the built form of human settlements to make them work effectively and to make them desirable places to inhabit among this reality described by Neruda. Designers can play a role in making spatial metaphors of cultural meanings for contemporary society with historic connections; or succumb to the easier packaging of pseudo-nostalgia, branded and easily marketed to people seeking security only in the *known*. Those metaphors are spatial constructions or compositions dancing with the stories, imprints, marks, and needs of humans and their settlements. We must understand both partners in the dance and seek out the creative forces offered by the dance. We must return to play, a free activity that enables us to engage creative actions in urban design problem-solving and engage design beyond the rhetoric.

I have had architecture and landscape architecture colleagues who refer to themselves as urban designers because they contribute to the generation of urban form in various ways. With all due respect, I ask them to look beyond the "scale" component of "urban" and the conventional models of design they too often over-utilize. I urge them and the students to engage the complexities of cultural, historic, time and spatial aspects of concepts of *urban or community—the CST matrix*. I urge them to let the design emerge from this complexity as a process of design discovery—not predetermined certainty. So, this book is also for them in the hope that the work can inspire an awareness of the creativity in addressing the meaning and functionality underlying urban design—the messy stuff—and of the rich underlying forces affecting spatial compositions.

As I discuss in Chapter 6 on typologies, there are established building and development configuration patterns that are used daily because they work and provide convention and effectiveness to the design and construction of the built environment. And some are obsolete yet repeated because they are known and market-tested (as in most residential subdivisions, from gated communities to co-housing). Some are devoid of meaning as in theme-towns, and others are relied upon in excess, becoming expedient and corporately franchised applications—they are deemed safe by investors. Our role as urban designers is to challenge that expediency, forging hybrids that reflect the contextual reality of communities to the best of our abilities.

I am truly appreciative of the many discussions with my graduate students in urban planning and design regarding the approach of this book: from the practical to the theoretical (or at least underlying philosophy). They are my audience as well as those planners and designers who still believe cities are for people—not just "smart" technology. And I thank my dear friend, colleague and business partner Professor Emeritus James Pettinari, University of Oregon, for his support and critical dialogue over the years. And of course, I dedicate this book to the emerging elements of play and creativity—my two grandchildren, Margot and Oscar. Oh yes and to my two wonderful Labrador retrievers, both of whom diligently slept at my feet during this process, keeping me company—Whidbey (now with the universe) and young Bacchus. Thank you all.

Part I

HUMAN SETTLEMENT DYNAMICS
FOUNDATIONS FOR SPATIAL COMPOSITIONS

Chapter 1

INTRODUCTION

My initial formal effort, beyond course work, to establish a stronger connection between urban planning/urban studies analyses and design composition/spatial structure resulted in the first edition of *Urban Design: The Composition of Complexity* (Routledge, 2011). This second edition is a complete revision of that effort that seeks to further strengthen the connections between key theoretical considerations of cities as complex living systems and the importance of design composition as a spatial language necessary to portray and interpret those considerations into real built form. Based on the living systems perspective, change is constant and outcomes are uncertain—and this as we will explore makes *design* even more critical in the city-building process. At the heart of this work is the desire to enable urban studies students—including and beyond established designers—to understand and actively participate in the making of built form through (urban) design.

The book also seeks to advance new ideas and methods in design composition that relate to the theoretical base associated with Complexity Theory and creative systems. There are those in the design professions who argue that complexity is not a theory, whereas I argue it is both a theory or set of phenomena affecting our cities and a state of condition in our cities. There are no formulae for success to be found in the book—it seeks to promote a creative problem-solving process, seeking discovery, novelty and innovation. It is a dialogue with interested students, practitioners and other urbanists about how design is inherent in this process, and a demonstration and experimentation of alternate approaches to urban design. Different from the first edition, this contains examples that I hope can stimulate and guide interested readers in engaging design. It is my hope that this dialogue can generate a myriad of other experimentation points among those readers.

Premise

All actions and decisions associated with the meaning and functionality of human settlements—the urban dynamic—have spatial manifestations; and these manifestations are inherent in and not separated from the analysis of that dynamic. Consequently, and regardless of the varying levels of expertise in design and planning among professionals, students and laypeople, all participants are better able to address complex contexts and affect the quality of the built environment through a basic understanding of the basic elements and principles of design composition. Urban design has a key role in not only the generation of ideas for the built form but in the testing and evaluation of those ideas and consequently the overall education and awareness of the public regarding a quality urban form.

Organization and flow of the book

Urban design is a field or domain of many facets. This book focuses on relationships between and among the following:

- the umbrella: creative (or living) systems theory relative to human settlements: complexity thinking and its implications for design

- basis for complexity in human settlements: the trialectic of culture/space/time—the CST matrix
- creative problem-solving (CPS): engaging complexity
- composition of complexity: the elements and principles of spatial organization and structure.

For those professionals, students and laypeople involved in decision-making regarding the built environment, being able to intentionally guide urban spatial structure is a critical aspiration and responsibility; beyond analysis and rhetoric. It requires a working knowledge of the dynamics of cities and (urban) design composition/compositional structure, particularly in light of the adaptive and emerging patterns within human settlements. Urban planning and urban studies provide the base means and methods to analyse and understand the complex interactions and resulting relationships of urban living. This provides the conventional basis for design determinants used by architects, landscape architects, urban designers and planners (including laypeople) to affect meaningful spatial structure, from the individual building and open space to the larger urban structure and composition.

Making the connection between those relationships (as outcomes of the CST matrix) and the built form is often diluted or compartmentalized and assigned to the "designers". Analysis and comprehensive understanding of urban issues and "design" often go in separate directions, resulting in fragmented or packaged urban design solutions. There is an increasing dependency on packaged outcomes, branded and market-suitable, as opposed to relevant and contextually responsive. And collaboration among disciplines does not seem sufficient to address these challenges. How can we improve this collaboration?

Mission 1: Explore complexity as a part of a creative urbanism, a distinct departure from established conventions; and redefine and make the connection for the role of urban design in this creative process.

This book discusses, explores and demonstrates ways and means to address complexity from a design perspective through creative problem-solving. *Complexity* comes from the Latin *plexus*, meaning *interwoven*, where a complex system has elements which interact and affect each other, making it difficult to separate the behavior of individual elements. The fields of urban study have tendencies to separate and specialize these elements for the efficient management of means and methods of analysis.

This book strives to explore the presence of design as an inherent part of this urban dynamic and to make the connection between design engagement and urban complexity (CST—the interactions of cultural, spatial and temporal forces) (Soja, 1996): designing for difference and creativity—for all participants in built environment-shaping. I have witnessed too many urban design-related studios where the planners are designated as the resource/analysis people and the architects and landscape architects as the *designers*— an immediate disconnect. Both groups fail to understand the inherent connections between comprehensive analysis and design composition and urban form; between divergent and convergent thinking; between linear or normative and creative problem-solving. Urban design is about *design* composition for this complexity, requiring all participants to engage in meaningful ways.

The detailed discussions of *complexity* incorporate work from many sources, including the emergent CTC domain—the complexity theory of cities that analyses them as complex self-organizing systems; a direction of study that grew exponentially as students and professionals in urban studies became engaged with this new paradigm of complexity and self-organization (Portugali et al., 2012).

And this is about more than improved coordination and communication among the various specializations of urban investigation; it is about the inherent and inseparable connections and interactions between (better) understanding of the complexities of urban living and ways to affect the qualitative spatial structure within which that living occurs. Yes, there are levels of experience and expertise in the design process; they will always remain. And the argument in this book is that the fundamental elements and principles of design (spatial) composition are not only available but required for all participants at appropriate levels who engage in related built environment decision-making—especially in complex situations.

Mission 2: Understand urban design composition as the inherent structural assemblage or order for the complex dynamics of human settlements.

(Urban) design composition forms the skeleton spatial framework for communities large and small. And as a result of the constantly changing nature of cities, this framework can influence quality spatial structure and resulting built form infill over extended time periods. Consequently, understanding the elements and principles of compositional structure is a necessary responsibility for all involved in urban design and planning, not just specialists. Design composition is explored in the book as the structural assemblage for the CST interactions, ever-changing in dynamic human settlements. This requires more in-depth response from the urban design community, not less.

Part II of the book establishes the basic fundamentals of design composition as functions of art, and also builds on the work of educator Friedrich Froebel, the "inventor" of kindergarten, an educational process involving play as a free activity that influenced Frank Lloyd Wright, Buckminster Fuller, Walter Gropius, Wassily Kandinsky, Zentrum Paul Klee, Johannes Itten and many more artists, architects and educators. Losing these principles in a tidal wave of technological means and methods has far-reaching impacts on creative solutions to urban challenges. This does not condemn technology but argues for a plurality of and appropriate use of means and methods in design. We revisit these principles in design composition.

Part II begins with basic exercises in design composition for the beginner and advances to compositional explorations of key and unique factors of complexity and "creative urbanism" dynamics, with a focus on creative problem-solving. The basic premise at work is that if a creative problem-solving process is engaged, then what are the nature and characteristics of the creative outcome—possibly novel and innovative? How do we forge design compositions with and for this creative outcome and its connections to the larger built environment?

More on this later in the book.

Mission 3: Describe the necessity of direct engagement in urban design composition in order to understand the dynamics of human settlements.

There is a significant difference in the rhetoric of urban design and a direct engagement in design-making. It is the difference between linear or normative problem-solving and creative problem-solving (Kasprisin, 2016). Urban planners who develop planning and design policy (statements of action) are at a disadvantage if they cannot perceive of the spatial ramifications and outcomes of that policy—much to the detriment of the built environment. Planning and urban design then become trapped or ensnared in forging regulations that are in response to poor or inadequate planning decisions—or the lack thereof.

Urban design is also a way in which community members can visualize, process and understand the spatial implications of urban development. And I don't mean the perspective views of baby carriages and balloons along a nice waterfront walkway. Urban design can increase the awareness of the public and stakeholders through a quality and meaningful spatial language that is accessible and interactive—achievable through a variety of appropriate representational forms.

> **Mission 4: Differentiate between the creative generation of urban design composition and its simulation through historical patterns, conventional typologies, and packaged models.**

As we go through design experimentation and examples, I make the distinction between creative outcomes responsive to need and context versus the convenient, packaged, often thematic or nostalgic models that are fully available to cities around the globe, contributing little to local authenticity. There is a tension between authenticity of a community's built form and one that is branded or contrived: the difference between a community that is creative in its process and one that brands itself as a "creative city" as a marketing ploy. Creative urbanism addresses a search for authenticity through the creative process with uncertain outcomes versus form applications devoid of significant contextual reality.

The reader can form his or her own opinions on these missions. They are the result of reflections on my years of experience in practice and teaching. I hope that these can be the foundations of an ongoing dialogue regarding the importance of urban design and its new directions.

Setting the stage for urban design: structuring human settlements

(The many) definitions and approaches to urban design

As I discussed in the first edition, when the definition of urban design is approached among design and planning colleagues, there are lots of viewpoints depending on their educational backgrounds and field experience, if any. And that is a good place to start for students and professionals alike. Why? Because the term elicits a wide array of agendas, points of view, approaches, theories, politics and philosophies of "urbanisms". Agendas can range from designing major portions of cities to public involvement and education to policy and regulatory perspectives. Specific foci can range from site design, downtown redevelopment, design guidelines, social justice and food production and distribution to cultural and behavioral principles; and all are valid components within the larger definition. As my graduate mentor Myer R. Wolfe (University of Washington, 1960s to 1980s) adequately impressed upon us: "Urban design is inherent in the comprehensive planning process."

As an architect and urban planner, I state at the beginning that urban design in the context of this book is defined as the spatial relationship between *urban*—the interactions of cultures, space and time—and *design*—the making of structural compositions and orders. Urban design as explored here is a design-based process founded in an urban studies context where design decisions emanate from awareness and understanding of complex urban forces. And *design* is inherent in every phase of that process.

Let's start with an overview of some basic definitions.

Urban. A word defining scale, meaning a physical "characteristic of the city as distinguished from the country"; "constituting a city or town". In this vein, terms such as "regional" and "rural" have the same importance to design simply at a different scale connotation. I often use the term "community design" because it defines a group of people in association or relationship or in social units within a space that is not scale-specific. Whatever scale term is used, the other side of the "urban" coin is its implication of complex interactions among cultural, social, economic, political, spatial, functional, time and historical elements within an urban scale.

Design. Essentially the act of conceiving and making something. The broader definitions range from conceiving an idea to fashioning a plan. In the context of this book, design refers to the generation, representation and making of forms and physical compositions that contribute to a structural or assembled urban part or system. Design is not style nor beautification; they are subcomponents.

Composition. Design is the assembling of a composition of elements (shapes and objects) in both an organized and a structural relationship: a building, a park, a residential block, an urban district. The elements are related by a series of principles, rules or spatial activators that impart meaning and functionality in an assemblage to the individual parts and elements.

- To make or create by putting together parts or elements.
- The arrangement of artistic parts so as to form a unified whole.
- The art or act of composing a work.
- Urban form as measured through geometry, the earth measure.
- The making of structural order guided by the elements and principles of art.

And here is a summary of basic approaches to urban design from various perspectives.

. . . physical quality of the environment
"Urban design is that part of the planning process that deals with the physical quality of the environment . . . it is the physical and spatial design of the environment." (Shirvani, 1985)

. . . about form and function
"Design is about considerations about both form and functions in new products, buildings, images and landscapes, drawing on technical, aesthetic and market considerations . . . the principal contributing professions and occupations include architecture, graphic design, industrial (product) design, interior design, fashion, landscape design, and urban design and planning." (Knox, 2011)

. . . arrangement of buildings into a single composition
"Urban design is allied to architecture and planning . . . the subject matter of urban design is the arrangement of many buildings so that they form a single composition . . . [and] is the study of the public realm as opposed to the private domain." (Moughtin, 2003, p. 2)

. . . city beautiful
"City beautification and monumental grandeur were the objectives of the City Beautiful Movement in the 1890s and early 1900s" (Burnham, 1893). Daniel Burnham and Frederick Law Olmsted designed the 'White City' exposition for the World's Columbian Exposition in Chicago, 1893.

. . . a symbolic attempt to express urban meaning in form
"We call urban design the symbolic attempt to express an accepted urban meaning in certain urban forms." (Castells, 1983, p. 304)

. . . no one's land
"[Urban design] has never been established as an independent profession . . . caught in the professional equivalent of no man's land, claimed by both (architecture and planning) and recognized by

neither . . . planning professions have also been reluctant to recognize 'physical design' largely because of an ideological commitment to social science based disciplines as the foundation for urban planning practice, a situation which has endured since 1970 . . . a one-dimensional approach to planning from which it has never fully recovered . . . [and] rendered standard planning practice unfit to deal with the current trend to project-based site planning . . . [making] planners . . . manifestly unfit to cope with the urban design process" (Cuthbert, 2003, p. 11).

That is a harsh indictment for planners wanting to be engaged in the urban design process. And a sobering reality. As I mentioned in the Foreword and Acknowledgments section, part of the reason for writing this book is to enable people interested in urban design, planners and designers, to actually engage in it and be able to understand and apply the elements and principles of design composition as it relates to the larger planning process: policy-making, development guidelines, growth strategies and more. Urban design does not have to be the sole domain of established design professions such as architecture and landscape architecture. And, subsequently, these design professions can expand their understanding of urban design through more engagement in the socio-cultural dynamics that are the foundation for design decisions.

. . . the architecture and urban environment of humanism
"[Gordon Cullen] complained in the introduction to his 1971 edition of *The Concise Townscape* that architects and planners had completely misunderstood his message with their banal use of cobbles and bollards . . . as his message was much deeper, it was about the architecture and urban environment of humanism . . . [and] urban designers must be able to design." (Gosling, 1996, p. 9)

. . . a collaborative art concerned with environmental change
". . . urban design is at its best a collaborative art . . . concerned with environmental change and the idea that environmental changes will yield as much public benefit as they can . . . [and] urban design is the ongoing process of shaping cities, their precincts, and their public realms . . . whether it is self-conscious or unselfconscious." (Lang, 1994, p. 76)

. . . designing with nature
And, of course, "designing with nature" (McHarg, 1969) now referred to as ecological design or "sustainable" design . . .

. . . design as biofunction
Dating back to the Olsmsted brothers (1898) and the design of the landscape as a function of natural processes such as water retention, dispersal, etc., the idea of design as a part of the biofunction of the landscape emerged as a dynamic approach in both environmental art and design. Artists like Lorna Jordan and Vicki Scurri of Seattle craft the landscape into a biofunctioning art piece, not as art *in* the landscape but as art *as* the landscape. Anne Spirn (1984) discusses the incorporation of biofunctions into the urban landscape, where design and environment work together to foster healthy urban environments.

. . . ecosystem design
Ecology's emergence on both the philosophical and scientific levels in the 1960s changed design as it had physics, introducing the integration of the sciences as part of a larger interactive relationship; and

challenged designers to move beyond master planning and goal-driven linear processes. John Tillman Lyle in *Design for Human Ecosystems* (1985) explores the need to employ the analysis of scientific information in the creative design process, focusing on the major components of the ecosystem (structure, function and location or context) as they relate to design.

... sustainable design

Urban planning has embraced the principles of sustainability as a way of preserving or protecting a desired outcome or state. But as Batty and Marshall (2012) argue, this assumes a level of predictability for the long-term future, not taking into account uncertainty and the adaptive capabilities of human settlements. Sustaining aspects of settlements and their environs can actually interfere with that settlement's ability to creatively deal with emerging challenges. Use of the term "sustainable" requires scrutiny so that it does not represent "carrying capacity" or goal-driven, long-term desired outcomes (predetermined).

... designing for human behavior

Designing for human behavior emerged in the 1960s as architects and planners began questioning the basic reasons driving urban design: form, social goals or human behavior? I remember in graduate school (1960s) being enamored with Robert Ardrey's *Territorial Imperative* (1966), as he explored the relationship between behavior and territorial dynamics—the occupation and defencse of territory. I certainly was admonished by psychologists in the late 1960s for both entering a field that was considered outside the realm of design and utilizing concepts of territoriality research conducted with animals other than humans. Nevertheless, the message resonated and opened up the urban design process to the need for interdisciplinary teams as the architect could not be all things in the process. Work by Robert Sommer (1969) regarding the issue of territoriality in office work spaces, Edward T. Hall's *The Silent Language* (1959) and *The Hidden Dimension* (1966), Robert Bechtel's *Enclosing Behavior* (1977), and many others began to increase designers' awareness of principles of human interactions with spatial environments based on social-behavioral dynamics. This awareness is an integral part of living systems design approaches regarding human behavior–spatial interactions and creative differences. They remain valuable resources to this day.

... as placemaking

The concept of place and placemaking stems from unusual, unique, specialized, even intimate interactions between and among people and locality (and the many variables associated with both). This is a challenging task as the behavior of people and their environments change constantly, altering the original use or intent of a "place" or having the original context altered by the changing built environment, affecting the behavior of occupants as time changes—possibly making the place indefensible or obsolete. Concerns exist regarding the standardization of placemaking with an over-reach of regulatory means, codes and standards. To this I add the replication of places, packaged and branded, as models and types out of context with little or no intimate potential. Arefi explores placemaking from three perspectives: need-based place, opportunity-based place, and asset-based place.

... neo-traditional and New Urbanism

The Congress for the New Urbanism, founded in 1993, is an international non-profit organization based in Chicago, IL, and Washington, DC, that advocates a return to historic urban forms with the following principles: walkability; connectivity; mixed use and diversity; mixed housing; quality architecture and urban design; traditional neighborhood structures; increased density; and green design. Names associated with the movement include Leon Krier, Christopher Alexander, Dan Soloman, Peter Calthorpe, Doug Kelbaugh, Duany, Plater-Zybeck and others. The principles are not new to New Urbanism and represent many urban design approaches. The New Urbanism movement has packaged and presented these ideas in workable formats for many communities.

These definitions are varied and often express political or philosophical approaches. As we explore in this book, aspects of all of these can be integrated into a coherent and creative approach to urban design. And urban design deals with all aspects of urban spatiality.

So, what is urban design?

Obviously, the domain encompasses most if not all of the above descriptions, and they range from the topical (placemaking) to spatial or structural compositions to various movements. The following is a description of the aspects of urban design that are closely related to the concepts and theories of complexity and a pursuit of a creative urbanism.

Urban design: spatial structure and order from meaning and functionality

Recognizing that "urban" is both a scale ladder (an interwoven scale mosaic) and a description of cultural spatial interactions in time, we begin our discussion of urban design as an integral spatial response to an array of meaning and functionality in human settlements, at multiple scales. And the spatial response takes the form of physical metaphors, different with an element of interconnectedness. Using Castells's words, "We call urban design the symbolic attempt to express an accepted urban meaning in certain urban forms" (1983, p. 304).

Difference is to be celebrated while being connected through creative compositions to a larger structural order. *Meaning* forms the foundation for the purpose in urban design processes: identifying, interpreting and transforming the richness and diversity of human activities into responsive and meaningful form and structure. Without this the process is abstract or detached, driven by models and franchised compositions that proliferate in our cities. The importance of "meaning" as well as functionality is explored in Chapter 2 and the discussions of designing for difference.

Urban design as directed intent, emergent (deviant) pattern, design through uncertainty for difference and novelty

Urban design is generated through various means, ranging from intentional (planning) toward a directed outcome; as emergent pattern that flows out of or emanates from underlying forces not totally perceivable or anticipated; and as novel solutions arising from a creative problem-solving process without predetermined outcomes. All have a role in fashioning urban form based on a specific context. They provide a perspective on urban design approaches given the complexity inherent in human settlements.

Established design practices fall under this category and are traditionally linear or normative problem-solving processes. They include master planning and comprehensive planning, supported by program analysis (problem and need identification and assessment), impact analysis (socio-economic–political–land use impacts), alternative development and testing, and cost–benefit analyses. At each stage in the process are spatial tests and simulations to aid in assessing the legitimacy of proposed policies and alternatives. Directed intent enables a process of coherency regarding established and preferred physical patterns and functional needs present and future for infrastructure. This method is also referred to as "rational", "comprehensive" and "synoptic" (Shirvani, 1985, pp. 109–110).

Basic steps in this process include but are not limited to:

- Step 1: data collection, survey of existing conditions (natural, built and socio-economic)
- Step 2: data analysis, identification of all opportunities and limitations
- Step 3: formulation of goals and objectives
- Step 4: generation of alternative concepts
- Step 5: elaboration of each concept into workable solutions
- Step 6: evaluation of alternative solutions
- Step 7: translation of solutions into policies, plans, guidelines and programs. (Shirvani, 1985, p. 111)

Aspects of this directed intent approach are transferable to a creative problem-solving process as is discussed in Chapter 3; comprising the basics of (information) processing or convergent methodologies in the larger design process (see Kasprisin, 2016).

Urban design as emergent pattern

This almost classifies as a serendipitous pattern, one that is discovered as it emerges from unseen or underlying forces and interactions through a creative and open process; subconscious, even subcultural—hidden but functioning as a group in response to underlying factors.

It forms the basis of creative patterning, whereby parts or systems of a human settlement form new patterns in response to complex interactions, in many cases not discernible until their impact is felt or observed as an unusual occurrence or even phenomenon.

Emergent patterns are essentially meta-determinant, uncertain in their existence until a certain level of physical manifestation occurs. Often referred to as "accidental", these emergent patterns are in fact the forerunners or indicators of significant creative change in existing systems. The shopping center, now universal as a model for retail development patterns, is an example of an emergent pattern internationally, beginning in North America in the 1960s. (This is not to discount the classic and original shopping streets, plazas and markets of historic cities . . . and the festival markets of Europe.) This refers more to a packaging and marketing pattern.

Basic steps in this process of emergent patterning include but are not limited to:

- Step 1: understanding adequate context (1): data collection, survey of existing conditions (natural, built and socio-economic), interdisciplinary socio-economic–political factors in time.
- Step 2: data analysis, identification of all opportunities and limitations, articulation of the polarity wheel (2), identification of the problem plurality (3).
- Step 3: formulation of stakeholder aspirations, needs and relational interactions (4).
- Step 4: creative capacity analysis for self-determination.
- Step 5: identification and assessment of emergent deviant patterns within coherent context.

- Step 6: generation of alternative concepts at multiple levels, including polarities.
- Step 7: elaboration and testing of each concept into workable solutions.
- Step 6: evaluation of alternative solutions.
- Step 7: translation of (tested) solutions into policies, plans, guidelines and programs.

Urban design as the design for difference and uncertainty

Obviously, these components are all related and are separated here for emphasis. Difference is defined here from the word *differ*: "to be dissimilar in nature, quality, amount, or form . . . a noticeable change or effect." Human settlements are systems of variation and difference, from ethnicity to politics to cultural preferences and patterns to spatial behaviors to color preference and on and on.

Currently in urban design, there is an increased emphasis on the active shaping of social and environmental visions along with the physical (Ganis, 2015). This is certainly supported by Soja (2000) and the CST interactions and underscores the imperative for designing for difference and uncertainty. From Ganis's perspective, an adaptive plan accommodates change in the people–place interaction and the resilient play that assimilates change in that interaction. The subtle difference is that in assimilation, "it is the conception of reality that is adjusted to fit existing schemes, whereas in accommodation, the existing scheme is adjusted to fit the reality" (Ganis, 2015, p. 3). As we approach difference and uncertainty, the challenge for all is to resist the urge to assimilate their dynamics into models, typologies and prepared packaged compositions. This is discussed further later in the book.

Urban design as a discovery of novelty

This approach to urban design is based in creative problem-solving as opposed to rational and linear problem-solving and underscored in the experiments and examples in later chapters. In *Play in Creative Problem-solving for Planners and Architects* (Kasprisin, 2016) I explored the role of play as a free activity without failure, where rules change as play progresses toward an uncertain outcome, as the glue or dynamic action in creative problem-solving. This applies to all aspects of planning and design. And yes, there is an outcome that results from the creative dynamics of the process, not something predetermined to be proven or disproven. Nor is the outcome something that is buried in the data—it is created by the process through discovery that leads to novelty and innovation.

In the examples that I constructed for students as guides, the very act of playing with, in this case, construction paper in semi-abstract constructs opened opportunities for design directions that were not perceived at the onset of the design process. The very act of play led to one composition after another. I am not concerned how the reader judges my efforts—I encourage the reader to be playful and let his or her imagination freely flow and experience this for themselves.

Urban design as a connectivity transaction

One of the more challenging aspects of urban design is its ability to make connections between and among differences in the built environment as creative solutions emerge. As I discuss in the later sections, our influence over specific architecture and other design statements is limited to guidelines, standards, and other regulatory factors. What urban design can focus on are the connections between and among the designed artifacts of the built form, the places where most human interaction occurs.

This connectivity can be expressed through building and open space typologies, or implied through the design composition with interlocking structures, solid/void polarities and others discussed in later chapters. One important part of connectivity is the connection through time: as diverse participants are involved in affecting the built form, with the challenge of maintaining a coherence in design with the variations brought to the process by differing forces.

I discuss alternatives to the conventional master-planning approach using in part probability trajectories, for example. Probability trajectories begin with similar aspirations as a master plan in that the need and direction for infrastructure, for example, is critical to identify in assessing resources and funds for a particular urban development over time. And yet, master plans change in many ways during that time, often unable to adjust to changes. The departure and role for urban design exists not in designating a set location of key elements but in the delineation of multiple spatial probabilities that respond to various divergent influences or potential catalysts, known and unknown, perceived as possible over a time duration. Challenging and a critical role for urban design as a testing mechanism—not predictive but projecting probability.

The following chapter discusses creative living systems, complexity theory and the impacts of these ideas on urban design.

Bibliography

Ardrey, Robert, 1966: *The Territorial Imperative: A Personal Inquiry into the Animal Origin of Property and Nations*: Atheneum, New York.

Arefi, Mahyar, 2014: *Deconstructing Placemaking: Needs, Opportunities, and Assets*: Routledge, Abingdon, Oxfordshire.

Batty, Michael and Marshall, Stephen, 2012: "The Origins of Complexity Theory in Cities and Planning." In Portugali, Juval, Meyer, Han, Stolk, Egbert and Tan, Ekim (eds): *Complexity Theories of Cities Have Come of Age*: Springer, Heidelberg, Dordrecht/London/New York.

Bechtel, Robert B., 1977: *Enclosing Behavior*: Dowden, Hutchinson & Ross, Inc., Stoudsburg, PA.

Burnham, Daniel, 1893: *Director of Works for the White City Exposition*: Chicago, IL.

Castells, Manuel, 1983: "The City and the Grassroots": University of California, Berkeley, CA. Reprinted in Cuthbert, Alexander R. (ed.), 2003: *Designing Cities: Critical Readings in Urban Design*: Blackwell Publishers, Cambridge, MA.

Cuthbert, Alexander R., 2003 (ed.): *Designing Cities: Critical Readings in Urban Design*: Blackwell Publishers, Cambridge, MA.

Ganis, Mary, 2015: *Planning Urban Places: Self-organizing Places with People in Mind*: Routledge, New York and London.

Gosling, David, 1996: *Gordon Cullen: Visions of Urban Design*: Academy Editions, London, UK.

Hall, Edward T., 1959: *The Silent Language*: Doubleday Co., New York.

Hall, Edward T., 1966: *The Hidden Dimension*: Doubleday Co., New York.

Kasprisin, Ron, 2016: *Play in Creative Problem-solving for Planners and Architects*: Routledge, Abingdon, Oxfordshire.

Knox, Paul L., 2011: *Cites and Design*: Routledge, Abingdon, Oxfordshire.

Lang, Jon, 1994: "Urban Design as a Discipline and as a Profession." In *Urban Design: The American Experience*: Van Nostrand Reinhold, New York. Reprinted in Larice, Michael and Macdonald, Elizabeth (eds), 2007: *The Urban Design Reader*: Routledge, Abingdon, Oxfordshire.

Lyle, John Tillman, 1985: *Design for Human Ecosystems: Landscape, Land Use, and Natural Resources*: Van Nostrand Reinhold, New York.

McHarg, Ian, 1969: *Design with Nature*: John Wiley & Sons, New York.

Moughtin, Cliff, 2003: *Urban Design: Street and Square* (3rd edition): Architectural Press, Oxford/ Burlington, MA.

Portugali, Juval, Meyer, Han, Stolk, Egbert, and Tan, Ekim (eds), 2012: *Complexity Theories of Cities Have Come of Age: An Overview with Implications to Urban Planning and Design*: Springer, Heidelberg, Germany/Dordrecht/London/New York.

Shirvani, Hamid, 1985: The *Urban Design Process*: Van Nostrand Reinhold Company, Inc., New York.

Soja, Edward W., 1996: *Thirdspace*: Blackwell Publishers Inc., Cambridge/Oxford.

Soja, Edward W., 2000: *Postmetropolis: Critical Studies of Cities and Regions*: Blackwell Publishers, Oxford.

Sommer, Robert, 1969: *Personal Space: The Behavioural Basics of Design*: Prentice-Hall, Englewood Cliffs, NJ.

Spirn, Anne Whiston, 1984: *The Granite Garden: Urban Nature and Human Design*: Basic Books, Inc. Publishers, New York.

Chapter 2

THEORETICAL CONSIDERATIONS (OR NOT)

Toward a creative urbanism: the larger picture

Another "urbanism"? No—an expanded "umbrella" for the role of design.

Theory is irrelevant, an impediment to creative design innovation.

(Speaks, 2005, p. 170)

As the reader will note, there is a divide within the design community, academia and practice especially regarding the validity and role of theory in design. To some, design is "a creative act, an unprecedented event, deductible from and reducible to no theory, but sprung from something necessary yet rarely referred to, namely courage" (Hatton, 2017, p. 174). Hatton goes on to argue that designers, not expected to be historians or theorists, can be articulate critics through their acts rather than words. And in reverse, if someone is to be a historian or theorist, they must have some knowledge of practice, the art of design.

Let's review the range of definitions for "theory", according to the *American Heritage Dictionary of the English Language* (2011): (1) a set of statements or principles devised to explain a group of facts or phenomena, especially one that has been repeatedly tested or is widely accepted and can be used to make predictions about natural phenomena; and (2) an assumption based on limited information or knowledge; a conjecture.

As the reader can deduce from the range of definitions of "theory", the notion that it can be an impediment to creative design innovation based on the statement "repeatedly tested . . . and can be used to make predictions" raises cautionary flags for design process—as well as basing theory on limited assumptions.

I am not a theorist nor a historian and view myself, in the words of others, as a "reflective practitioner". I respect theory/theories as a guide for design process, one that is based on the observation, perception and experimentation of unusual indicators of the changing dynamics within human settlements. I expand on this in a discussion of the cultural/spatial/time (CST) matrix in this chapter. And I am seeking ways to bridge the gap between theoretical insulation and design crafting. In other words, I argue that all participants in the making of cities require both a sense of a larger guiding framework and an engagement with the making of urban form.

And I use principles from physics, biology and ecology as a basis for that guiding framework related to design application.

Premise

The complexity of the state of being or condition resulting from the myriad interactions within human settlements requires new approaches for urban designers in order to creatively influence the evolving built environment with its complex dynamics. I introduce creative problem-solving as an alternate to linear or normative problem-solving as a means of diverging from the conventional "predictive . . . master-planned" approach to design and planning. Cities are alive and are not predictive at all scales.

Creative problem-solving processes can provide the means and methods necessary to address the acknowledged complexity (by theorists and practitioners) of cities/human settlements—seeking creative outcomes through a process of discovery: novel and innovative. If novel and innovative outcomes are indeed possible, then they can constitute and contribute to an emergent creative urbanism at varying scales; distanced from packaged, branded and franchised outcomes. A creative problem-solving process is not disconnected from reality; it is inherent in and derived from creative systems.

Subsequently, complexity as a state of being and a theoretical viewing lens arises from the interactions of culture, space and time (CST) integrally not as separate components forming complex relationships at multiple levels in settlements. Opportunities and potentials for new means and methods in urban design arise from creative or living systems perspectives emanating from physics, biology, mathematics and philosophy—ecology as a process of complex interactions.

The chicken or the egg?

Presenting a discussion and dialogue of this larger perspective and relating it to the acts of design, making urban form and structure, is my mission. It is a challenge, from the varying terminologies of the sciences and philosophies to the need to bridge the abstract with applied reality. The major components of this larger umbrella for design can be presented in different ways and they are integral, not separable, components. So bear with me as this practitioner finds his way in this metaphorical lush forest of possibilities to explore new design directions (or reinforce and expand coherent existing directions).

As a means of presenting this larger "umbrella framework", I have focused on six major components for discussion.

1   The umbrella for an approach to a creative urbanism: creative (or living) systems theory relative to human settlements.
2   The trialectic of culture/space/time—the CST matrix—as the basis for an articulation of the elements and principles (and uncertainties) within this creative system (of human settlements), forming complex interactions (and patterns) of human activity.
3   Complexity thinking and the theory of complexity to engage these interactions and the implications for urban design.
4   Seeking "thirdspace": the creative outcomes within human settlements, using:
    •   creative problem-solving (CPS): engaging complexity in urban design
    •   play as a free activity of discovery
    •   the uncertainty principle.
5   Implications for urban design: means and methods:
    •   a multi-level view or perspective of human settlement spatial dynamics
    •   designing for constantly changing realities
    •   incremental design contributions to the emergent whole
    •   larger-term probability design trajectories (as an alternative to the master-plan approach)
    •   connectivity between and among emergent (possibly creative) spatial patterns.

6   Composition of complexity: the elements and principles of spatial organization and structure—where urban design is used as an exploratory, informative, demonstrative, evaluative and ordering process.

The umbrella: creative (or living) systems theory relative to human settlements

Cities can be viewed as artifacts, with infrastructure, buildings and open-space components. Human settlements are the places where people live, work and play—they are alive. I make this distinction as the discussion of "smart cities" wafts among the new wave of planners and designers devising ways to solve urban problems with new technologies.

Based on the "aliveness" perspective of human settlements, I begin with an overview of creative systems theory (living systems) as it applies to human settlements and their design. Creative or living systems emerged from the domains of physics, biology, mathematics and the overall field of ecology as a means of dealing with the nature of reality—complex, with many variables and uncertainties, multiple existence and has major implications for domains such as design and planning.

> The systems view looks at the world in terms of relationships and integration. Systems are integrated wholes whose properties cannot be reduced to those of smaller units. Instead of concentrating on basic building blocks or basic substances, the systems approach emphasizes basic principles of organization.
>
> (Capra, 1982, p. 266)

In essence we are designing for relationships in meaning and functionality seeking to infuse human settlements with these basic principles of organization—a living, changing order. It acknowledges at various scales the objects such as buildings, roads, sewers, houses; and argues that those objects exist within and as parts of complex relationships, not simply as artifacts to be weighed, measured and compared.

> The activity of systems involves a process known as *transaction*—the simultaneous and mutually interdependent interaction between multiple components. Systemic properties are destroyed when a system is dissected, either physically or theoretically, into isolated elements. Although we can discern individual parts in any system, the nature of the whole is always different from the mere sum of its parts.
>
> (Capra, 1982, p. 267)

This by now is a well-repeated phrase. In physics, this transaction is referred to as the "aha!" moment, the time or point when all things come together. It may also be the same process when a person experiences an urban space as a "place", not based on evaluation or measurement but on the interdependent interaction between multiple components: climate, orientation, materials, spatial order, other people, sounds, smells, etc.—aha!

Another term used in defining creative systems is "creative causality" (Johnston, 1991), meaning both change and relationship are formative dynamics, where reality is composed of ongoing, interwoven processes of creative self-organization. This does not exclude the designer from this creative process and challenges and changes the role of the designer. This is also the basis for the use of terms such as "emergent reality", where the design/planning process learns to recognize, identify and focus on phenomena resulting from these formative dynamics. The implications for urban design processes are unlimited and not limited to pre-packaged outcomes.

Creative systems theory essentially states that reality is fundamentally creative and adds to traditional theory in key ways: first, it provides a big picture based on science; second, it offers ways and means to understand complicated, messy and complex interactions and relationships; and third, it delves into a new cultural maturity needed to survive the future.

This language has been around since the 1960s, along with the emergence of a general recognition of the concept and principles of ecology and quantum theory. Too often, it remains in an abstract state with little connection or applications in various domains. That has changed significantly in recent decades with applications in psychology and psychiatry (dealing with relationships in individuals and groups including corporations and institutions), business, and urban planning and design, as we will discuss in the next section. Remember, this language and the principles discussed below are based in physics and distinguish creative causality from the mystical and material cause-and-effect models.

Key principles and terminology of creative systems theory

The exploration of atomic and subatomic worlds drastically changed the way physicists and other scientists observed reality.

> In the twentieth century . . . physicists faced . . . a serious challenge to their ability to understand the universe. Every time they asked nature a question in an atomic experiment, nature answered with a paradox, and the more they tried to clarify the situation, the sharper the paradoxes became. In their struggle to grasp this new reality, scientists became painfully aware that their basic concepts, their language, and their whole way of thinking were inadequate to describe atomic phenomena.
>
> (Capra, 1982, p. 76)

Enter a new way of thinking that has filtered down and through many domains.

Critical to our discussion on new directions for urban design is the basic principle identified by physicist Niels Bohr in 1913 (see Bohr, 2008): isolated material particles are abstractions and their properties can only be defined and observed through their interaction with other systems. For planning and design, this brings the work of Henri Lefebvre (1992), Edward Soja (1996) and others into the discussion with the trialectic of cultural, spatial, and time/historical components of human settlements, where the reality of those settlements can only be understood through the interaction of all three, not one or two. In other words, what is critical is the resulting relationship or outcome formed by the interactions that define what is occurring; and what is the focus of our design efforts. We deal with objects or particles constantly and can easily get lost or distracted by their shininess. Importantly, their resulting interactions with themselves and other aspects of context are what reveals "meaning" and what we are really designing for and why. I refer to this as the CST matrix and discuss its importance later in this chapter.

The terminology of the new physics and biology can be daunting and confusing, particularly as we apply it to design and planning. I am no physicist and want to engage as many readers in this emerging dialogue as possible, hoping that each reader asks how these terms and principles can be applied to urban design. All the terms that follow are part of the theory and dialogue on creative/living systems, a category that includes the human settlements we inhabit. They obviously are parts of a larger integrated discussion and are summarized here for reference purposes and as an introduction to a different use of terms from the planning and design domains. Again, I hope they stimulate the urban design community to explore and transfer these principles to the design of human settlements. I include some thoughts and observations after many of the terms on the possible transference to the urban design domain. Listed below are key phrases and principles that are characteristics of this terminology and language.

P1: Self-organizing system

A living systems order, its structure (assemblage) and organization (functional relationships) are determined by the system itself, from within, not imposed by the surrounding environment with its organization; yes, environment has influence, but structural changes result from the internal dynamics of the system itself.

 Urban design implications: This has implications when we discuss "creative capacities" of communities, and impacts the way planners and designers approach and work with communities—working from within, not imposing top-down expertise from without. Does this exclude designers? Quite the contrary, as designers and planners are or need to be within the system—a part of it and its processes. Designers bring experience, technical and compositional knowledge to the table, case studies and design experimentation and exploration skills. And this begins to redefine the role of urban designers as key participants (not top-down experts) in the process. This approach may conflict with conventional wisdom regarding the role of the planner and designer, requires more time during the process, and promises less compromise in the outcomes.

P2: Self-renewal

A dynamic phenomenon that is the ability to continuously renew and recycle components while maintaining the integrity of the overall structure; this also involves the principle of creative coherence, keeping what works and changing what does not. This principle can be embedded in an ongoing assessment process as the community evolves.

 Urban design implications: As a part of a self-organizing process, a community can (continuously or periodically) assess its health and creative capacity, being aware of the CST interactions that function properly and those with symptoms of descendancy. This is well within the current practices of urban planning and requires an interdisciplinary approach to planning, going beyond infrastructure, going beyond last-minute reactions to emerging urban challenges.

P3: Uncertainty principle and complementarity

The uncertainty principle emerges from the sciences, particularly physics, and psychology in relation to creativity and creative problem-solving processes; essentially the dynamics of the process are constantly maintained and the outcome emerges from that process—it is not a solution that exists or is embedded in the data, nor is it an anticipated outcome, and its uncertainty promotes outcomes that can be creative, unique, not predetermined or expected—novel and innovative.

 Urban design implications: The uncertainty principle works on all levels of urban or community design, from the conduct of workshops and charrettes to the making of design compositions. Students have difficulty with this concept in that they often work to specify and further define an initial design concept as if it is a solution. The final solution is not evident until manifested through the process, emerging, changing, evolving in different ways—it is called *flow*. I can begin the process with "notions" and if I allow them to mature and evolve instead of forcing them to a set or anticipated outcome, they can produce novel solutions. As the design process progresses within a creative problem-solving dynamic, the design composition begins to manifest itself. I can prepare for a community workshop with background information, input, case studies, a solid data base—and enter the workshop process with the mission of allowing the process itself, through dialogue, explorations, etc., to determine the outcome, or at least advance the process enough for the next workshop. The old convention of entering the process with *n*-alternatives and seeing which one stands up to general critique or a charming sales pitch by the designers asks for problems and compromises, and has no chance of being creative. This requires skill and training in *interactive* facilitation.

P4: Dynamic context

Dynamic means constantly in motion, vigorous, energetic, as in creative energy. Basic patterns and relationships (in human settlements) are understood in terms of their CST context—the reality of the moment. These contexts are constantly in motion, characterized in part by multiple interactions among their components, the connections between and among those interactions (emerging as relationships), and the resulting transformations. This relates directly to the CST matrix, again where culture represents the socio-economic–political forces of human interaction, spatial represents the locality and context of that interaction, and time represents the periods within which human interactions and events occur, currently and historically.

   Urban design implications: For urban design, the implications are significant—we are designing for change, not static situations; we are designing with elements that still remain viable (coherence) and explore hybrids and alternatives that are responsive to the changing patterns. "Packaged" solutions may not be sufficient to address these dynamic contexts. The very interaction of people with their natural and built environments alters and changes that context, subtly and in dramatic ways that we may not be aware of unless directed. This again is about training for expanded observation skills. Periodically, a former student from my watercolor class will comment on how much more color and value they perceive in daily life as a result of the painting experience. The same applies for the perception of the dynamics of context.

P5: Quantum theory

A theory of atomic phenomena: the origin of many of the principles of creative or living systems. Many of these principles are relevant to urban design, urban form and building cities.

P6: Creative causality

Creative causality represents a perspective where causality is creative, separate from the cause as mythical/spiritual and from the cause as materialistic, linear; where both change and relationship are dynamic forces of reality, and reality is composed of ongoing, interwoven processes of creative self-organization (Johnston, 1991). The principles of creative causality, including creative differentiation and capacitance, are effective foundations for planning and design applications particularly with public involvement and inclusive interactive participation.

   We work with many of these principles in the book as an effort to bridge between theory and design application. Creative capacitance, for example, involves the ability of the community itself to deal with and resolve challenges to its CST composition, not relying on outside monies and experts as the prime problem-solvers. If a community's creative capacity is diminished or corrupted, all the money and expertise available will not solve underlying and systemic problems.

Urban design implications: This principle challenges what we are looking for in our urban planning and design analysis, going beyond the linear cause–effect approach—causality is a creative dynamic action. We are designing objects not as static elements but as representations of emerging relationships in our settlements.

P7: Self-transcendence

A dynamic phenomenon that is the ability to be creative beyond mental and physical boundaries in the processes of learning, development and evolution; this is the foundation for creativity and creative problem-solving.

P8: Open systems

Systems that maintain a continuous exchange (in and out) of energy and matter with their environment in order to survive; this is known as "metabolism" that maintains the system in a state of non-equilibrium, essentially putting it always "at work"—distanced from equilibrium or static states. This represents in part the important connections or portals between and among human settlement parts or smaller systems, districts, clusters of compatible relationships.

Urban design implications: Many assume that a state of equilibrium is desirable for human settlement systems when in fact the system or settlement is continually "vibrating", alive with an active or dynamic metabolism "at work". Defining and working with this metabolism poses an intriguing approach for urban design. The "urban metabolism" refers to the process of a settlement breaking down or synthesizing forms of energy to sustain itself.

P9: Systems order

An order achieved by coordinating activities that do not rigidly constrain the parts, allowing for flexibility and variation, even unique and irregular, that enables living systems to adapt to new circumstances.

Urban design implications: This may be the antithesis of the "master plan", where outcomes are committed to over long periods of time with little flexibility, predictive and expected to accommodate unforeseen changes that unexpectedly occur and can lead to compromises in the system. Given an awareness in the systems order regarding flexibility and variation, unusual phenomena, these unexpected changes can be better engaged with the system adapting to rather than accommodating them. This systems order is at the core of creative compositions, where the urban order, physical and spatial, has an adaptability factor that enables flexibility and non-linear changeability.

P10: Coherence

Equilibrium is not stability; the stability of self-organizing systems is dynamic and non-linear, and maintains its overall structure with what is healthy and simultaneously makes changes to and replaces any components that are not working or contributing—what works (in context) is retained and what does not work is changed or replaced over time. I use the term "in context" because what works is not a foreign, imported or invasive typology but an integral part of the context of the larger system. And the stability of a system is not absolute—it will maintain that stability when fluctuations are below a critical size or state and is always ready to transform and evolve. Do not confuse this with "sustainability" as they are separate and distinct principles—"coherence" continues the system with ongoing changes and "sustainability" continues the system with the maintenance of the existing, underlying resources or components.

Urban design implications: As urban designers, we already address many aspects of the community sector or district under study as "givens", identifying positive elements to be supported and built upon. Coherence asks us to go beyond this identification and investigate the relationships of the parts of a human settlement that are contributing and coherent to the larger whole—and why! They are not isolated parts and do not act in isolation of other parts of the settlement or community.

P11: Evolution

Evolution is an open and ongoing non-linear process that continually creates its own purpose and whose outcome is inherently uncertain—based in the creativity of the emerging reality. The general pattern of evolution can be recognized and is comprehensible with characteristics that include the progressive increase of complexity, coordination, and interdependence; the integration of multi-level systems; and a continual refinement of certain functions and behaviors, within limits.

Urban design implications: For planning and design, this is a twofold challenge: there is a recognizable pattern of structural and organizational change in human settlements and, the recognition of changes in emerging purpose, needs, functions and patterns. They are not necessarily linear and, as in creative causality, can alter the course of living systems in unknown or unexpected directions. This reinforces the concept of uncertainty, not relying on a predictive outcome process.

P12: Complexity

The result of a state of multi-level interactions that arise from the coevolution of living systems and environment at all levels as both are "alive"—transactions. It is a state of being that is complicated with multiple unknowns, not static or stable; the multi-level interactions result in a myriad of emergent relationships that are the connections within human settlements—the basis for urban design foci that defy simple analytics.

Urban design implications: From my perspective, this complexity represents the richness of quality and diversity in human settlements, and the need for urban design to engage this complexity, forming or composing spatial metaphors that respond to that richness. The notion of a design composition changes dramatically regarding this complexity formed by the interactions and relationships within the CST matrix. And to engage this complexity as urban order or compositions, the urbanist must understand the elements and principles of design composition.

P13: Homeostasis

A state where the system appears in equilibrium and is always in a state of fluctuation even when it is not apparent; the system has great flexibility, always with extensive options for interacting with its environment, and it is self-regulating.

Urban design implications: Imagine observing an urban park, set in concrete and vegetation, over a period when the environment, climate, and human activities constantly interact with its physicality; always in a state of fluctuation, subtle or substantial—it may appear "stable" or in equilibrium and is constantly changing. A larger scenario is a neighborhood sector, apparently stable, yet constantly undergoing changes that can be observed, indicating emerging patterns or ascendancy or descendancy (in its creative capacitance).

P14: Adaptability/resilience

Adaptability is a system changing as needed to various influences, whereas resilience absorbs and accommodates changes within the existing structure, resisting major changes. In prolonged environmental changes, a system may amplify or use certain deviations as catalysts for change or adaptation rather than resilience or resistance to that change.

Urban design implications: Resilience to change may result, for example, in defensive variations of community development, from alternative cohousing to gated communities, to regulatory approaches that react to and defend community from various forms of development transgressions, in many cases compromised actions. An adaptable approach seeks third and distinct creative paths, seeking novel and innovative outcomes.

P15: Non-linearity

Not in a straight line, course, or direction, i.e. deviant, varying effects within a system that are not proportional to their causes; a movement with an unknown direction and outcome; or initial known direction or trajectory that is changed and altered by deviant effects.

P16: Stratified order

A multi-level, multi-layered system that is composed of integrated, self-organizing wholes with smaller parts that act as parts of the larger whole, resulting in various levels of complexity. This term reflects the human settlement system.

P17: Entropy

The steady and inevitable deterioration of a closed system; in an open system, entropy is an opportunity for renewal and variability within the system as it deconstructs from its "completeness" and renews.

Urban design implications: As the urban designer identifies elements and patterns of deterioration within a human settlement, a larger question emerges via entropy: what are the underlying causes and what opportunities for positive change exist or are possible in the pattern of deterioration? How can that entropy lead to form or direction of renewal? In many cases, it may simply be a matter of identifying the questions surrounding that deterioration. Again, symptoms are not the problem, they are indicators of a systemic issue.

P18: Polarities and bridging

Relationships that are opposite in tendencies and characteristics, yet complementary. Similar to a color wheel wherein color opposites contain combinations and exclusions of the primary colors and as a result are complementary in their relation to the larger whole—red and yellow make orange, with the excluded

ᴶlue the opposite and complementary; red and blue make purple and the excluded and
ᴵᴼʳ is orange; yellow and blue make green and the complementary opposite or polarity is red.
ᴸban design implications: In planning and design, polarities assist in recognizing the temporary
ᴶ or boundaries of community attitudes, pursuits, tensions that define the nature of a dialogue, until
ᴬᴼse polarities undergo changes resulting from the dialogue—referred to as bridging polarities—working
past the tensions of the original limits or opposites to a new and distinctly different place—"thirdspace"—
and allowing the process (not the facilitators) to create new patterns. I have used this extensively in public
involvement processes associated with urban design projects; it requires more time (and budget), and an
interactive interdisciplinary approach.

P19: Thirdspace

The term "thirdspace" has a number of definitions that apply to planning and design: 1) a third and
distinctly different outcome that can embody the principles of the initially opposing entities that are
in tension—advancing the dialogue to a creative non-compromising outcome where the key principles
of each initial tension are incorporated into a new and third dialogue; 2) the resulting relationship(s)
among historical, social/cultural and spatial interactions/transactions; 3) an unknown at the outset of a
planning and design process, at times located in the margins (Soja, 1996) and at other times non-existent
until forged by a creative process; 4) in physics, the "aha!" moment or event of discovery through creative
processes.

   This is discussed at length in later sections of the book.

P20: Probability trajectories (versus planned expectations)

Trajectories are paths or chosen courses of action characterized by an object or system that experiences an
initial propulsion, setting the objects or systems in motion over time along an anticipated path/destination
(curve). "Probable" is a key term in that the destination is not predictive, likely but uncertain. In planning
and design, they can be viewed as self-organizing impulses (propulsion) that have initial direction, movement, initial meaning and inevitable impact(s). I use the word "initial" because once in movement they
begin to change and alter their characteristics based on the changing context within which they move,
and the dynamics of both internal and external forces—thus, the term probability trajectories. They can
be deviant or errant and can serve as catalysts, intended or aligned catalysts for change, and can lead to
new emergent trajectories—new, non-linear directions for change. These trajectories are probability-based,
with uncertain (even though intended) impact locations and outcomes. Probability trajectories are time-
sensitive, altering course and direction based on contextual changes with a non-linear, evolving re-entry
phenomenon.

   Urban design implications: The trajectories represent multiple scenarios of probable outcomes in
urban planning/design—nothing new. The trajectory presents a key role for urban design in that the three-
dimensional nature of an urban design scenario, a visualized probability with buildings (or form-based
massing), landscape elements and principles, compositional order and connectivity components, provides
a community and its stakeholders with educational tools regarding development impacts, possible catalysts
and hybrids. The more scenario trajectories, the greater the range of probabilities that can be assessed. In
many ways, the architectural/urban design competition is an example of multiple probability outcomes
from which a community can learn, test and experiment its built-form path.

P21: Place—the outcome of phenomena between and among people and context

In living systems, incremental spatial outcomes are emergent capsulations of reality, with some outcomes, intentional or not, given special recognition as "place", based on the perception of the space by the individual and his/her experiences in that space over time. This is a critical definition of place from a creative urban perspective in that the 'quality' of the place is based on the observer's perception—not on material objects and compositions alone. Another characteristic of place is 'participatory place' (Ganis, 2015), which can be viewed as creative place that is based on lived experiences that change and evolve into new and differing realities over time. Consequently, "place" can be historic, a current special lived experience, and an evolving and uncertain future based on a changing context.

P22: Transaction

The act of conducting or carrying on activities and communications with two or more other entities—actions associated with relationships and interactions between and among two or more entities. In living systems a transaction is a simultaneous and mutually interdependent interaction between multiple components resulting in the emergence of specific structures (Capra, 1982, p. 267).

Urban design implications: This is a way and perspective of viewing the nature of urban patterns. When a person enters a specific space, it is not just the objects in the space that are experienced; it is the simultaneous sensory experience of temperature, arrangement, color, smell, sounds, etc. that transact in a sensory experience. The designer can assess the composition in its context, not as an isolated object or form but as a "living" system.

P23: Emergent realities

A new and different pattern emerges from changes resulting from multiple, often unnoticed interactions over time, representing a deviation or departure from the ongoing system. In planning and design, they can be represented by symptoms (of change), emergent hybrids: for example, "big box" retail stores in response to shopping malls that integrate a warehousing typology with bulk retail goods under one roof; homeless encampments; "smart" cities.

Urban design implications: Emergent realities in human settlements occur throughout the CST matrix, from changing cultural patterns to their spatial manifestations over time. As designers seek out opportunities and determinants for design in their analysis, these emerging realities, in some cases unusual phenomena, can indicate future changes in established patterns of urban form—the first primitive shopping center or warehouse retail facility or intercept retail center, for example.

P24: Self-similarities (fractals)

An object whose parts at infinitely many levels of magnification appear geometrically similar. The fractal influences the form and characteristics of the larger whole; and its effects are not limited to natural forms. The brick, for example, has characteristics that are reflected in the larger whole (right angles, cube derivative, etc.). Fractals also describe the tracks and marks left by the passage of dynamic activities; they record the images of movement in space and can be viewed as the geometry between dimensions (Briggs, 1992). To many people, the word "geometry" refers to circles, arcs, cubes, etc., when in fact it stands for "earth measure". Fractal geometry offers a framework in which a simple process with a basic operation repeated many times, resulting in a highly irregular pattern. The French-American polymath Benoit Mandelbrot coined the term "fractal" as a general description of a large class of irregular objects (Falconer, 2013).

Urban design implications: This can be the topic of a whole new work—the use of fractals as a design tool in human settlements. I have applied the von Koch curve to building massing studies. The Sierpinski triangle offers visually complex new patterns for development patterns, originating from the repetition of simple patterns.

P25: Watersheds within watersheds—places within places

Watersheds are spatial systems composed directly from the natural relationships within the ecosystem, in this case the flow and direction of water with the landscape and its inhabitants, humans included. Each is a unique phenomenon and related to a larger system, displaying special physical and cultural aspects. The many river watersheds of the Pacific Northwest in Washington State, a part of a larger bioregion, were given specific identities and characterized by the indigenous Salish inhabitants as the Snohomish, the Stillaguamish, the Swinomish, and others—all individual and interrelated. The term "places within places" highlights the transference of this principle to human settlements and urban design regarding the people–context phenomena.

Urban design implications: These watersheds, nested realities, places within places have their own identities based on their individual ecosystems and relate to surrounding and outlying watersheds, all part of a larger system, transferring information and energies (metabolism) to and from one another. What are the boundaries of a project area?

P26: Creative differentiation

This principle has applications to the overall creative process and to the creative potentials within individual people and groups such as communities. Regarding the creative process, it represents in this discussion four different formative aspects of the creative cycle: a sequencing that has two halves and four periods of change. The first half is the differentiation phase, as a new entity separates from its original context, evolves or matures, and assumes a unique form. In the second phase, the entity integrates back into its creative context, forming a new and larger whole—thus a differentiation phase and an integration phase. The four phases of evolution that also apply to human personalities (all with creative potential) include: pre-axis—an elemental language of the body; early-axis—symbolic, metaphorical, visual imagery, inspirational characteristics; middle-axis—the "sweat/work" phase, confronting the reality of the creative entity, its evaluation; and late-axis—moving from the mystery of the formless (pre-axis) to a reality that has both possibility and first form (early-axis) to the challenge to solidify the entity form (middle-axis) to the phase of giving that form its final expression; followed by its integration back into its creative context (Johnston, 1991).

Working with people, we discuss the creative potentials of all personality patterns.

Urban design implications: When sitting around a table of stakeholders in a workshop, for example, all appearing similar in basic cultural patterns, all have a creative-difference potential and may view the same challenge in many contrasting ways. Recognizing these differences is an important beginning to a real dialogue on community issues. The same concept applies to sectors of the city, appearing similar and defined by differences that need to be recognized and incorporated into any design analysis.

P27: Creative capacity

The creative capacity of a system is its potential and ability to be creative within itself, with the implication of the system's capability to heal and change itself as a self-organizing entity. In applications to planning and design, I discuss the use of creative capacitance as a primary focus for planners and designers, not merely the symptoms that are indicators of a decrease in that capacitance.

P28: Simulation

To imitate, to fashion a representation or model of an existing situation (or design).

Urban design implications: Simulating a design is not equal to generating a design: one is a representation of a style, model, etc. (a "Georgetown" residential typology in Portland, Oregon); the other is novel.

P29: Perception

The organization, identification and interpretation of sensory information in order to represent and understand a given situation or environment (see Arnheim, 1969).

P30: Perceptual horizon

A minimum perception of "design" required to engage design: knowing its elements and principles and how they can be applied; the need to go beyond rhetoric, urban form/design history as a basis for design participation.

P31: Phase transition

Transitions exist as connections. In physics, phase transitions are transformations of matter from one state to another, i.e. water to ice. Transition is a structural change between levels of relative stability or order in a human settlement, where structure and function change during transition and the system or community takes on new properties (de Roo and Rauws, 2012).

P32: Bifurcation

Occurrences in dynamic systems triggered by small changes in parts of the system that cause sudden "qualitative" or "topological" change in systems behavior.

Urban design implications: One example is that of the catalytic approach to urban design (Attoe and Logan, 1989), where a small change inserted into the larger system can cause significant changes in the built form.

The dynamics of human settlements: the trialectic of culture/space/time—the CST matrix

Human settlements, as living systems, are imbued with ongoing interactions among three broad categories of human activity: culture (C), space (S) and time (T). Culture represents the social, economic, political, and behavioral forces of settlements; space represents the natural and manufactured objects and spatial patterns defining these settlements; and time represents the historic and event periods of human activity. They all interact simultaneously, not in separate or partial engagements, generating complex relationships and situations. It is these relationships, not simply buildings and infrastructure objects or isolated functions, that urban design needs to engage. This is part of a discussion, a dialogue on directions and approaches I have seen emerging over the last 42 years of practice and decades of teaching urban design. I argue that we as designers need to expand our experimentation with means and methods needed to engage complex CST relationships in real contexts. The CST matrix is the basis for the forces or dynamics of human settlements—challenging urban designers to create and adapt compositional orders that respond to these relationships.

The demonstrations and experiments in later chapters are not based on set "rules" and are guided by principles from the arts as starting spatial activators. They are experiments in creative problem-solving that can test theory and lead to new directions in perspective, approach, means, and methods.

Theory is a set of well-developed concepts related through statements or expressions of relationship, which together constitute an integrated framework that can be used to explain or predict phenomena (Strauss and Corbin, 1998, p. 15). These *concepts* are generalized ideas or abstract notions, not formulae, and are therefore speculative, based on conclusions resulting from observations of unusual or emerging occurrences in communities and their larger civilizations. Theory provides the practice of urban design with starting points and initial direction: principles that guide process and discovery of new or novel solutions. These are not absolute and are functions of the workings of civilization, its arts, science and philosophies. And they are constantly changing.

Theory is only as good as its application to reality (living systems) and does not exist in an academic vacuum. It evolves from the dynamics of the multiple dimensions of reality, responding to emerging patterns, and in turn is altered by the interaction with those patterns as they mature. Urban design's strength is that it provides a series of tests as physical/spatial constructs within community contexts that assist communities in increasing their capability to self-organize and evolve—always challenging current theories.

Consequently, as we explore living systems theory as a foundation and umbrella *guide* for urban planning and design processes, we need to understand the basis for the complexity resulting from the myriad of multi-level interactions in human settlements as this complexity is the catalyst for urban design composition and order.

The complexity matrix (CST)

CST and the n-dimensional matrix

The CST matrix, derived in part from the work of Soja and Lefebvre, symbolizes the basic essences of human settlements as defined through the resulting relationships of culture, space and time/history: the trialectics of spatiality—the production of space. As in Figure 2.1, we are designing for the resultant relationships of dynamic interactions that emanate from the trialectic of CST, not one or two but all three aspects of community. This obviously is not easy and requires interdisciplinary best practices to identify and engage these complex relationships—the strength and contribution of urban planning domains. Spatiality is a key ingredient and not separate from culture and time/history—the strength of the design domains. They require integration in their analytical approaches and processes. And the implications for urban design are clear: packaged solutions or applications used as plug-ins with little regard to context are not contributing

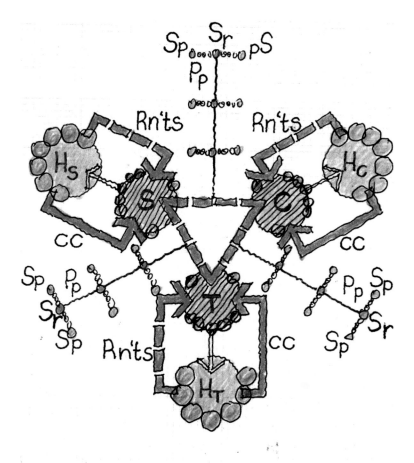

Figure 2.1. CST design complexity diagram. *Culture, space, and time are necessary integral parts of the design process for human settlements. Not one, nor two, but all three are part of settlement analysis, thus increasing complexity as a state of being. As space and culture, space and time, and culture and time are explored and assessed, relationships between and among the forces of CST are identified as significant interactions (Sr) and significant polarities (Sp). Each level of polarities has contextual characteristics (scale relevant: global, national, regional, metropolitan, city, district, neighborhood, etc.). Within each level, space-program elements are identified, including those within the significant polarities for testing. The larger view also assesses the historic/time aspect of the CST forces (Hs, Hc, Ht) for coherent or continuing contributions (CC) to the meaning and functionality of settlements, and those remnants (Rn'ts) that exist and may have potential for reinvention into and as a critical part of contemporary emergent design compositions.*

to a creative process; they are simulations at best. So, let us begin the CST discussion with context as the underlying container for CST.

Context—the game board

Context is not synonymous with background or setting, as in a stage set. A word that is often misused in planning and design, context represents the state of reality for a given time, location, environment, and level of human activity. It is not just physical, not just social, and not just an historical pattern—in the words of Lefebvre and Soja; it is perceived space, conceived space, and lived space. When context is observed from this perspective, the game board changes dramatically for urban design analysis, requiring collaborative and interdisciplinary approaches to design processes.

Context can be viewed as the historic and current urban form with layers of cultural and historic meaning, relating culture to form as best as possible; and providing clues as to the trajectories of future form patterns.

Culture

Culture is the core of the CST trialectic or matrix, representing the patterned behavior of peoples over time in space representing social-economic–political and behavioral interactions within human settlements. Culture can be established or traditional, transitional, emergent, deviant and in the margins of community, as in Soja's discussion of Los Angeles (Soja, 1996, 2000). The needs, demands, characteristics, and expressions of culture all contribute to a complexity of context that cannot be ignored or bottom-lined in the design process. To address housing issues in a city, for example, as limited to the percentage of deteriorated houses on a block, crime occurrences in a neighborhood, single-parent households, and renters versus owner-occupied houses is scratching the surface, as it does not address relationships between and among the CST factors.

And in the culture of modern cities there is a tension among design for design's sake, design for social benefit and design as a tool of corporate marketing. As stated by Knox (2011, p. 6), an important function of design is in social reproduction, where it creates settings and images that structure and challenge community values and world-views of different class factions and contribute to "moral geographies" that express particular or specific value systems in material form—creating relevant spatial metaphors. These moral geographies celebrate difference, diversity, creativity, and authenticity.

The role of corporate capitalism and marketing as a part of contemporary cultural patterns is a major challenge for designers, creating a polarity between communities of authenticity and "cathedrals of consumption" (Knox, 2011, p. 9). Cities are branded for marketing purposes, i.e. "creative cities movement" (Mould, 2017) as a classification of cities as opposed to cities that are inherently creative.

> Therefore, Creative City policies such as rebranding, focusing on creative industry activity, attracting the creative class, building Cultural Quarters and Media Cities, beautifying public spaces around cultural and creative rhetoric, generally espousing an aura of "cool"—they have all become all too obvious markers of a homogeneous strategy of capitalistic accumulation.
>
> (Mould, 2017, p. 165)

This marketing of culture is reinforced in *Cities of Difference* (Fincher and Jacobs, 1998), wherein the notion of "aestheticization" is discussed as the self-conscious exploitation of cultural capital. Jacobs identifies and characterizes a new cultural logic of development "exploiting cultural differences as events-led planning, gentrification, the process of selling a city image, the expansion of sites of consumption, and even the rise of urban design as the new planning common sense" (Fincher and Jacobs, 1998, p. 252).

Our focus on culture is on a search for and understanding of real urban behavior as opposed to inauthentic diversity (Fincher and Jacobs, 1998). A point of beginning is to understand what has been appropriated for consumptive goals versus what components and relationships within culture(s) retain their unique differences and identities. Consumptive cultural exploitation may always be a part of city dynamics, and there is a need to reinforce and celebrate the politics of differentiation—a place of creative potentials. Many practitioners, myself included, with good intentions, used cultural differences for urban design forms to celebrate differences, selectively using the local and the past in reassembling the desired elements in an orchestrated pastiche as solutions—festival spaces and sanitized and exoticized ethnic enclaves (Fincher and Jacobs, 1998).

Does this mean we, as urban designers, can't propose or design festival spaces, event places, etc.? Hardly. What is requiresd is a clear and interactive involvement with these cultural differences within cities, where the design solutions emanate from the community, possibly with smaller, even messier (almost spontaneous) places and spaces that actually serve the community rather than advertise it—localized urban design projects forged through local political will, not from the outside, where they are smaller, localized and articulated by the community. The urban designer is a key and important element of this localized process, assisting the cultures of difference in understanding, testing and forming authentic projects, possibly approaching an "otherness" resulting from a creative problem-solving process. This is the beginning phase of the designer's assistance in the strengthening of a community's creative capacitance.

Simplified methods, packaged models, franchise designs and applications are no longer sufficient to deal with this complexity in cultural differences. And since *design is a function of culture* (Lazano et al., 1990), it needs to address the dynamics of culture, including its politics in design metaphors. Design remains the "making of composition and form" where decisions on physical/spatial orders and outcomes are needed by communities. The design process becomes personal (the designer is a part of and immersed in the process) as well as a part of the larger public (and private) dialogue, and results in incremental contributions and changes to the ever-changing urban reality. And these incremental resolutions are then connected to adjacent and nearby urban components involving a form of connectivity design (more on this later). This is not about diminishing the designer's role but greatly expanding the scope and responsibility of that role: engaging with the different set of localities, histories, cultures, and social issues.

> *Principle: culture has or leaves an imprint and patterning on the built form and continues as an evolving and emergent response to itself and surrounding context, coupled with the newly obsolescent and the newly emergent.*
> *Principle: within a larger culture of a civilization, there are multiple levels of cultural "watersheds," cells, places or containers each with their own identities and patterns and directly or loosely interconnected; the authenticity of these watersheds is critical to forging a responsive and responsible urban form.*
> *Principle: culture exists in an interactive relationship with space over time, not in a vacuum or absolute state.*

Space

Space has many dimensions based particularly in how it is perceived by the observer(s): geographer, planner, urban designer, architect and landscape architect, regulator, psychologist, politician and participant–resident etc. It is natural, comprised of organic parts, i.e. a watershed; social/cultural (imprinted from human interactions over time); practical, as in a street—symbolic, metaphorical, remnant and left over. It ranges from creative/unique/novel to packaged, franchised and reproduced. According to Lefebvre (1992), space can be perceived (made aware of/understood), conceived (imagined/intentional/planned), and lived (engaged/experienced). It can be both a cherished personal space and a commodity for branding and marketing—for capturing the consumer, as in shopping mall typologies. The craftspeople who make a space leave an imprint through their tools and methods (and cultures); users leave their imprint, from feelings of a sharing or need fulfilled to territorial markings through various forms of graffiti. In this manner, space is coveted for various reasons, occupied and defended (Ardrey, 1966).

During the 1960s and 1970s, architects and designers experimented with the relationship of human behavior to space, from concepts of territoriality (Ardrey, Sommer, Hall) to the work of Christopher Alexander (*Pattern Language*, 1977). In *Enclosing Behavior* (1977), Robert Bechtel argues that "there is no such thing as the design of space or spaces. *Behavior*, not space, is enclosed by architecture" (p. vii). These concepts were not new but the means and methods to analyze them were emerging in non-design fields. Bechtel argued for techniques based in ecological psychology, including behavior-setting surveys. More currently, studies in creative differences (Johnston, 1991 and others) address the relationship of behavior through personality to space. Over time the fields of psychology and psychiatry took the lead in behavioral aspects of human–space relations. The point here is that the study of space has taken on a complexity well beyond the experiences of planners and designers, and underscores the multi-dimensional nature of "spatiality", and argues against franchised approaches to design.

Let's go back to basics: space is physical and material, composed of objects in compositional relationships, composed of vertical, tilted, and horizontal planes, enclosing and representing values, economies, politics, emotions, stories and needs. As *place*, space is an assembled metaphor for urban meaning and functionality in real, often raw or coarse, contexts. The metaphors range from compromised space to space with special meaning as *place*; from spaces of dominance and power to those on the periphery, resistant to that dominance and open to creative actions. As explored in this work, meaningful space requires a discovery process within the creative capacity of a particular community—a process of self-organization that transcends "master planning" and goal planning with "predictive physical outcomes"—a non-linear evolutionary process.

Lefebvre discusses the distinction between the "problematic of space" and "spatial practice", where the former can be formulated on a theoretical level and the latter is empirically observable. The "problematic" consists of questions about mental and social space and their interconnections, and links with nature and with "pure" forms. As urban designers, we deal with spatial practice—where space is observed, described, analyzed, and manufactured. And yet, the problematic aspect of space underlies the nature and meaning of spatial compositions. Space is both personal and political, one being a form of self-awareness and management and the other a place of tensions and conflicts.

Some key principles:

Principle: every human action has a spatial outcome and manifestation.

This seems obvious and yet is overlooked by many professionals who find it convenient to isolate or separate human action from spatial interaction for the ease of analysis. The object of the analysis is the relationship between and among culture/space/time, not each category.

An experiment that I give beginning planning students: where there are three or more housemates in a dwelling, related or not, observe, record, and visually diagram how each housemate undertakes certain key activities related to the spatial construct of the dwelling. Does one study in the living room with music and people around? Does another require quiet and insulation from the general activities? Does one study in a space adjacent to, somewhat separated from, yet semi-involved with group activities? This is only one layer of observation that can be done to underscore the relationship of activity to space construct—and what various individuals do to manipulate a generic space (a house with four bedrooms, etc.) in order to accommodate a specific activity.

Principle: space as outcome is uncertain at the beginning of the design process, even though initially intended or instigated by a set of desires and needs, particularly over time.

Spatial compositions are intentional constructs that go through three major phases of "being": the act of designing/composing, complete with its own divergent aspects related to context and community input and diverse authorship; the act of being placed into, engaged and tested by contextual forces; and the act of being changed or altered by that testing, leading to uncertainty. This uncertainty may not be observable in the immediate aftermath of the design-context placement and becomes more apparent over time—a new learning opportunity.

Principle: human space emerges as a built environment, a physical form (composition in context), pauses and generally meets its specified intended needs and aspirations, and recedes into obsolescence or obscurity.

Space can be understood as an emergent phenomenon as the human actions (and those of related life forms and earth functions) generate and manipulate the spatial environment, from the ant hill to the gated community to the skyscraper. All spatial compositions are held accountable to the reality and principles of physics and biology: they grow, pause, or sustain for a brief time, then degrade, collapse, and reconfigure. Space is emergent with the polarity of decadency.

Principle: space is influenced by the dynamics of its location in the CST system or matrix:

- center: stable (through a dynamic balance—not dormant), static, convergent
- mid-ground: working, managed
- periphery: less stable, resistant, transforming, divergent
- adjacent: in tension or alignment
- nearby: associative
- remote: detached or disengaged, deviant, errant.

The CST matrix of community interactions affects the nature of space and the dynamics or capacity of that space to be creative. In the social districts or containers of human settlements, the established centers are stable or static, the former as a center in dynamic balance, the latter not dynamic, possibly lacking in an ability to change and be creative relevant to evolving forces in society. Space is open to political impacts, i.e. the catastrophic impacts of shopping malls or intercept centers on small community downtown retail districts—often the results of political and economic decisions—where "There is no unspatialized social reality" (Soja, 1996, p. 46)—from land use to design standards to zoning. And the power is often at the center—dominant. The interaction of cells or parts within the CST matrix is influenced by the intensity of interaction among those parts as they move farther from the center. Various relationships exist and change, with levels of intensity of interaction ranging from analogous compatibility to tension to contrast and conflict. The further out toward the periphery, the more internal demand for change and the more creative and divergent the forces for change.

Space then is composed of multiple dimensions, beginning with the physical and material, layered with a functionality and a social/cultural logic and imprint; again, layered with personal and community meaning—a form of hyperspace (Kaku, 1994), a dynamic vibration. It remains revered or at least appreciated and antiseptic or speculative. For the urban designer, space is inherently related to culture and time/history, carrying meaning and function in a coherent pattern, and changing and being manipulated by the dynamics of culture and time/history. We explore and experiment with compositional structures that can go beyond the accepted and conventional transformations of form, engaging new patterns as they emerge, identifying and incorporating remnant patterns that linger from previous time periods, through connecting and bridging actions—pursuing creative novel design solutions.

Time/history

Time is a measurement of reality, incorporated with the three known space coordinates (x, y, z, n), making space and time intricately and intimately connected to form a continuum known as "space-time", where space can never be discussed without time, and vice versa. Time is something (a dimension) that acts to define the "stuff" of experience as much as the space coordinates . . . every act or idea has a place in time, as time (Johnston, 1984/1986). Since time always has a place in time, it is an ever-changing measurement where time frames the emergence, pausing (dynamic balance), and receding of all human actions. The creation and erasure of spatial patterns in the changing settlement landscape occur within event-periods. In human settlements, these event-periods mark a cultural–spatial relationship that leaves its mark in traditions, means and methods, and physical "handprints" in space.

Principle: history is knowledge expressed in behavioral/cultural patterns, physical artifacts and spatial patterns.

Past event-periods are expressed in elements and patterns remembered and/or remaining in the built environment. They have/had a physical presence and may or may not have current relevance. They can be preserved in stories, as monuments, as cultural reminders or celebrations, or incorporated into new emergent patterns as bridges to the future, with new meaning and functionality. Their historical dynamics remain incorporated in the present realities to varying degrees.

Principle: current time represents a bridging between the past and the future, ranging from the measurement of stable dynamics to emergent catalysts or catastrophic changes.

All current time events are emergent, pausing, or descendant. The pausing state is a short-lived dynamic balance highlighted by periods of alignment and coherence that are always on the verge of flux.

Principle: future time is uncertain, containing probabilities at most, not predictions or guarantees, essentially non-existent.

Time is a dimension inherent in every human action and its spatial manifestation.

The CST matrix provides a guide to the relationships within human settlements resulting from the reality of multiple interactions between and among cultural, spatial and time forces. These interactions produce realities that are complex, complicated, political, in tension and multi-directional regarding "next steps". How do we as urban designers address and design within this complexity?

Complexity thinking and complexity theory—means and methods to engage the human settlements as self-organizing living systems

Historically, planning and design focused on the identification of the urban dynamics of human settlements in order to solve urban problems (Portugali et al., 2012). Planning and the design fields of architecture and landscape architecture have for years separated and evaluated aspects of urban dynamics, dealing with comprehensive planning as opposed to integrative planning (and design). Given the nature of the basis for human settlement complexity (discussed in the next section regarding the CST matrix), new approaches have filtered down from the study of creative or living systems that deal with urban dynamics for their own sake—as interactive and integral relationships where design is inherent in the process. Key principles applicable to these emergent methods include:

- the unpredictability of cities as complex systems
- urban dynamics as nonlinear and ever-emergent
- human settlements have the capability to be self-organizing entities
- the need to develop pluralistic processes with means and methods relevant to collaborative strategies of planning and design
- embrace the uncertainty, ambiguity, and openness of creative problem-solving as a nonlinear path to discovery, novelty and innovation for human settlements.

There are differing approaches to studying and applying creative systems theory to urban planning and design that provide a current framework for this overview. Two are discussed here.

Quantitative approach
Santa Fe Institute (North America)
CTC (complexity theory for cities—Europe)
Characteristics: simulation models, scientific evaluations

Qualitative approach
Capra (1982)
Johnston, Institute for Creative Development (North America)
CPS (creative problem-solving—North America)
Characteristics: generation, openness, uncertainty, creative

This list can be expanded and serves as a starting point for this discussion.

Theory of complexity for human settlements

Complexity as a state of being and a theory

As is discussed in the following section, the interactions or urban dynamics of culture (social, economic, political, behavioral aspects), space (physical elements and compositions), and time (history, time events or periodicities) produce a reality that is complex: ranging from messy and disheveled to novel and innovative, often interwoven in the same tapestry. This constitutes a state of reality that urbanists of all backgrounds are confronted with on a daily basis: it is not separated, categorized and neatly packaged. In the larger related context, primarily through physics going back to the 1920s, a body of work emerges that addresses the complexity with complex living systems, the multi-variable and unknowns previously avoided through convenient, not relevant methodologies—the emergence of complexity theory.

Years ago, I was introduced to the movie *Mindwalk* (Bernt Amadeus Capra, 1990), starring Liv Ullman, John Hurt and Sam Waterston, and the work of physicist Fritjof Capra (*Tao of Physics*, 1991 and *The Turning Point*, 1982), Bernt's brother, regarding living systems and ecology. For me, it initiated a fascinating exploration of systems and complexity theory emanating from physics, at times dizzying (Kaku, 1994) and at times directly connected to planning and design.

They say there is no such thing as coincidence. Possibly correct: years ago, after flirting with Capra's literature, I sat on the curb of our dead-end street in Seattle for a break during a neighborhood volleyball game. My new neighbor sat next to me and we began the usual new friend conversations. My neighbor was/is Charles (Charlie) Johnston, MD, founder and director of the Institute for Creative Development (ICD), a psychiatrist and author of, at that time, *The Creative Imperative* (1989) and, later, *Necessary Wisdom* (1991). Both books made the connection between living systems and human relationships—work that I was able to incorporate into my urban planning and design public involvement processes. Another door opened.

From there other readings contributed to this new direction, with questions on their impacts for how professionals approached urban design. Examples of these readings include Waldrop's *Complexity* (1992), where I was introduced to the concept of *spontaneous self-organization*, *insight* as the ability to see connections not just isolated problems in the built form, and the *edge of chaos* as the balance point where the components never quite lock into place but never reach turbulence; and the complexity approach—made of patterns that change and partly, but never quite repeat, that are always new and different. And a thought that I cherish—complexity, where new ideas and innovative genotypes are forever nibbling away at the edges of the status quo. I discuss this further in the section on coherence.

Another contributor at that time: Mark Ward (*Beyond Chaos*, 2001):

Universality implies that our desire to know everything is doomed to failure. It shows that many complex systems that make up and punctuate our lives are essentially unpredictable. We should not strive to understand what will forever remain unpredictable. Change is part of the deal, so we would do well to get used to it. If you are looking for certainties you have come to the wrong existence.

(Ward, 2001, p. 294)

Others: *The Background of Ecology: Concept and Theory* (McIntosh, 1985), *Quantum Reality: Beyond the New Physics* (Herbert, 1985), and many more. As one can observe, this material can be abstract and very distant from the planning and design of cities. And it has generated a new paradigm that challenges the means and methods of planning and design. And it has raised new questions on how and why we design.

Enter the CTC: complexity theory for cities and the Sante Fe Institute

I think it is safe to say that current complexity theory is not a monolithic theory, but has rather become a tool box for dealing with complex systems, e.g. the growth of cities, population dynamics, etc. . . . [and] that a close cooperation between experimentalists, observers . . . and theoreticians . . . will be the most important thing for the further development to this field.

(Haken, 2012, p. 19)

As in the previously mentioned references, complexity theories emerged from questioning scientists in the 1960s, with Capra, Haken and Prigogine, among others, examining physical-material systems that exhibit phenomena of emergence and self-organization that were previously regarded as typifying organic or even socio-cultural systems, but not material systems (Portugali et al., 2012). Thus began the studies of cities as complex, self-organizing systems, and the theories affect all domains of study, urban planning and design. The CTC movement is led by theorists such as Juval Portugali, Hermann Haken, Peter M. Allen, Stephen Read, Han Meyer, Egbert Stolk, Ekim Tan and others in Europe (see Portugali et al., 2012). The list is extensive, the range of applications is broad, and again the door has been opened with the question for all urbanists: how can urban *design* be redefined and applied in light of these new directions and principles?

The Sante Fe Institute, founded in 1984, Sante Fe, New Mexico, is an independent theoretical research institute focusing on the multidisciplinary study of the fundamental principles of complex adaptive systems.

While uncertainty is a constant in assessing urban futures, action is still required to shape the built form in ways that meet the needs of the populace and enable creative capacities in human settlements. Cities are intrinsically unpredictable; a future city cannot simply be the built-out product of a creator's imagination (e.g. master planning) in the way a building can be, nor is it growing like an organism as there is no knowable optimal form of target organism to steer towards (Batty and Marshall, 2012). Thus, the reference to an evolving non-linear system—creative.

Complexity theory is inherent to creative or living systems, based on the myriad interactions of the many parts within the systems, and the uncertain and unpredictable outcomes emerging from those inter-actions. The following section explores principles within creative systems that in my opinion and experience have direct applicability to urban planning and design.

A summary of those principles (P) is as follows:

- spontaneous self-organizing entities (communities)
- adaptive versus resilient entities/accommodation versus assimilation: the "holon"
- an open process, at times ambiguous, with uncertain outcomes evolving through a dynamic process
- trajectories of probable possibilities versus predictable outcomes
- place as a participant and transactional process
- connected increments: the power of connectivity—a fundamental role for urban design.

Creative problem-solving: engaging complexity in urban design

Creative problem-solving (CPS) is a non-linear evolutionary process characterized by discovery forging novel solutions that can lead to innovation—and creative outcomes. I explored CPS in *Play in Creative Problem-solving for Planners and Architects* (Kasprisin, 2016) as it relates to the design domains, in particular urban design, planning, architecture and landscape architecture. As a part of that process, the concept of play as a free activity without failure was integrated into the process as the spark for discovery in CPS. As we search for additional means and methods to address the complex interactions in human settlements, we gain from a departure from linear or normative problem-solving, increasing our creative capacities to arrive at meaningful "solutions" to urban challenges. I focus on play as both a process and a means throughout the demonstrations and experiments in later chapters.

Creative problem-solving is a generative process, divergent (away from the center) in polarity to assimilation/convergent process of bringing together ideas and information (for analysis). Both are neces-sary aspects of design thinking. Generation is not the uncovering of something that exists (in the informa-tion and context); it is the creation of something novel arising from a dynamic process. Consequently, *design* is a process that is particularly suited to be a driving force that can address complex urban challenges—and it involves the "making of something real".

As I discuss in *Play in Creative Problem-solving for Planners and Architects*, the work of psychologists Cropley and Cropley provided the foundation for the application of CPS to the design domains. The fol-lowing principles and characteristics of creative problem-solving are based on the writings of the Cropleys, Edward Soja, Henri Lefebvre, Charles Johnston, and others.

Principles of creative problem-solving

1   CPS generates ideas based on the construction of theories rather than the testing of a given theory: avoiding established "models", "beliefs", clichés and conventions.

2   CPS has available and employs the analytical tools for the handling of masses of raw data from the CST awareness matrix using both qualitative and quantitative methodologies from within crafting and digital methods, skills and tools.

3   CPS evaluates those ideas that include the consideration of alternative meanings and phenomena, and exhibits an awareness of emergent realities and phenomena.

4   CPS is systemic and creative simultaneously, and utilizes visual thinking processes to organize and structure relationships and emergent ideas.

5   CPS identifies, develops and relates the concepts that are the building blocks of (new) theory.

6   CPS exploits the novelty resulting from those ideas and/or theories—leading to innovation.

(Adapted from Kasprisin, 2016, pp. 16–18)

These are a combination of CPS principles or basic rules for both product-generation (making something) and use in grounded theory research. A CPS process requires different approaches and methods from those now practiced in most educational institutions and design offices to deal with complex, multi-layered sets of information and idea discovery. This path toward creativity applies to all fields and not just those of traditional (urban) design. CPS also requires a solid foundation of knowledge or historical information assembled as relationships of meaning and functionality in order for that idea discovery to emerge. Creativity does not occur in a void. All information is viewed as emergent or descending, based on the cultural, spatial and time/history forces (CST matrix) at the heart of those relationships.

Essential characteristics of CPS

Key characteristics or descriptions of CPS include the following:

1   Cognition (gaining knowledge through awareness, reasoning and judgement) that utilizes an integration of analytical and symbolic/imaginal processes through a whole mind–body thought process of intellectual and sensory thought or perception (thinking with the senses).

2   A recognition of *problem-in-context* that is evolutionary and emergent, not predetermined—a matrix of problems to be recognized.

3   A process that is prolonged and demanding.

4   A process that combines abstract thinking with real-life experiences and case studies.

5   A process that requires developed skills which are usually domain specific, i.e. architecture and urban design, with special materials, tools and techniques.

6   A process that requires practice in skill and methodology.

7   A process that contains symbolic object-learning through "play" as an energizer and experimentation activity, activated by compositional principles.

8   A process that has a definitive product, something that is made, i.e., fashioned, composed, strategized, etc.

(Adapted from Kasprisin, 2016)

These principles and characteristics are the foundation for the compositional exercises later in the book.

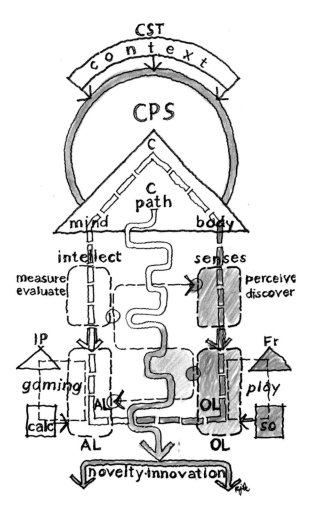

Figure 2.2. Creative problem-solving diagram. *As a guide to the major components of the CPS process, the diagram highlights the major elements in relationship. CST (culture, space, time); CPS—Cpath (creativity path)—Mind (intellect)—AL (analytical learning)— calc (the "calculator")—Gaming—Body (senses)—Fr (Froebel)—OL (object learning)—SO (symbolic object)—Play.*

Implications for urban design

This book explores alternate means and methods leading to meaningful and contextually relevant urban form. This section highlights key principles that can be used to enrich existing urban design processes. It is not inclusive and hopefully can assist in a continuing dialogue in the design community regarding complexity and creative approaches to urban problems and challenges. And the pursuit of creative solutions to urban situations does not mean new formulated or packaged typologies.

- Implications for urban design: means and methods:
  - a multi-level view or perspective of human settlement spatial dynamics
  - designing for constantly changing realities
  - incremental design contributions to the emergent whole
  - longer-term probability design trajectories (as an alternative to the master plan approach)
  - connectivity between and among emergent (possibly creative) spatial patterns
  - a multi-level view or perspective of human settlement spatial dynamics.

HUMAN SETTLEMENT DYNAMICS

Human settlements are self-organizing, potentially creative entities—comprising dynamic interactions of CST

Creative urbanism is founded on principles of creative processes that lead to relevant, unique or novel solutions for human settlements (implied in "urbanism"), as opposed to conventions, typologies, models and franchised products. The former is context relevant and the latter is contextually blind based on narrow parameters such as economics, political compromises or design styles. By placing the word "creative" on the table, the process of urban design takes on new and dynamic meaning for all who are engaged in city-building.

Creative urbanism is a unique spatial response to the CST matrix, an anomaly, localized within an adequate context (human settlement watershed) with center(s), mass, edges and edge energy.

The word "creative" is loaded as we pursue the notion that a creative problem-solving process can result in a creative urban outcome—unique and innovative; and it can contain conventions and typologies that adhere to a principle of relevant coherence. More on this later.

A key underlying principle of creative urbanism is the self-organizing capability of human settlements to change in structure and (meaning) from within, through various reactions to the relationships of and among people and their environments.

It is not an absolute or universal principle and is dependent on a key characteristic within the settlement: a capacity for creativity and creative actions. Creative capacity is enabled by an open-ended process with uncertain outcomes, essentially tolerating a state of ambiguity within the process; the capability to adapt to relational interchanges; an acceptance that rules and principles change as the creative process evolves; and the challenge of maintaining the integrity of the dynamics of the creative process. This has significant implications for spatial orders and compositions.

Within the "urbanism" aspect of the creative settlement are key characteristics such as scale hierarchy (watersheds within watersheds); diversity; multiple dimensions which we define as the CST matrix; and the complexity that emerges from the interactions of the CST matrix.

Let's explore the key characteristics and dynamics of creative urbanism as we prepare to make the connection between this concept of human settlements and design—the making of spatial order, structure and composition in consort with that uniqueness. These include:

- the CST matrix: dynamic relationships within human settlements
- scale hierarchy: human settlement watersheds within the larger whole
- complexity as a state of being resulting from intricate, complicated interconnected parts and a theory of emerging order and structure in complex systems
- self-organizing/structuring capability
- coherence (and departure)
  - coherence can rely on selected typologies that have integrity and viability
  - departure is divergence through discovery of novel and innovative outcomes
- creative capacity
- emergent realities
- spatial structure and order
  - probability-based composition
  - beyond typology and urban form history (identifying typologies is not sufficient to address changing and emerging patterns and forces in human settlements)

- – history of urban form provides guidelines regarding typologies and are less relevant as design tools because they are displaced from original context
- – diffused composition and emergent compositions
- – catalytic events and resulting energy
- • connectivity within the scale hierarchy
- • probability strategies.

Creative capacity and differences

For a system to engage challenges and ongoing change, creative problem-solving is essential in arriving at the next plateau of uniqueness and innovation. That problem-solving requires an ability or capacity for creative actions on the part of a community's inhabitants. This also includes an acceptance and tolerance for creative differences that can lead to creative discovery, innovation and a larger creative urbanism.

Designing for constantly changing realities

As discussed earlier, urban design needs to address human settlements as constantly changing realities, not relying on conventions or typologies in the long run, constantly assessing changes to the spatial structure and order of communities. Typologies have a viable role as starting points in the design process and are also constantly changing and adapting to the CST matrix.

Incremental design contributions to the emergent whole

The formation of cities and settlements requires the making and construction of buildings, open space, and infrastructure on a constant and daily basis. These are incremental contributions to a larger evolving whole always in process. Each design element needs to be viewed in relationship to the emergent whole, not as a separate stable island, even when the emergent whole is uncertain—a daunting challenge to say the least. This is why the process needs to be dynamic, always active. "Smart" cities, for example, need to be smart beyond the technological monitoring of infrastructure, where the aspects of culture and time are incorporated into that "smart" monitoring and assessment.

Longer-term probability design trajectories (as an alternative to the master plan approach)

Issues for discussion:

- • Planning for the future—are comprehensive and master planning obsolete?
- • Integral "planning".
- • Nested realities or islands in the sky?
- • Probability trajectories and catalytic start-ups (implants).

Integral planning and design are in practice in many communities where the design of elements is assessed with the changing reality (ascendant or descendant) of context. This is not an easy task as separate domains can be in conflict or competition regarding various problems and challenges. The technology exists to integrate not simply coordinate the relationships involved in the impacts of current activities and long-term implications of those activities. Let us take the idea of "smart" cities and expand that notion to the larger CST matrix.

Development and the emergent urban form are usually associated with districts, neighborhoods, definable areas, city sectors, etc. and can be viewed as urban watersheds or "nested realities", each acting or forming within itself and yet connected to adjacent or nearby sectors with varying relationships that go beyond their own borders. When defining a "project area", the adequate area or context may go well beyond the initial or obvious context. (A project in a given neighborhood may have an adequate context of five surrounding and nearby neighborhoods, based on aspects of the CST matrix.)

The master plan is and has been a valuable guide for the development of city sectors for infrastructure and other development components. Their value is in the short term rather than the long term due to the changing nature of cities and the CST relationships. An idea for consideration relates to probability trajectories (Miller, 2017), wherein Miller describes the *formless trajectory* as defined by projects that "resist the certainties and confidences of previously dominant paradigms surrounding architectural form. Design work associated with this trajectory intentionally avoids formal order, lacks bravado and disrupts visual and spatial coherence" (p. 50). Order is not defined by "formal", and the parts are favored over the wholes as their creativity contributes to the wholes. This, explains Miller, is a shift from topological clarity and uniform geometric resolution toward indefinite patterning and localized order. It can be viewed as a pursuit of disorder within spatial principles.

A trajectory is an action with initiation force, propulsion, movement, direction, and impact forming either a dispersal effect or catalytic effect. Here are key aspects of trajectories useful in urban design strategies (all probability trajectories have a core structure with variable connectors, a core variability with organizing principles, that do not abide by a dominant paradigm and have multiple outcome hybrids).

- *Diffusive trajectories*
  The impact is widespread, impacting a larger number of people, not intense.
- *Errant trajectories*
  Open-ended, free flowing, experimental.
- *Emergent trajectories*
  Based on emergent patterns, often differing from established context.
- *Catalytic trajectories*
  Intended to cause certain impact actions or reactions to a specific context.
- *Deviant trajectories*
  Intentional trajectories intended to disrupt or divert conventional patterns with uncertain results.
- *Preservation trajectories*
  Builds on historic remnants as bridges to the future, explores new forms of preservation.

Impact areas for trajectories are viewed as probable compositions based on multiple hybrids and can be self-organizing once in motion.

So, how can this work? Urban design has the advantage of visualizing probabilities in semi-abstract to realistic representations. I may begin with a predictive trajectory, the conventional and articulated master plan scenario, complete with infrastructure, buildings and open space. I can then take the same space-program/CST components and compose as close to a polarity as possible. I now have two viewpoints with the same underlying program. I can also begin with a predictive trajectory and with community participation, add catalysts or deviations to that plan, and compose a responding design trajectory in a series and sequence of time periods.

At a minimum, this process provides a growing understanding within the community as to the possibilities and changeability of long-term planning/design process, better preparing the community for change and increasing its creative capacity.

Connectivity between and among emergent (possibly creative) spatial patterns

Connected incrementalism—bridging and connectivity

Design and constructed built form are ongoing in our cities and settlements. Two key roles of urban design are the bridging between built-form actions and the connectivity between and among those actions. In many ways, the key characteristic of connectivity is the concept of *edge*—the line of intersection of two surfaces; the beginning and end of a shape or object; a relationship between two or more entities; a dynamic interplay of two distinctly different entities (the wave crashing on the sand beach). Edge energies are physical/spatial interactions or dynamics between two or more different entities.

As mentioned earlier, human settlements have nested realities or watersheds, all different in cultural makeup and ascendant and descendant characteristics, yet all are related in time to one another. Some relationships are immediate and direct—adjacent, nearby, competitive—while others are remote, further away. In a settlement, with their differences they still have common or shared characteristics: they may have various loci, centers of intense activity and/or neighborhood idiosyncrasies that can act as catalysts, and edge conditions and energies. These edge energies can be interactive, with various forms of feedback emanating from the edge back through the nested reality and its loci. These dynamics provide key feedback mechanisms for urban design and can be the locations for emergent patterns (in response to both the internal workings of the reality or community sector and the interaction with other nested realities) and design catalysts. These edge interactions are a key source of connectivity between and among community sectors.

This connectivity is active within the full-scale ladder, from regional to urban block patterns. This again is where urban design has its strongest role: providing that connectivity between and among the dynamics of economics, politics, architecture and landscape architecture that are constantly ongoing within the built form.

Connectivity within the spatial scale hierarchy

Edge energies, a place of dynamic change and connectivity:

- adjacent (rigid/separate)
- blurred (in flux)
- mingling (reforming, containing relational aspects of each side's essential characteristics)
- positive/negative
- solid/void
- protective
- aggressive
- resistant

- hard and soft
- harmonious
- contentious—in relation to internal structure.

The many compositional methods to connect entities via edge conditions is described in Chapter 4 and highlighted in the demonstrations and experiments. Some key methods and principles are:

- adjacent—static and less dynamic
- interlocking—alternating penetration by each edge, for example
- blurred or soft—undefined, transitionary
- merging or mingling—components of each are mingled and form new variations and retain existing characteristics
- hard and soft/lost and found—a combination of defined and less defined or undefined physical edge
- positive/negative—concave/convex
- bridging—connecting two entities with the elements and principles of each retained in the process
- pass through energies, infusion and exchange (transportation systems)
- locational intercept places as possible connective loci.

Composition of complexity: elements and principles of design composition

Part II of the book is a dialogue on the connection between urban design philosophies and the act of design, through demonstrations and examples. It makes the connection between understanding the complex relationships in human settlements and the act of giving meaningful form to those relationships. This is a challenge, as being open to creative solutions requires letting go of established formulae and conventions as the primary sources of problem-solving—albeit enlisting them if and when they meet the requirements of contextual responsiveness. This does not mean that new design solutions replicate contextual patterns as they can also be stark departures to that context—with meaning.

Part II begins with a discussion of the basic elements and principles of design composition as they relate to urban design. At the core of this discussion is the power of compositional structures to form and assemble the physical/spatial elements of human settlements. For example, the circle is both a shape and a compositional structure where the structure may be the ordering framework for many differing shapes in a coherent circular pattern.

The compositional demonstrations and examples in Part II explore ways to address and engage complexity that results in spatial structure and order, not restricted to formal order, the essential role of urban design.

Bibliography

Alexander, Christopher, 1977: *Pattern Language*: Oxford University Press, Oxford.

American Heritage Dictionary of the English Language, 5th edition, 2011: Houghton Mifflin Harcourt, Boston and New York.

Ardrey, Robert, 1966: *The Territorial Imperative: A Personal Inquiry into the Animal Origin of Property and Nation*: Atheneum, New York.

Arefi, Mahyar, 2014: *Deconstructing Placemaking: Needs, Opportunities, and Assets*: Routledge, Abingdon, Oxfordshire.

Arnheim, Rudolph, 1969: *Visual Thinking*: University of California Press, Berkeley and Los Angeles, CA.

Attoe, Wayne and Logan, Donn, 1989: *American Urban Architecture: Catalysts in the Design of Cities*: University of California Press, Berkeley/Los Angeles/London.

Batty, Michael and Marshall, Stephen, 2012: "The Origins of Complexity Theory in Cities and Planning." In Portugali, Juval, Meyer, Han, Stolk, Egbert and Tan, Ekim (eds): *Complexity Theories of Cities Have Come of Age*: Springer, Heidelberg, Dordrecht/London/New York.

Bechtel, Robert B., 1977: *Enclosing Behavior*: Dowden, Hutchinson & Ross, Inc., Stoudsburg, PA.

Bohr, Niels, 2008: *Work on Atomic Physics*, vol. 3, ed. Ulrich Hoyer: Dowden, Hutchingson & Ross, Inc., Stroudsburg, PA.

Briggs, John, 1992: *Fractals: The Patterns of Chaos*: Touchstone, Simon & Schuster, NY.

Capra, Fritjof, 1982: *The Turning Point: Science, Society and the Rising Culture*: Simon & Schuster, New York.

Cropley, Arthur and Cropley, David, 2009: *Fostering Creativity*: Hampton Press, Inc., Cresskill, NJ.

de Roo, Gert and Rauws, Ward S., 2012: "Positioning Planning in the World of Order, Chaos and Complexity: On Perspectives, Behaviour and Interventions in a Non-linear Environment." In Portugali, Juval, Meyer, Han, Stolk, Egbert and Tan, Ekim (eds): *Complexity Theories of Cities Have Come of Age: An Overview with Implications to Urban Planning and Design*: Springer, Heidelberg/Dordrecht/London/New York.

Falconer, Kenneth, 2013: *Fractals: A Very Short Introduction*: Oxford University Press, Oxford.

Fincher, Ruth and Jacobs, Jane M. (eds), 1998: *Cities of Difference*: The Guilford Press, New York.

Ganis, Mary, 2015: *Planning Urban Places: Self-organizing Places with People in Mind*: Routledge, New York and London.

Haken, Hermann, 2012: "Complexity and Complexity Theories: Do These Concepts Make Sense?" In Portugali, Juval, Meyer, Han, Stolk, Egbert and Tan, Ekim (eds): *Complexity Theories of Cities Have Come of Age: An Overview with Implications to Urban Planning and Design*: Springer, Heidelberg/Dordrecht/London/New York.

Hall, Edward T., 1966: *The Hidden Dimension*: Doubleday and Co., New York.

Hatton, Brian, 2017: "Repositioning: This Think Called Crit. . . ." In Stoppani, Teresa, Ponzo, Giorgio and Themistokleous, George (eds), *This Thing Called Theory*: Routledge, Abingdon, Oxfordshire.

Herbert, Nick, 1985: *Quantum Reality: Beyond the New Physics*: Anchor Books, New York.

Johnston, Charles, MD, 1984/1986: *The Creative Imperative*: Celestial Arts, Berkeley, CA.

Johnston, Charles, MD, 1991: *Necessary Wisdom*: ICD Press, Seattle, in association with Celestial Press, Berkeley, CA.

Kaku, Michio, 1994: *Hyperspace*: Oxford University Press, Oxford.

Knox, Paul L., 2011: *Cites and Design*: Routledge, Abingdon, Oxfordshire.

Lazano, Ediardo, 1990: *Community Design and the Culture of Cities*: Cambridge University Press, Cambridge, MA.

Lefebvre, Henri, 1992: *The Production of Space* (trans. Donald Nicholson-Smith): Wiley-Blackwell, New York.

Marshall, Stephen, 2012: "Planning, Design and the Complexity of Cities." In Portugali, Juval, Meyer, Han, Stolk, Egbert and Tan, Ekim (eds): *Complexity Theories of Cities Have Come of Age: An Overview with Implications to Urban Planning and Design*: Springer, Heidelberg/Dordrecht/London/New York.

McIntosh, Robert P., 1985: *The Background of Ecology: Concept and Theory*: Cambridge University Press.

Miller, Kyle, 2017: "Repositioning Before Theory." In Stoppani, Teresa, Ponzo, Giorgio and Themistokleous, George (eds), *This Thing Called Theory*: Routledge, Abingdon, Oxfordshire.

Mould, Oli, 2017: *Urban Subversion and the Creative City*: Routledge, Abingdon, Oxfordshire.

Portugali, Juval, Meyer, Han, Stolk, Egbert and Tan, Ekim (eds), 2012: *Complexity Theories of Cities Have Come of Age: An Overview with Implications to Urban Planning and Design*: Springer, Heidelberg/Dordrecht/London/New York.

Shirvani, Hamid, 1985: *The Urban Design Process*: Van Nostrand Reinhold Company, Inc., New York.

Soja, Edward W., 1996: *Thirdspace*: Blackwell Publishers Inc., Cambridge/Oxford.

Soja, Edward W., 2000: *Postmetropolis: Critical Studies of Cities and Regions*: Blackwell Publishers, Oxford.

Sommer, Robert, 1969: *Personal Space: The Behavioural Basis of Design*: Prentice-Hall, Englewood, NJ.

Speaks, Michael 2005: "After Theory", *Architectural Record* 193 no. 6: 72–75.

Strauss, Anselm and Corbin, Juliet, 1998: *Basics of Qualitative Research*: Sage Publications, Inc., Thousand Oaks, CA.

Waldrop, M. Mitchell, 1992: *Complexity: The Emerging Science at the Edge of Order and Chaos*: Touchstone, Simon & Schuster, NY.

Ward, Mark, 2001: *Beyond Chaos*: Thomas Dunne Books, St Martin's Press, New York.

Part II

THE MAKING OF SPATIAL COMPOSITION AND STRUCTURAL ORDER

Chapter 3

ENGAGING DESIGN

Design: as a noun it is a graphic representation of something conceived or invented; and as an action or verb, it is the making of something physical in space with a reasoned purpose or intent.

In urban design, the actions include designing physical constructs (open space, building configurations, etc.); testing ideas, proposals and policies; and helping communities understand the "why" of form regarding the ramifications of planning and design decisions. Urban design is inherent in every aspect of human settlement interactions, in all aspects of comprehensive planning, from building houses to political decisions. Consequently, people who engage in any aspect of urban design require a basic level of understanding of design, its elements and principles, in order to make meaningful decisions beyond clichés, conventions and packaged models. They need to engage the act of design.

Some will protest this argument as unreasonable or unnecessary, supporting the notion of segregated domains of expertise in urban planning and design. I argue that one does not need to be an expert to understand the language and principles involved at the minimum, enabling one to be an active and contributing participant in design decisions. Engaging the spatial language of design can open a myriad of "doors" and new directions.

In order to engage design, all participants—stakeholders, students and professionals—must confront challenges to the unique properties of design, namely, an unknown outcome, an evolutionary process of exploration and experimentation—in many cases non-linear, with skill development (acquisition and practice), ambiguity and, if truly engaged in the design process, a personal connection to the act or contribution of making a design—and opening oneself up to criticism. Design requires the individual(s) to go beyond the "talking head" stage: intelligent and well-meaning, unwilling or unable to engage in tasks of design relative to spatial thinking due to a lack of skill development, a reticence to admit it, and in turn seeking diversions and avoidance of design out of fear.

And if one is to be an urban designer, in any capacity, one must have knowledge of design's relationship to art, history, culture and theory/theories, as well as a knowledge of its practice, including means, methods, and the elements and principles of spatial composition . . . and be able to engage in self-reflection through criticism. "To design requires courage, regardless of criticism . . . and an acceptance of inevitable failure . . . passionately regarded as another starting point, cherished, not wasted" (Hatton, 2017, p. 168).

Why is this relevant? The participation in the design of human settlements is serious business, affecting the lives of all participants. A major shift has occurred in the design of cities: the franchised packaging of models and typologies that are replicated, producing "cathedrals of consumption" characterized by shopping malls, chain stores, franchised outlets, thematic districts and towns based on marketing objectives rather than the underlying meaning and functional requirements of a given settlement. And for urban designers, due to the rise of digital (processing) methodologies we urgently need a reality check that includes the reclaiming of the art and craft of building—reclaiming them from the reaches of dry, disengaged theory (Adler, 2017, p. 179); or from the void created by any thoughtful foundation, leading to packaged, pre-programmed cities. A city can be "smart" regarding its technological infrastructure but that does not mean it is sensual or alive. Disneyland and Disneyworld were "smart" from the 1960s on and they were/are not cities.

It is in the community, its history and emergent cultures and values, that shapes the theory of design and design practice. History can foster and feed multiple theories for design but it is the existing pre-emergent and emergent interactions of community where urban design has a need to assemble structure, spatial order and composition that translate, integrate, and support the socio-political economic forces of community—requiring meaningful design.

When I taught watercolor painting at the university level in the architecture program, I found it important to educate myself again to better guide students in the relationship between design and art. Handing out older exercises did not suffice as I redid them again and learned more each time—going beyond the "knowledge" of watercolor painting and engaging the physical connection to the medium. Why is this important? My re-engagement with the methods improved my interactions with students with a fresh and meaningful understanding of the medium.

I taught watercolor as a fine art, not a representational medium—one that sought to integrate philosophies of approach with creative means, methods and tools. And it represented the direct engagement of artist, medium and tool—a dynamic personal experience that was frightening to some students.

Consequently, in order to reach out to readers of this book who want to engage design, I revisited design composition means and methods, revisiting the design exercises and examples to better assist the reader in experimenting with the design principles and elements.

The reader has many means and tools at his or her disposal when doing the suggested exercises—ranging from crafting to digital tools and techniques. As I discuss at length in *Play in Creative Problem-solving for Planners and Architects* (Kasprisin, 2016), there is a role for both—and they are different. Generating ideas requires *divergent* thinking—away from the stable center, on the edge and it benefits from a crafting process where discovery through sensual manipulation of physical materials is more prevalent. Processing ideas, testing and evaluating them in particular, is a function of *convergent* thinking—bringing together ideas and information for assessment. This is reinforced with the means and methods of digital technologies that can simulate ideas and information. Design encompasses both in a creative problem-solving process, going beyond being effective—seeking creative outcomes.

I utilize drawing and physical modeling techniques (paper constructs with scissors and glue—pretty simple) because they are fast, three-dimensional, and playful—leading to discoveries of novel solutions. Each student can assess what techniques they are most comfortable using—keeping in mind the differences between divergent and convergent thinking processes. Other fast techniques include color markers, color pencils, pastels, and three-dimensional collage work. Set aside the fine-point pen, the technical pen and the pencil, as they are by nature detailed and slow.

I ask students not to get "precious" about the design exercises—treat them as fast experiments or sketch problems, not finished or complete projects. In addition, we do not have the benefit of the CST matrix analysis of context, making the focus of the exercises on compositional formation.

Design as creative problem-solving requires an understanding and appreciation of the elements and principles of design composition—along with a proficiency with various skills that are part of the process and in themselves require practice through repetition. Let's put the "talking heads" and packaged programs on the shelf and engage design—play and discovery.

Let's explore skills before we embark on the larger mission with material from Phillip D. Tomporoski's *The Psychology of Skill* (2003). Skill is the ability to use knowledge effectively and readily in the execution of performance. This requires motor skills (body elements and functions) and cognitive skills such as problem-solving, memory, and thinking with the senses. Skills also require motivation and are domain-specific. This motivation is also directly connected to how you design, re: play and the concept of *functionlust* (if I enjoy doing something I am likely to do it again)—the pleasure of doing something.

According to Tomporoski, skills are learned and conducted as a result of dynamic processes that involve contributions of the body, the mind, and the spirit. Skills require practice and training through repetition as well as conscious and unconscious mental processes. I discuss this in more detail in *Play in Creative Problem-solving for Planners and Architects* (Kasprisin, 2016). The area of skill-necessity in design processes can intimidate many students and practitioners, leading them to crutches—new "apps" that make the process easier. Design requires practiced skill in a pluralism of methods, from crafting to digital technologies, not one all-encompassing method.

Bibliography

Adler, Gerald, 2017: "Pragmatics: Towards a Theory of Things." In Stoppani, Teresa, Ponzo, Giorgio and Themistokleous, George (eds), *This Thing Called Theory*: Routledge, Abingdon, Oxfordshire.

Capra, Fritjof, 1991: *The Tao of Physics*: Shambala Publications Inc. Boston, MA.

Hatton, Brian, 2017: "Repositioning: This Think Called Crit. . . ." In Stoppani, Teresa, Ponzo, Giorgio and Themistokleous, George (eds), *This Thing Called Theory*: Routledge, Abingdon, Oxfordshire.

Johnston, Charles, 1989: *The Creative Imperative*: Celestial Press, Berkeley, CA.

Kaku, Michio, 1994: *Hyperspace*: Oxford University Press, Oxford.

Kasprisin, Ron, 2016: *Play in Creative Problem-solving for Planners and Architects*: Routledge, New York.

May, Rollo, 1975: *The Courage to Create*: W.W. Norton & Company, Inc., New York.

Tomporoski, Phillip D., 2003: *The Psychology of Skill*: Praeger Publishing, Westport, CT, and London.

Waldrop, M. Mitchell, 1992: *Complexity: The Emerging Science at the Edge of Order and Chaos*: Touchstone, Simon & Schuster, NY.

Chapter 4

DESIGN COMPOSITION
RELATIONSHIPS, ELEMENTS, PRINCIPLES AND STRUCTURE

Form as community content and relationship

The urban design process is often referred to as "place making", an interpretation of urban meaning and urban functionality in form (Castells, 1983), as spatial metaphors and sensory and sensual built environments considered special by the observer. As we engage the factors and relationships inherent in the CST matrix, the making of meaningful compositions becomes increasingly challenging and complex. In many cases, urban designers are confronted with two options: undergo a creative problem-solving process fraught with unknowns, which is time-consuming and ambiguous; or fall back on franchised, packaged design models and types that appear to resolve a design problem.

As a result of observing students struggle with and often avoid engaging in a creative design process, I developed a graduate-level course in urban design composition (UW) that introduced them to the elements and principles of design composition to enable their immersion in a creative problem-solving process. This required a learning process involving the spatial language of design, the principles of design as functions of art, and an understanding of the connection between design composition and community content and relationships. The progress was significant, once initial fears were recognized and engaged.

Along with this learning process is the necessary act of artful play (see Kasprisin, 2016), design experimentation, and the process of discovery and novelty through a crafting process. I talk about the crafting process often in this book and it is not in competition with technological digital processes but a part of the pluralistic approach to creativity. As I discuss later, and it bears repeating, there is an appropriate time for crafting (generation) and technological (processing).

Before we discuss the spatial language of design composition, let's review the larger relationships that comprise every composition: organization and structure.

Organizational and structural relationships in composition

Before discussing the elements and principles of design composition, it is important to underscore what the major parts of a composition are—organizational and structural relationships. The elements and principles, the shapes and spatial activators, or the nouns and verbs of the spatial language are incorporated into these relationships as compositional wholes.

Composing is to put something in proper order and form, assembling a larger physical entity from smaller relational groupings, clusters or systems; it is an aesthetically harmonious arrangement of smaller nested systems for a defined period. Aesthetics of course are relative to culture and social agendas; and they are major variables in design composition. In basic design, regardless of aesthetics, composition consists of the arrangement of organizational relationships that represent essential functions that reflect the needs of community. When organizational relationships are integrated with a structural order, the resulting composition begins to define spatial metaphors, meanings, stories articulated in its physical dimensions and relationships.

Let's explore *design as a composed organizational relationship*:

- Design always has meaning(s), stories told through design as spatial metaphor whether in art, architecture, or urban design; shape is content (Arnheim, 1969).
- Design comprises "parts" in relationship where the parts are in effect smaller systems that range in ordered shapes from columns (capital, shaft, pedestal) to socio-cultural orders and patterns reflecting needs from compatible interactions of CST.
- The "parts" in relationship do not constitute the final design, but rather the functional needs of the design, often expressed in physical typologies (double loaded corridor residential building, for example). Or the "chair": with a basic organizational relationship composed of a horizontal seat, a back support and vertical supporting elements. These are critical needs organized to produce a functioning and generic "chair" as organizational relationship. The "chair" becomes real and has an identity when "structure" specifies what it is made of and how it is assembled, giving it form.
- Consequently, design is also the structure or assemblage or organizational needs and relationships. Structure and organization thus become dance partners initiated by need, influenced by context and material requirements, and assembled into a distinct pattern, i.e. designed.

Organizational relationships

Let's approach composition from the starting point of "relationship", where function and meaning are integrated and manifested in form—the eidetic vision. Compositional relationships are presented as a set of two relational clusters: *organizational* and *structural*. *Organizational* refers to the operations and functions of a composition whereas *structural* refers to the nature of assemblage of those organizations into a physical, material whole.

As in the chair example, "parts" are arranged in relationships between and among other parts to fulfill a need or aspiration. These needs emanate from social-cultural–political interactions in human settlements. They represent the essence of urban meaning and function, or the drama created between or among people in dialogue. We can view these organizational relationships as functional directives for a design or art work. They are critical in design when we bridge the gap between need and spatial accommodation of that need. Urban designers and planners often overlook this critical "space program" bridge between statement of need and the implementation of a design in context. Conversely, some in the fields spend inordinate amounts of energy with the identification of "space programs" and barely engage the assemblage phase of composing—design.

In the design of the master plan for Tanana Valley Community College in Fairbanks, Alaska (Bettisworth and Kasprisin, 1982), the team interviewed each department and catalogued projected needs for its successful functioning over a period of time. Within each department, "parts" or smaller systems were identified as functional requirements: classrooms for (x) students with specific functions, offices, meeting rooms, laboratories, studios, support services, etc., all with quantitative requirements and dimensions, etc. These parts were then arranged in beneficial or compatible relationships with other parts to form a larger departmental system.

Each was then arranged with other departmental system parts in search of a larger and compatible relationship of needs. At this stage, basic site context input was added, influencing the larger relational whole (overall site size and configuration and access points). In many cases, the organizational relationship diagram can hint at semi-abstract forms—the value of the semiotic diagram.

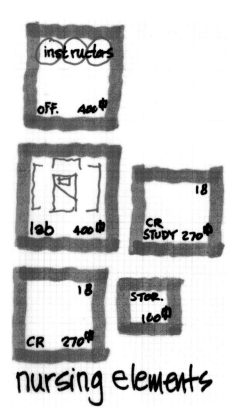

nursing elements

Figure 4.1. Departmental "pieces" and needed elements. *Before relational assemblies occur, the basic needs and elements (spaces, objects, tools) are identified, made into lists and diagrams of what, how much and what size. They are objects not yet in relationship, essentially "what" and "how much".*

Figure 4.2. Departmental organizational relationship diagrams. *"Tanana Valley Community College Master Plan" (Fairbanks, Alaska), organizational diagram of the General Science Labs—a smaller system or part of the whole.*

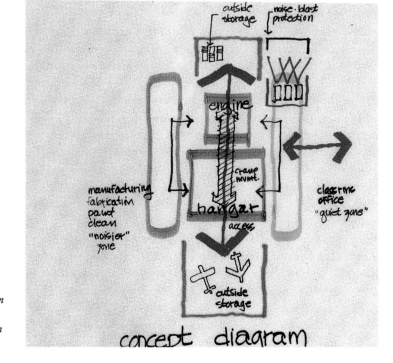

concept diagram

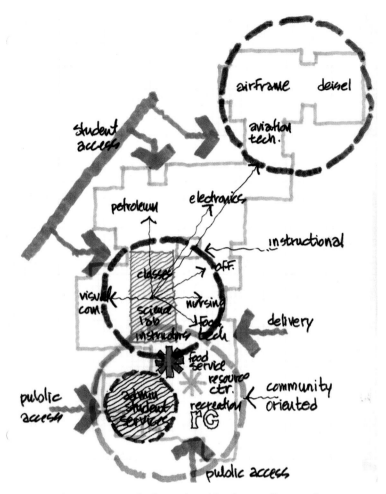

Figure 4.3. Facility-wide organizational relationship. *This diagram illustrates the convergence of all academic departments and supporting facilities as an organizational relationship with initial contextual response.*

Structural relationships

The structural relationship component in a composition assembles the functional, operational and contextual relationships into a physical spatial composition using the elements and principles, the spatial nouns and verbs, of design. At the heart of the composition are driving or dominant structural principles that frame the objects within the composition. Complex compositions have multiple structures in relationship, all performing a supportive action within the larger one.

These structural relationships are the beginning stages of design composition and represent a phase in design where form takes on responsible and responsive meaning. In the following illustration, the Tanana Valley Community College organizational relationships are coalesced into a structural relationship both in initial diagram form and subsequent three-dimensional massing. The diagram is one of many that were explored as possible structural constructs to accommodate the organizational aspects.

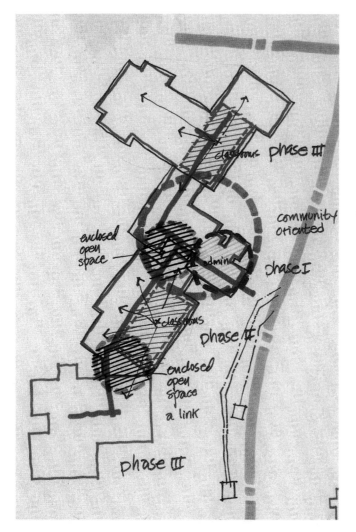

Figure 4.4. TVCC structural diagram option. *The diagram explores various ways of structuring or assembling the organizational relationships into a composition relative to site context. The larger composition emerges as a system of structures integrating buildings, uses, open space and site context. This is one of six such options generated from the organizational diagrams.*

The spatial language of design composition: "nouns" and "verbs"

Design elements: "the nouns"

As I build up the elements and principles of composition to a more complex level of application, I use examples that are initially abstract in nature, increasing in complexity and realism as we proceed.

    Element: a basic or fundamental component, part, or quality (of space)—an object.

    Elements constitute the basics for the graphic design alphabet of spatial compositions. We use symbols and shapes to represent a spatial language; we use shapes as elements to form spatial compositions. As an initial requirement in architecture school, my colleagues and I were asked to construct the Roman alphabet, letter by letter, with compass, triangle, etc. Needless to say, we gained an understanding not of "A" but of the lines, circles, and straight lines that made up that "A" (as constructed by the Romans).

The beautiful formal geometry of the alphabet characters as comprised of circles, angles, and straight lines became apparent.

What is important for the beginning designer is an understanding of the flexibility and ability to manipulate these basic elements into meaningful form (and language). The essential element is the shape.

Shape (also a relationship of area to edge): any discernible bounded area defined by line or contour, value change, color extent, intensity change, and/or texture and their contrasts or some combinations; composed of a specified area, extent, or field and contained or marked by a boundary or edge. A shape can be direct, as in the square or circle; semi-direct, as in the "L"; or implied, as in the separation of space formed by two or more elements, similar or different, in relative close association.

Shapes define the physical world and constitute a visual language. They can be:

- Geometric (earth measure—implying a mathematical foundation as in geometry).
- Organic (living systems, fractal, changing in response to environmental conditions).
- Primary (first in order of development, from which others are derived—circle, square and line).
- Derivatives (traceable to another primary source).
- Polarities (positive and negative, figure and ground, solid and void, lost and found, black and white).
- Ambiguous (uncertain, changing, evolving).

The diagrams are basic and indicate a beginning complexity that can be attained with manipulation exercises for each primary shape. I assign paper collage exercises to students so that they can practice this manipulation with fast and easy methods—a valuable lesson for later composition exercises.

Let's begin with the basic elements as shapes in art and design.

Dot: a point, small mark, or small circular shape, represented in other scales as:

- point
- circle
- sphere
- star.

Line: a thin (relatively) elongated shape characterized by a length that is substantially more than its width, also represented at many scales, beginning with pen/stylus-made marks and going to and beyond rivers and freeways.

The line acts as a contour and as a compositional structure, such as the axis. In some applications, it is a direct statement, such as a contour or outline of a shape; and it is implied, such as the edge of a painted shape, existing by the ending of a stroke or wash. Example characteristics include:

- implying length over width
- contour, edge
- straight, curvilinear, broken, intermittent, flowing, falling
- vertical (column, flagpole, skyscraper, comet tail)
- horizontal (axis, highway, coastline)
- directional (arrow, vector, graph, ramp).

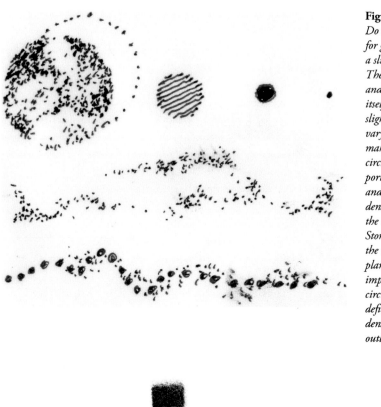

Figure 4.5. The dot. *Do not take the dot for granted—a speck, a slight circular mark. The dot is shape-defining and density-relevant. By itself, it is the speck or slight mark. In clusters of varying density, the dot makes shapes (squares and circles, for example) and portrays value in lights and darks based on dot density. At larger scales, the dot becomes the circle: Stonehenge from the air, the top of a cylinder, a planetarium—pretty impressive for a small circular speck. Practice defining shapes with dot density as opposed to outlines or contours.*

Figure 4.6. Dot density. *Dots are effective symbols for affecting density in various shapes. The diagram shows varying densities using dots in a spattering technique.*

Square: a primary shape with four equal sides all at right angles to one another, with two pairs of parallel lines.

The square, as discussed in compositional structures, has essential characteristics that define its geometry: four equally separated corners, four equal sides, four right angles, equal diagonals, a center point equidistant to each of the four sides.

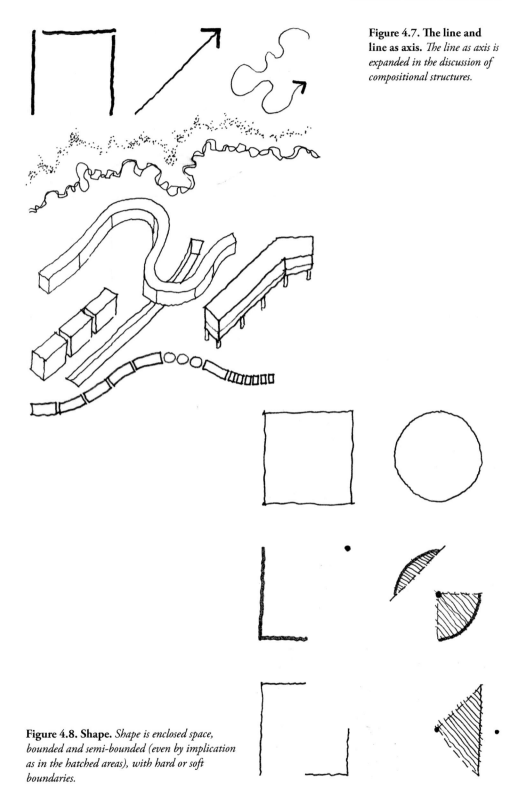

Figure 4.7. The line and line as axis. *The line as axis is expanded in the discussion of compositional structures.*

Figure 4.8. Shape. *Shape is enclosed space, bounded and semi-bounded (even by implication as in the hatched areas), with hard or soft boundaries.*

Figure 4.9. Square.
The square is one of the primary shapes with many derivatives. There are many ways to represent the square without fully defining its four equal sides: as four equally separated corners with parallel sides; two sides and a corner; four connecting equal and parallel sides; two triangular shapes; and on and on and on. I have students construct paper renditions of the many ways the square (as well as the circle and line) can be manipulated without losing their identity.

Derivatives of the square, a primary source, include:

- rectangle
- triangle
- diamond
- parallel lines.

These derivatives constitute the majority of shapes used in design. They are flexible, capable of extensive manipulation, as we shall explore in later chapters.

Circle: a primary shape everywhere equidistant from a given fixed point or center.

The circle has physical characteristics both as a shape and as a compositional structure that enable it to be expressed in different ways, direct and implied. These include the arc (implying two or more radii), the radius, diameter, circumference or portions thereof.

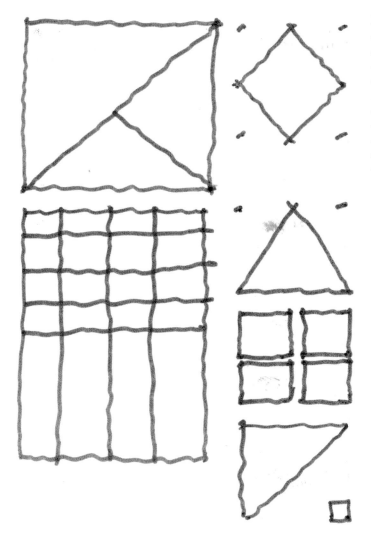

Figure 4.10. Derivatives of the square. *The square is "parent" to many conventional shapes used in design, from the rectangle to the triangle. Learning how to manipulate them in various ways helps the student understand how to add complexity to conventional shapes.*

Derivatives of the circle, a primary source, include:

* radial burst
* ellipse (two-centered curved shape)
* curvilinear forms.

Other shapes in design:

* polygon (enclosed shape, especially with more than four sides)
* trapezoid (four-sided shape with two parallel sides)
* trapezium (four-sided shape with no parallel sides)
* fractal (an object whose parts appear similar at many different levels, reflected in the larger whole).

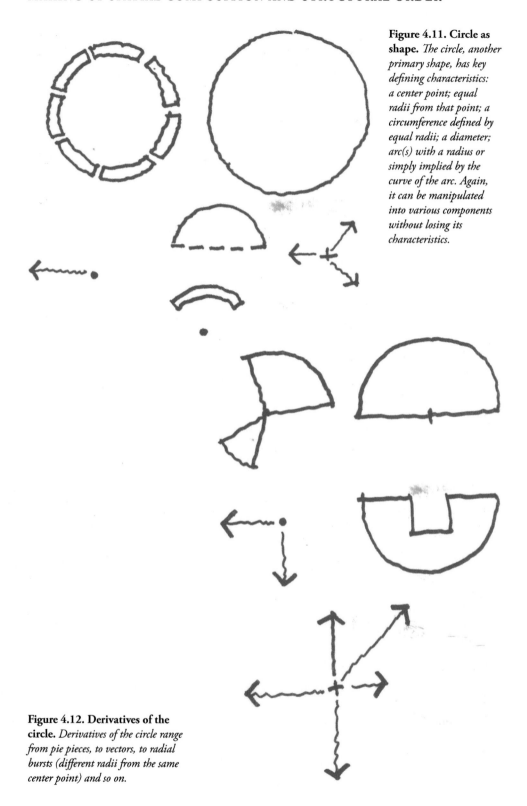

Figure 4.11. Circle as shape. *The circle, another primary shape, has key defining characteristics: a center point; equal radii from that point; a circumference defined by equal radii; a diameter; arc(s) with a radius or simply implied by the curve of the arc. Again, it can be manipulated into various components without losing its characteristics.*

Figure 4.12. Derivatives of the circle. *Derivatives of the circle range from pie pieces, to vectors, to radial bursts (different radii from the same center point) and so on.*

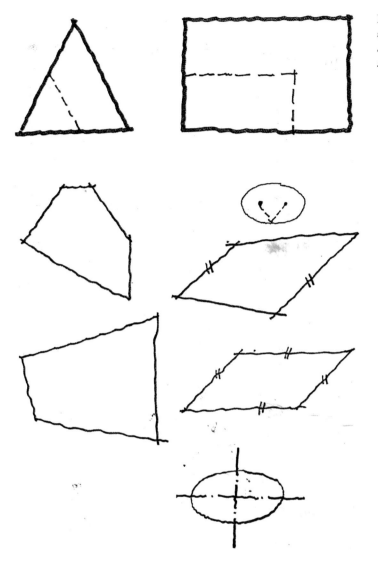

Figure 4.13. Other shapes in design. *Shapes derived from the primary shapes and departures.*

As we complete this overview of spatial "nouns"—the elements and shapes of the visual language—let's review additional characteristics applicable to those elements. These all influence how shapes are incorporated into compositions:

- *Size*: dimensional appearance in relation to other shapes.
- *Texture*: a surface characteristic implying a touch response or visual appearance as a surface interacts with light or other variations to its surface features.
- *Grain*: a density of surface characteristics (dots per inch/centimeter, for example).
- *Direction*: a movement to or from somewhere (N, S, E, W); horizontal, vertical, diagonal, circular.
- *Transparency*: light and image are apparent through a material.
- *Translucency*: light is apparent with diffused image through a material.

- *Opacity*: light and image are prevented from passing through material, either absorbed or reflected.
- *Position*: location in relation to other shapes; see "Focus or center of interest".
- *Orientation*: exposure, implies direction and position.
- *Stability*: relationship to ground plane, gravity, lack of motion (stability can also be a state of dynamic action in balance—stable).

The use of these basic shapes is readily discernible in the later, more complex project examples. The student can also refer to *Play in Creative Problem-solving* (Kasprisin, 2016) for detailed examples and exercises.

Elements as planes and volumes: shape constructs from basic elements

The basic elements combine to shape both the spatial alphabet into spatial constructs (planes) and planes into volumes. In design, these constructs are the building blocks of architecture, landscape architecture and urban design. They begin with two-dimensional constructs (planes, axes, fields) and assemble into three-dimensional constructs as volumes.

   Planar shape (plane): a flat surface; a surface containing all the straight lines that connect any two points on it:

- overhead (ceiling, roof)
- vertical (wall, fence, window)
- horizontal (footprint, floor, path, lying down, prostrate)
- oblique or angular (tilted or inclined, ramp, shed roof, slope)
- multiple vertical and horizontal planes in relationship
    - L-shape
    - ramp-landing
    - parallel
    - orthographic
    - oblique
    - U-shaped
    - enclosed
- curved vertical and horizontal planes in relationship
    - equal radii
    - arcs
    - undulating (changing radii) and/or changing centers
    - S-shapes (repeating but reversed equal radii)
    - enclosed cylinder
    - enclosed sphere.

   Axis (line): an unlimited line, half-line, or line segment serving to orient a space or geometric object:

- overhead (contrail, power line, trellis component, light string)
- vertical (elevator shaft, rocket exhaust, skyscraper, flagpole)

- horizontal (corridor, street, sidewalk, rowhouses)
- oblique (off ramp-landing, switchback).

Field or pattern (dots):

- pebble field
- rock wall
- texture
- grain.

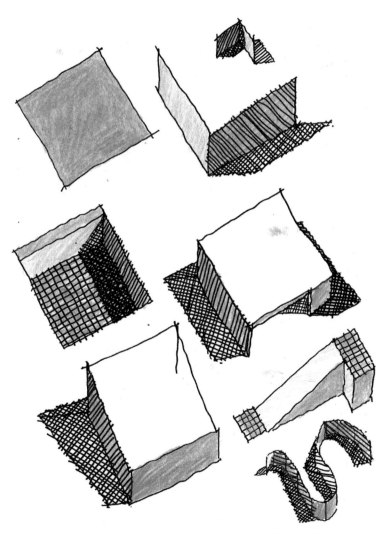

Figure 4.14. Planar shapes. *The combinations of planar shapes create volume, enclosed and semi-enclosed, or bounded space.*

Seem obvious? Many people are oblivious as to the makeup of their surroundings.

Volumes: three dimensional shapes constructed from combinations of planes where at least three elements or planes define length, depth, and width or breadth:

- space displaced or defined by mass (solid, such as a bowling or soccer ball)
- space contained or enclosed by planes or mass (stadium, dome, channel, tunnel, building)
- sphere
- prism
- cone
- cylinder
- pyramid
- cube.

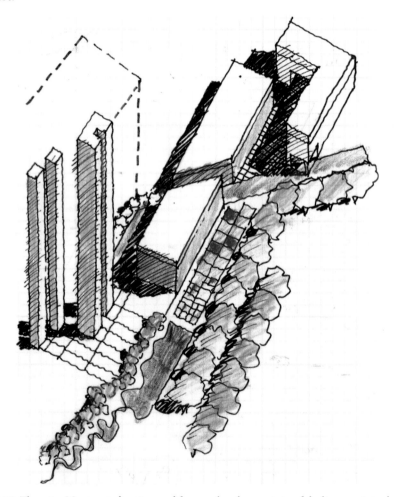

Figure 4.15. The axis. *Movement, direction, and force are key characteristics of the line or axis in design. As discussed in compositional structures, the axis assembles and structures composition. The axis can consist of horizontal pathways, waterways, landscape elements, linear building mass, and vertical elements, such as elevators and buildings.*

Descriptors or characteristics of planes and volumes

Planes and volumes are shapes and have additive descriptors that affect their use and appearance:

- *Size*: dimensional appearance or description in relation to other shapes.
- *Texture*: a surface characteristic implying a touch response or visual appearance as a surface interacts with light or touch or other variations to its surface features.
- *Grain*: a density of surface characteristics (number of dots per unit of measure).
- *Direction*: a movement to or from somewhere (N, S, E, W); horizontal, vertical, diagonal, circular.
- *Transparency*: light and image are apparent through a material.
- *Translucency*: light is apparent, image is diffused through a material.
- *Position*: location in relation to other shapes.
- *Opacity*: light and image are prevented from passing through material, either absorbed or reflected.
- *Orientation*: exposure, implies direction.
- *Stability*: relationship to ground plane, gravity.

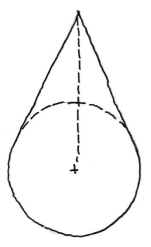
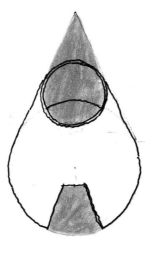

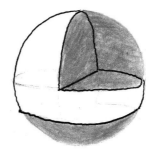

Figure 4.16. Volumes A. *These are the volumes that constitute our built environment in primary and hybridized forms. Sphere: any round body with a surface equally distant from the center at all points. Prism: a solid whose ends are equal and parallel polygons and whose sides are parallelograms. Cone: a solid with a circle as a base and a curved surface tapering to a point. Cylinder: a solid with parallel and equal circles as ends. Pyramid: a solid with a square base and four sloping sides meeting at a point. Cube: a solid with six equal square sides.*

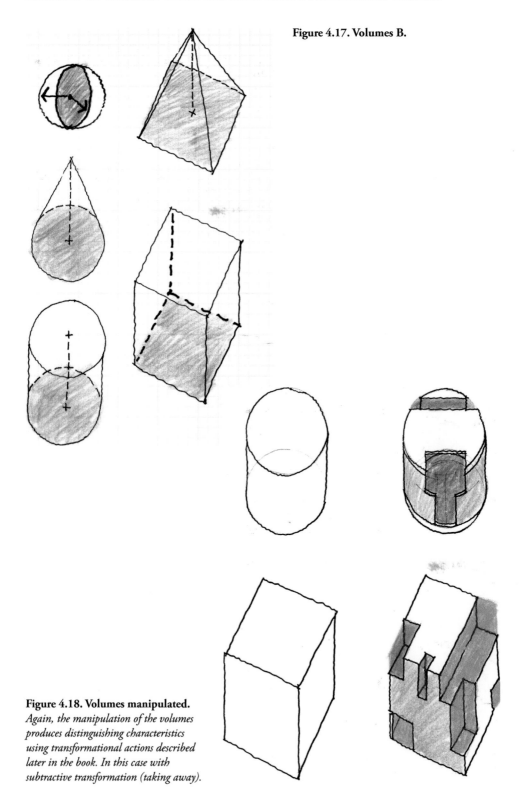

Figure 4.17. Volumes B.

Figure 4.18. Volumes manipulated.
Again, the manipulation of the volumes produces distinguishing characteristics using transformational actions described later in the book. In this case with subtractive transformation (taking away).

Focus or center of interest

Focus or center of interest (CI) is often overlooked in design and emanates from the golden mean, a point or area of emphasis in a composition, two- or three-dimensional. The CI can be the climax, the point of most drama, the "aha!" and is supported by the other elements and principles in composition.

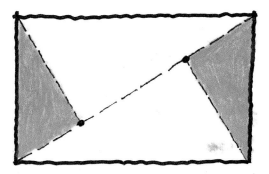

Figure 4.19. Focus or center of interest in plan. *Center of interest (CI) is the "aha!" point of highest drama, or main aspect of a design stor. In painting the CI is usually located at one of the quadrant centers or at a location along any diagonal where a perpendicular line intersects the diagonal from any corner.*

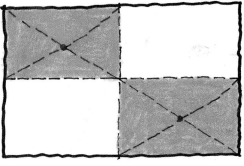

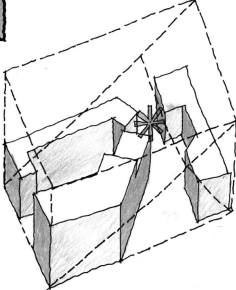

Figure 4.20. Focus or center of interest in three dimensions. *This example comes straight out of the art of composition and has interesting potentials.*

CI

Design principles: the "verbs" of spatial language

Principles are rules of conduct, fundamental laws (not absolute) that explain an action. They are often perceived as outcomes when in reality they are the conduct or activator that causes the outcome. In design composition, principles instruct and guide elements into relationships—organizational and structural. The following principles result from centuries of artistic exploration and apply directly to most aspects of design, including urban design. They can assist the beginning designer as well as the practitioner in activating objects, elements or shapes into dramatic arrangements. As in all matters of creative problem-solving, the development of skills, means and methods requires practice, not memorization. Portions of this chapter deal with exercises in these verbs or activators and are critical for advancement to more complex explorations.

"Verbs" or activators of the spatial language (obviously not all verbs but includes terms that direct actions):

- *Alternating*: the repeated use of two or more shapes, sizes, etc. usually in succession as in ABABABAB.
- *Angle of view(ing)*: the amount, range, dimension or extent of view framed by two straight lines that meet, forming an angle of view; the space between those lines defined by an extension to the horizon; angle of view from the focal point, the observer.
- *Balancing*: a state of equilibrium of a total work; balance and weight are similar expressions of the same principle; balance is not static but a dynamic interaction that is stable.
- *Bridging*: the act of integrating polarities and contrasts, conflicts with minimal or no compromise (unity, separation, blending).
- *Compression*: to make more compact by pressing objects together, also resulting in a force or resistance.
- *Conflicting*: a state of disagreement or disharmony; a disturbance (distraction) resulting from the opposition of simultaneous functioning of mutually exclusive relationships or elements.
- *Contrasting*: setting into opposition in order to demonstrate differences; call attention to based on opposing elements or features.
- *Datum*: things known or assumed; a common reference point that can represent or exist as a design principle—an organizing reference within a design composition.
- *Directing*: showing or indicating a way.
- *Dominating*: an action, element or pattern having a recognizable strength or importance over others usually through size, value, weight, placement.
- *Edge energies*: the energies, forces, dynamics of the coming together of two or more shapes, elements, patterns, relationships; the end of something and the beginning of something else.
- *Gradation/grading*: an increment chang(ing) in value, color, temperature, key or intensity, density, etc. within a given shape or pattern or among a group of shapes.
- *Harmony*: an arrangement (or arranging) into an agreeable whole; benchmarks are needed to establish what harmony is for design related to the context of the design.
- *Merging/mingling*: bridging two or more elements, compositions, relationships together at their edge transitions, creating a third and distinct edge transition where the essential characteristics or principles of the originals remain and are integrated with a new original element.
- *Patterning*: repeated use of elements and compositions forming a larger whole; often composed of clusters of smaller design principles such as repetition with variety, gradation, etc.
- *Polarity actions*: establishing the limits of the design, dialogue, and shape potential, or design actions within a specific context—subject to change and evolution; often represented by tension, contrast, and confrontation defining the temporary limits.

- *Procession/processing*: making something come closer, be seen, larger shapes, darker values, brighter and warmer colors, for example.
- *Recession/recessing*: making something recede, go further away in distance, smaller shapes, lighter and cooler colors, for example.
- *Repeating*: a recurring element or relationship or pattern at regular intervals.
- *Repetition with variety*: usually the same element repeated with variations in size, color, or other physical characteristic: AaAa or repeated circles, each of diminishing size.
- *Rhythm*: a repetition that is alternating in various and consistent intervals: AaaAaaAaa or AaaBBbAaaBBb.
- *Symmetry/asymmetry*: similarity of form or arrangement on either side of a dividing line or shape, or a relationship with correspondence or similarity between entities or parts (symmetry); the absence of similarity in form or arrangement (asymmetry).
- *Tension*: a force or tendency to stretch or make taut; the interplay of conflicting elements wherein a tightness or tautness occurs between them, often resulting in a force of pulling away.
- *Transformations*: changing shapes and compositions by a number of actions such as additive, subtractive, dimensional change, merging, and others.
- *Unifying*: to consolidate or bring together as one or a unit.
- *Varying/variety*: something that is distinguished from others of the same kind by a specific characteristic or set of characteristics.

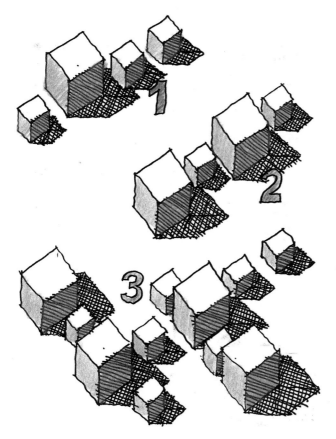

Figure 4.21. Alternation (A).
Two or more choices, repeating patterns composed of two or more elements alternating as every other or in sets or clusters of patterns. Alternation can be valuable when seeking coherence or consistency in complicated building form environments; and it can break up monotonous forms in the manner of the alternation. Two different clusters of alternation forms (1) and (2) are combined in a 1, 2, 2 sequence (3).

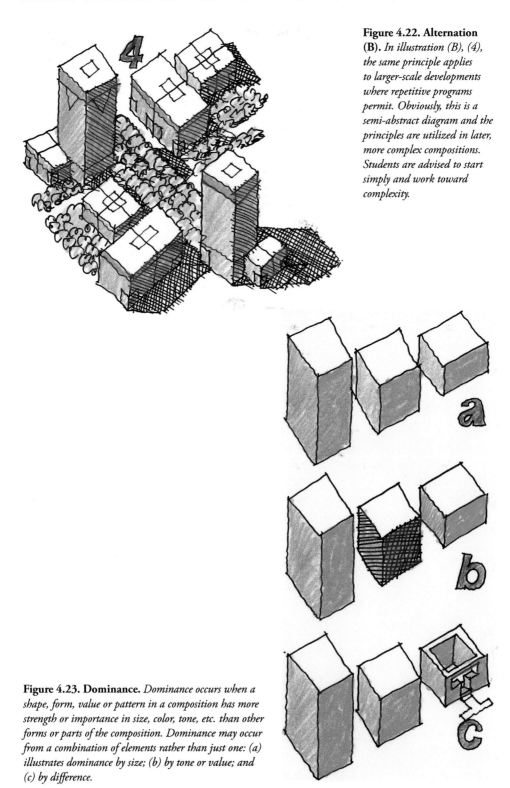

Figure 4.22. Alternation (B). *In illustration (B), (4), the same principle applies to larger-scale developments where repetitive programs permit. Obviously, this is a semi-abstract diagram and the principles are utilized in later, more complex compositions. Students are advised to start simply and work toward complexity.*

Figure 4.23. Dominance. *Dominance occurs when a shape, form, value or pattern in a composition has more strength or importance in size, color, tone, etc. than other forms or parts of the composition. Dominance may occur from a combination of elements rather than just one: (a) illustrates dominance by size; (b) by tone or value; and (c) by difference.*

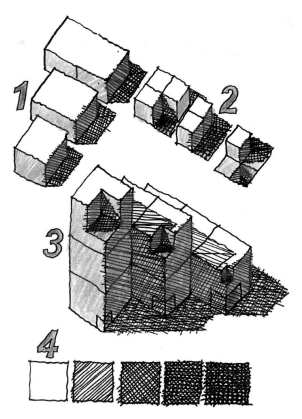

Figure 4.24. Gradation and repetition with variety (and value). *The cube is repeated at different sizes (dimensional transformation) for a gradual increase in horizontal width (1); changed in increasing complexity using positive and negative quarter volumes (2); and graded vertically in both overall volume and component details (subtractive transformations) (3). Gradation occurs in light patterns from light to dark. In art and design, a five-value scale is used ranging from light, mid-light, mid-, mid-dark, to dark (4).*

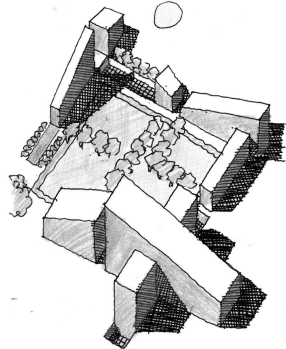

Figure 4.25. Harmony. *In painting, harmony can be achieved by using the same family or palette of colors dominating the composition. In design, a repetition of a family of volumes, like the sheds in the illustration, augmented by a directional movement and hierarchy of sizes, can also instill harmony to the composition.*

73

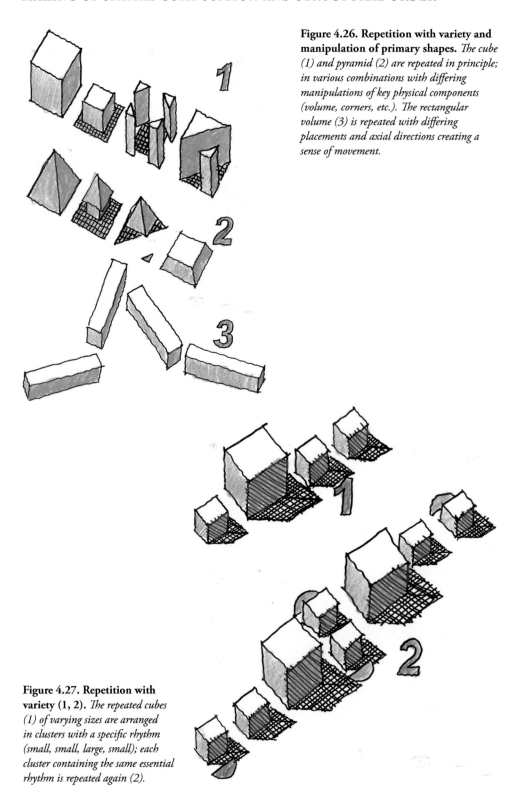

Figure 4.26. Repetition with variety and manipulation of primary shapes. *The cube (1) and pyramid (2) are repeated in principle; in various combinations with differing manipulations of key physical components (volume, corners, etc.). The rectangular volume (3) is repeated with differing placements and axial directions creating a sense of movement.*

Figure 4.27. Repetition with variety (1, 2). *The repeated cubes (1) of varying sizes are arranged in clusters with a specific rhythm (small, small, large, small); each cluster containing the same essential rhythm is repeated again (2).*

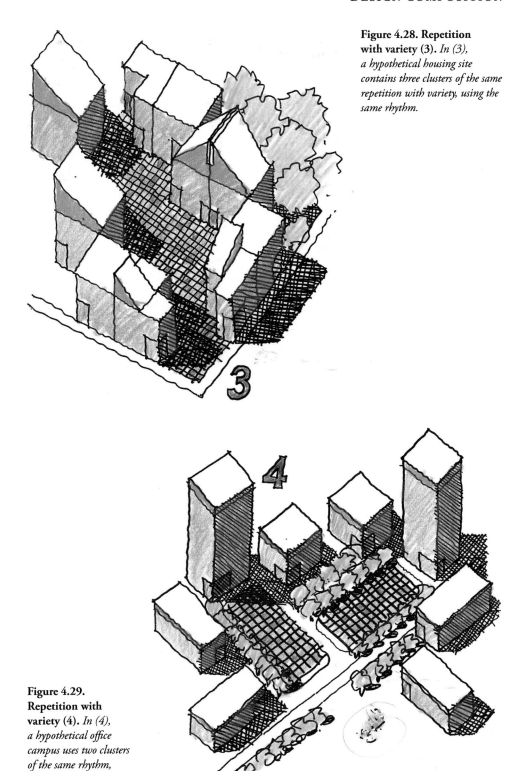

Figure 4.28. Repetition with variety (3). *In (3), a hypothetical housing site contains three clusters of the same repetition with variety, using the same rhythm.*

Figure 4.29. Repetition with variety (4). *In (4), a hypothetical office campus uses two clusters of the same rhythm, repeated in clusters.*

Compositional structures: the overall ordering spatial mechanisms

Note: this section may be confusing to the student at first, as it may appear to be iterative of the previous discussion on shapes. This section is about shape as a compositional structure, an assembling force of multiple shapes. Subsequently, I revisit characteristics of shapes as structuring forces.

Now the square, circle and line become more than elements, objects or shapes; they become structuring forces or mechanisms for complex compositions—forceful and malleable.

Arnheim (1969) states that there are only two basic structural compositions—circle and square—from which all other structuring mechanisms emanate. I add to this the line or axis as it is inherent in both the circle and square, albeit not always evident, and is a powerful structuring mechanism in and of itself. Hybrids of each major structuring form include but are not limited to rectangles, grids, radii, and axes. These are explored here and in exercises in later chapters.

The student may ask: Why are these important? Because they provide the *dynamic principles* for assembling and framing organizing functions and their material characteristics, giving specification to organizational relationships. It becomes the difference between the competent arrangement of shape/uses in space and the dynamic ordering of those shape/uses in a coherent spatial metaphor.

Let's review the various characteristics and derivatives of the three basic compositional structures as described earlier in the chapter. Why do something that seems so obvious?

The primary shapes provide a mathematical foundation for forms, and they are the basis for complex configurations that bring order and structure to urban compositions. Remember, order—"a condition of logical or comprehensible arrangement among separate elements of a group . . . such that proper functioning or appearance is achieved" (*American Heritage Dictionary of the English Language*, 2011).

As an important exercise for students, I have them construct with paper variations of each primary shape to gain an understanding of their flexibility and malleable natures. Begin with the basic or obvious characteristics of each and begin to image the shape as more abstract or implied, then move on to its derivatives with the same approach: basic and abstract or implied. I include "implied" as it introduces the concept of flexible or manipulated use of the primary shapes.

Square characteristics

Square: a plane figure having four equal sides, forming four right angles.
   Basic characteristics:

- four equal sides
- four equidistant corners
- center point equidistant from each corner and similarly to each side
- sides connected by right angles.

   Implied characteristics:

- four- to five-dot pattern (center point plus four corner points)
- opposite right-angle corners
- two parallel lines distant by their own measurement
- four identical quarter shapes

- two identical half shapes (rectangular or triangular)
- a cross of two equal lines implying four quarters
- an "X" of two equal lines implying four corners.

Square derivatives

Grid:

- square or rectangular repetitions in adjacency
- orthographic pattern
- vertical and horizontal patterns
- types:
    - standard square grid
    - standard rectangular grid
    - broken grid
    - meandering grid
    - hybrid grid.

Rectangle:

- multiple squares
- portions of a square
- two pairs of parallel lines, each pair of different lengths.

Triangle:

- connecting three points not in a straight line by straight line segments
- three-sided shape
- three points.

Diamond:

- intersection of vertical and horizontal lines each with a different dimension
- a composition of triangles
- four points forming four non-right angles.

Cross:

- two (or more) intersecting lines.

Diagonals:

- non-perpendicular, angular
- implied movement and direction
- 45-degree-angle orientation.

Horizontal/vertical:

- the center line of a square in either a vertical or horizontal orientation
- lying down/standing up—straight.

The "L":

- a vertical and horizontal configuration of two connected lines or shapes
- a corner
- deflection.

Let's explore these compositional structures through exercises and examples: the more you engage the greater your understanding of their flexibility.

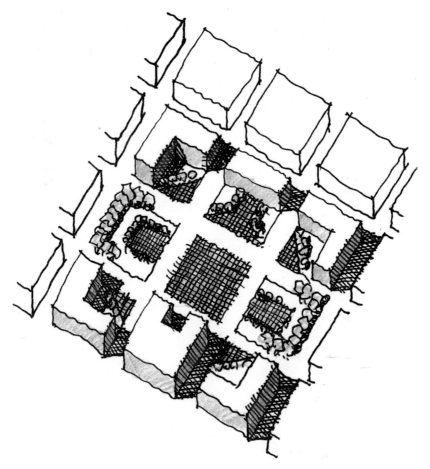

Figure 4.30. Compositional structure: the square. *The square is a powerful structuring mechanism for other shapes and elements in urban form, reflected here in the conventional block grid and the assemblage of buildings and open spaces within that grid.*

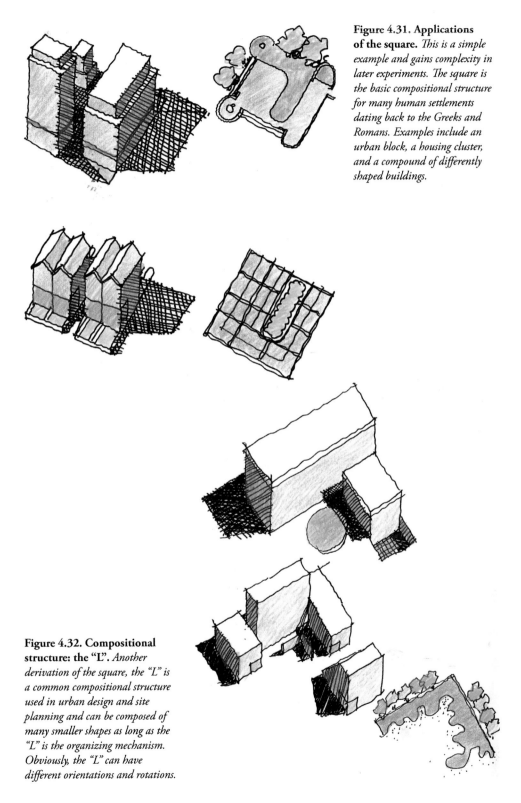

Figure 4.31. Applications of the square. *This is a simple example and gains complexity in later experiments. The square is the basic compositional structure for many human settlements dating back to the Greeks and Romans. Examples include an urban block, a housing cluster, and a compound of differently shaped buildings.*

Figure 4.32. Compositional structure: the "L". *Another derivation of the square, the "L" is a common compositional structure used in urban design and site planning and can be composed of many smaller shapes as long as the "L" is the organizing mechanism. Obviously, the "L" can have different orientations and rotations.*

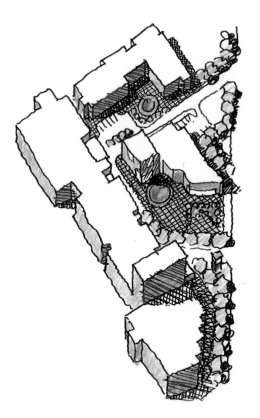

Figure 4.33. "L" as leisure retail center. *The "L" has many applications especially on small or tight sites. This illustrates a small leisure retail center on a triangular site, with one "L" nested in another.*

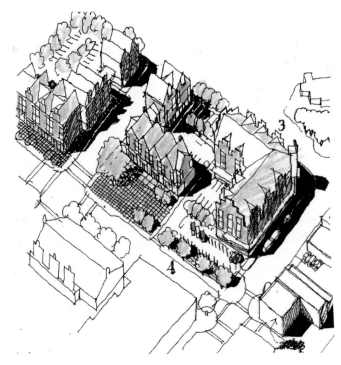

Figure 4.34. "L" as mixed-use block. *In this illustration, three "L" structures of residential/retail buildings comprise a mixed-use complex, dramatized with varying setbacks, creating diversity of form with one compositional structure repeated three times.*

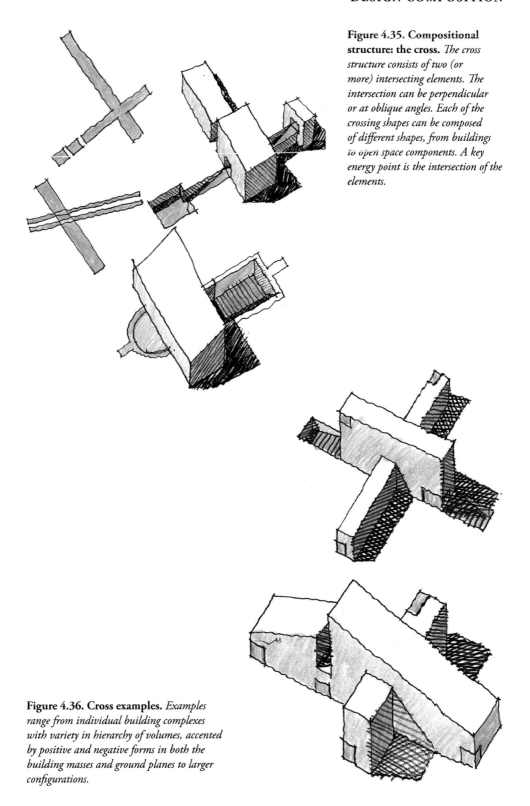

Figure 4.35. Compositional structure: the cross. *The cross structure consists of two (or more) intersecting elements. The intersection can be perpendicular or at oblique angles. Each of the crossing shapes can be composed of different shapes, from buildings to open space components. A key energy point is the intersection of the elements.*

Figure 4.36. Cross examples. *Examples range from individual building complexes with variety in hierarchy of volumes, accented by positive and negative forms in both the building masses and ground planes to larger configurations.*

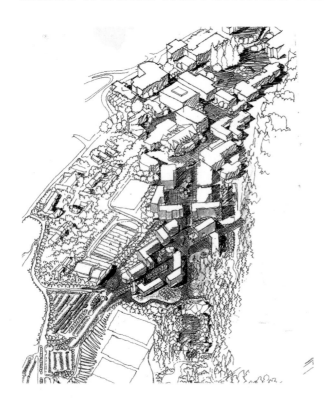

Figure 4.37. Cross complexes.
In large compositions, such as Western Washington University expansion option, a crossing axis with courtyards assembles and connects new development to the existing campus pattern.

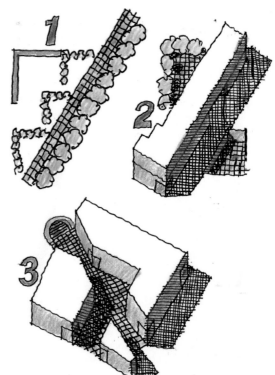

Figure 4.38. Compositional structure: the diagonal. *The diagonal is another derivation of the square and provides both a sense of direction and movement. As in the illustration, the diagonal can be an axis for movement in relation to an orthographic pattern, or it can appear as a positive building mass orientation against the grid, or as a negative void within a building mass complex. I use it extensively in later, more complex examples.*

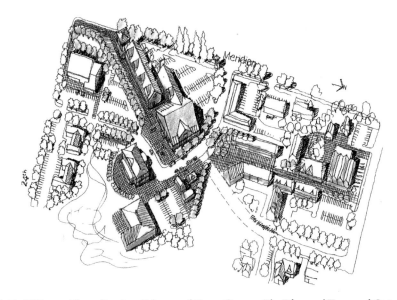

Figure 4.39. "Diagonal" application: Edgewood Town Center. *The Edgewood Town and Civic Center is connected to the main street intersection and related off-site new developments with an axial diagonal pedestrian concourse that directs movement toward a new city hall site. Civic buildings, new mixed-use commercial buildings, and a historic farm complex are visually and physically assembled parallel to and at the termination of the diagonal axis. As in all compositions, trees and landscape elements define space rather than simply occur within space—the trees strengthen and highlight the diagonal structure.*

Circle characteristics

Circle: a plane curve everywhere equidistant from a given fixed point, the center.

    Basic characteristics:

- center point
- perimeter equidistant from same point, circumference
- radii all equal length
- arc: indicating at least two intersecting radii perpendicular to the arc.

    Implied characteristics:

- center point and radius
- radius
- arc
- three dots along circumference.

Circle derivates

Radial burst structure:

- circular relationship in which the radii are different lengths emanating from same center, implying movement and direction and an irregular perimeter.

Curvilinear dominance:

- curves and spirals predominant
- serpentine, arcs, ovals, motion.

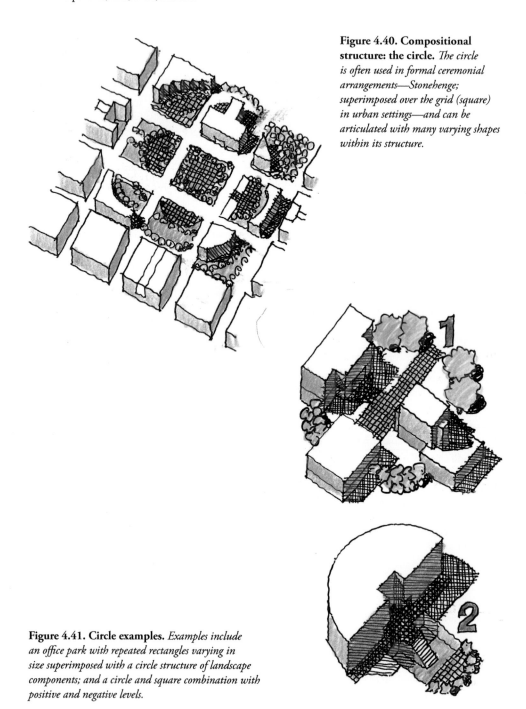

Figure 4.40. Compositional structure: the circle. *The circle is often used in formal ceremonial arrangements—Stonehenge; superimposed over the grid (square) in urban settings—and can be articulated with many varying shapes within its structure.*

Figure 4.41. Circle examples. *Examples include an office park with repeated rectangles varying in size superimposed with a circle structure of landscape components; and a circle and square combination with positive and negative levels.*

Town Center Community Focus: Civic Center

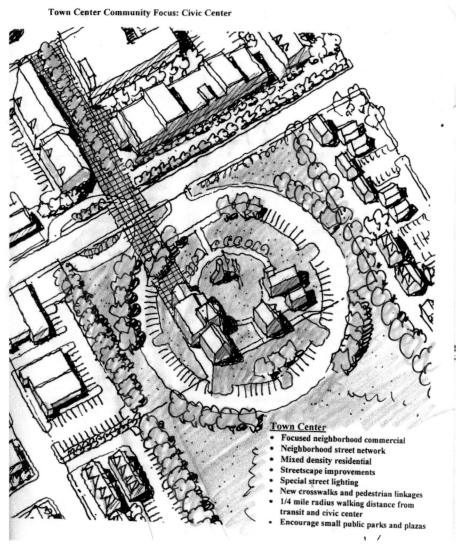

Town Center
- Focused neighborhood commercial
- Neighborhood street network
- Mixed density residential
- Streetscape improvements
- Special street lighting
- New crosswalks and pedestrian linkages
- 1/4 mile radius walking distance from transit and civic center
- Encourage small public parks and plazas

Figure 4.42. Town center circle structure. *In Edgewood Town Center, a circular structure defined by the parking area provides a phase one framework for a civic and town center with future phases responding to the outer edge of the circle (not shown).*

Line characteristics

Line: a geometric figure formed by a point moving along a fixed direction and the reverse direction.
Basic characteristics:

- length is longer than width
- directional movement indicator
- a border, boundary, contour.

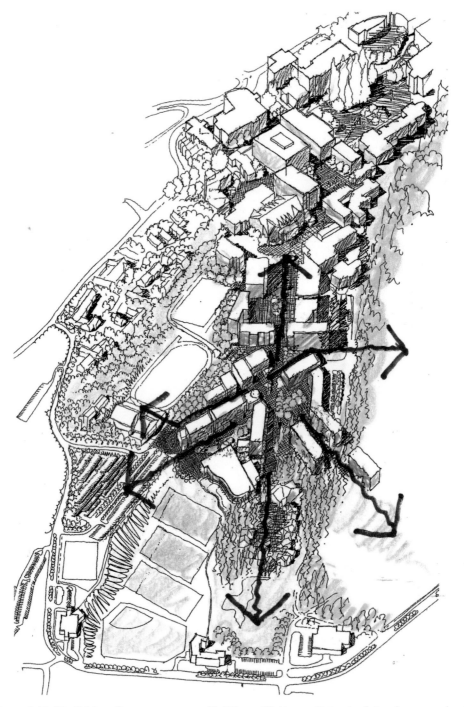

Figure 4.43. "Radial burst" campus concept. *The Western Washington University design charrette explored a radial burst structure to connect educational pods within the southern sector of campus, connecting new and existing facilities with a radial burst pedestrian pattern emanating from a key intersection open space.*

Implied characteristics:

- the axis
- two or more connected dots
- an arrow: movement and direction
- beginning and an end
- solid
- broken
- straight
- curvilinear
- intermittent.

The axis is a powerful structuring mechanism usually combined with other compositional structures. An axis is not limited to a straight line. It can change direction and is often used in design configurations, from straight to curvilinear to broken, etc. Suggested angles of change include: 0–180, 90, 45–45, 45–22.5, 30–60/60–30.

Other angles of directional change are certainly valid. The conventional angles listed above provide workable mathematics in form without getting unnecessarily complicated. In order to challenge the rules or guides, learn the basics first.

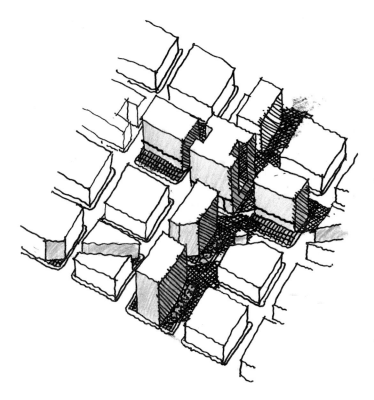

Figure 4.44.
Compositional structure: the axis. *Streets in the grid are axes, as is a river and a freeway—a powerful linear force that assembles functional relationships within and along its movement and direction. In urban settings, they provide direction and penetration into and through dense building masses for orientation, reference, and movement—both with the grid and at angles to the grid. A progressive or graded axis structures the main avenue in the grid and diagonals cut across the grid.*

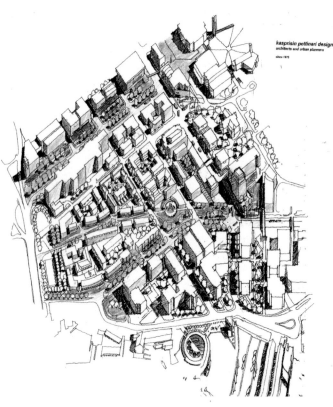

kasprisin pettinari design
architects and urban planners
since 1975

Figure 4.45. Formal and informal axes in urban contexts. *The axis provides order and orientation to dense urban areas. In the southwest UW campus plan axonometric, axes occur as formal boulevards, casual and curving streets, and pedestrian concourses— connections between courtyard typologies and the basic street grid.*

Figure 4.46. Axis as pedestrian concourse. *At the human scale, the axis as pedestrian concourse connects people to their immediate environments within the larger urban core. It also attracts uses and features along its edges, activating the concourse experience and providing connections between and among downtown components.*

Other compositional structures

Other compositional structures include bridging, cantilever, superimposition, clustering, merging, and interlocking mechanisms.

Bridging structure

- Often two or more centers or foci joined by a connecting element or relationship.
- Bridging structures can be elevated, depressed, at grade level, and even vertical, as in an elevator or funicular, such as an elevated sidewalk/skybridge, underground concourse, or inclined elevator.
- Most bridging mechanisms are physical but can also be implied via cultural histories related to a specific site or historic cultural pattern with remains of past infrastructure, buildings, or natural features (a disappearing forest recharge area, for example).
- Bridging can be implied through a placement of opposites (solid/void, complementary and opposite colors, positive/negative).

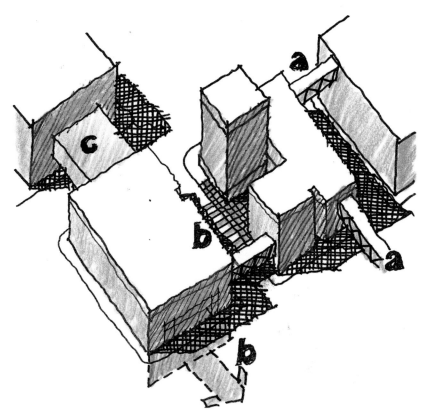

Figure 4.47. Compositional structure: classic bridging. *Bridging can occur with a conventional crossing (over and, in its polarity, tunneling under) of physical features (water bodies, freeways, urban blocks, etc.). In the illustration, (a) represents skybridges, often in cold weather urban areas; (b) represents at-grade crossings as a common bridging mechanism; and (c) represents a building component as the bridging mechanism.*

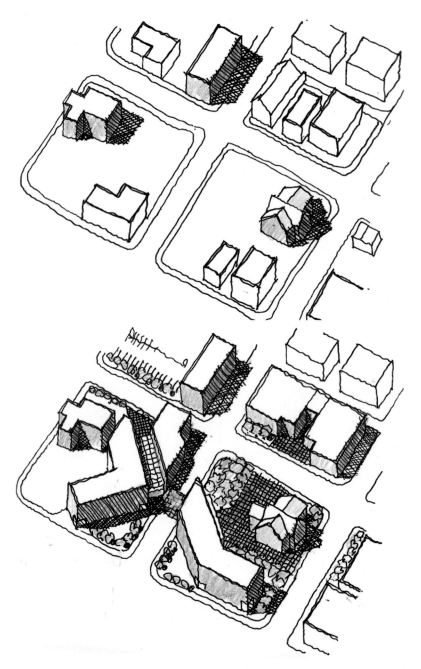

Figure 4.48. Bridging as connecting mechanism. *Most bridging mechanisms have a connecting function and can be effective in linking existing significant features, such as historic buildings, to new development. The orange represents existing civic uses and the blue represents an historic/heritage building. Bridging and connectivity are nearly synonymous, as we shall see later in the book. This simple example underscores the importance of connecting or bridging key features within the built form to new development, possibly with design guidelines or overlay policy.*

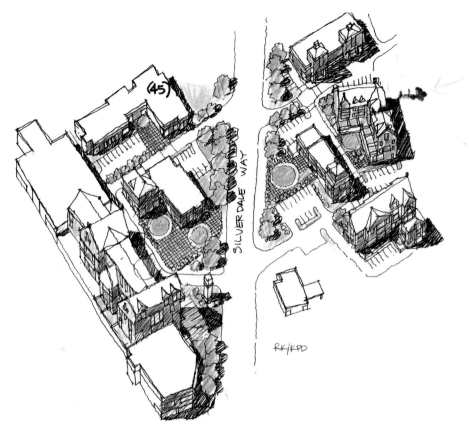

Figure 4.49. Bridging between developments. *Bridging can be effective in both connecting two sides of a major arterial and different development entities with open space features, building orientations, repeated elements, etc.*

Cantilever structure

- A projecting structure that is supported at a point closer to one end and carrying a load at the other end or along its length.
- Usually used in support of other structures and relationships.

Superimposition structure

- To superimpose is to lay one element or pattern over another. The principle can also imply the dominance of one element over another.
- Superimposition can be a space, e.g., a circle structure over a square structure, a sphere within a cube, etc.
- Two spatial relationships brought together in an overlay pattern, including two conflicting or opposing relationships seeking a new outcome through superimposition.

Figure 4.50. Compositional structure: cantilever A. *The cantilever is a suspension in space at one end of an element or composition, in this example, extending out and over a lower space as in observation decks. Even though this is an object— cantilevered deck—the concept can be expanded to a cantilevered waterfront walkway along the larger waterfront, for example.*

Figure 4.51. Compositional structure: cantilever B. *In this example, the cantilever is a waterfront dining area extended out over the water, and an observation platform over a protected urban habitat area.*

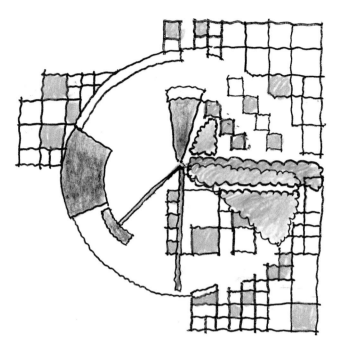

Figure 4.52. Compositional structure: superimposition A. *Superimposing two or more different spatial structures can lead to new integrated compositional resolutions as illustrated here with square, rectangle and axis overlain on to a circular form.*

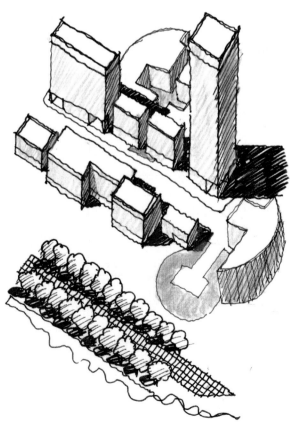

Figure 4.53. Two compositional structures: superimposition B. *This example takes a linear building axis and superimposes circular structures over the axis at key locations.*

Clustering structure

- Clusters are groups of spatial elements arranged around a common or shared feature(s) or facility, in close or compact arrangements, with open space among them. They are typically connected to a larger framework, such as additional clusters, by axial elements (roads, paths, alleys, mews, etc.). Clusters can assume the form of other compositional structures (circles, squares, etc.) that guide the arrangements of their interior elements.
- They can range in type from courtyard housing to office compounds in a campus setting, and can be composed of the same building typologies or mixed-building (and -density) types such as farmsteads and other mixed-density housing projects (illustrated later in the book).

Merging structure

- Merging is to combine or unite elements and structures into a single entity.
- Merging is effective if the characteristics of each original element or structure are retained within the merge as well as the blending of those initial characteristics into new elements or structures, a form of bridging.
- A metaphor example is the merging of two parent entities that form a new outcome and have their characteristics retained in the new pattern.
- Merging is a valuable tool for treating edge conditions between and among development phases and types.

Figure 4.54. Compositional structure: clustering. *In this illustration, courtyard clusters are combined with an axial open space/wetland structure (Edgewood Meadows) to assemble and frame a new town center connected to a new civic center: The Meadows of Edgewood.*

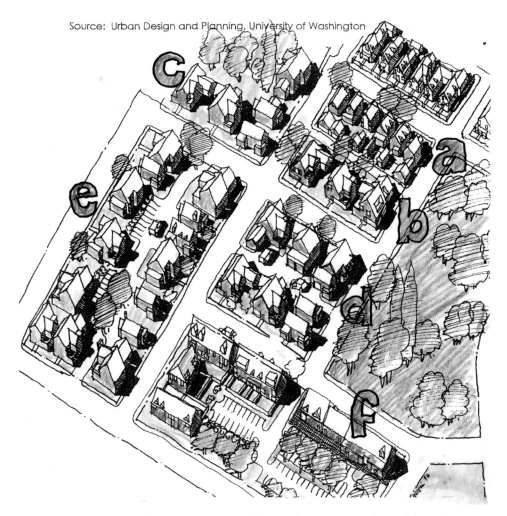

Source: Urban Design and Planning, University of Washington

Figure 4.55. Compositional structure: merging. *The example experiments with mixed-density housing types to address edge conditions between different density and typology developments, mixing and merging types at key edges.*

Interlocking structure

- Interlocking is the integration of two or more shapes, patterns, or structures into one another using a positive/negative, projection/concave interaction.
- Take the fingers of each hand and bring them together in an interlock or saw-tooth versus adjacent position.

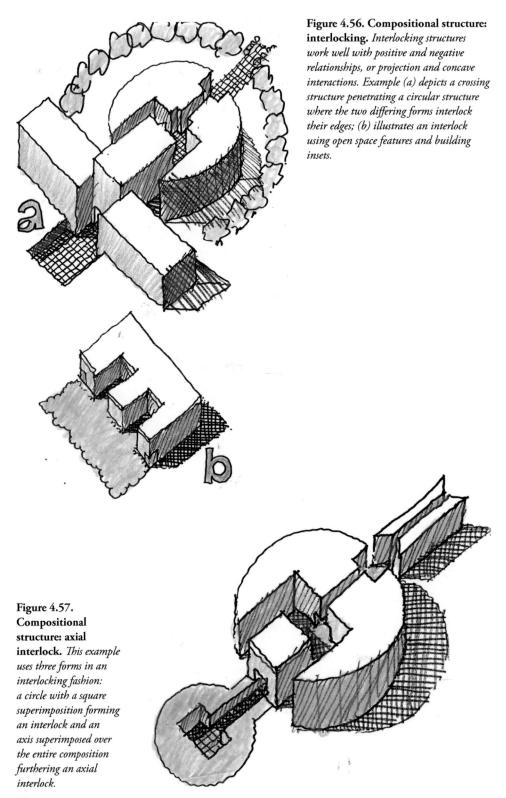

Figure 4.56. Compositional structure: interlocking. *Interlocking structures work well with positive and negative relationships, or projection and concave interactions. Example (a) depicts a crossing structure penetrating a circular structure where the two differing forms interlock their edges; (b) illustrates an interlock using open space features and building insets.*

Figure 4.57. Compositional structure: axial interlock. *This example uses three forms in an interlocking fashion: a circle with a square superimposition forming an interlock and an axis superimposed over the entire composition furthering an axial interlock.*

Spatial frameworks: underlying guides for composition

Guides for composition: spatial frameworks

Spatial frameworks are guides that assist in assembling compositional structures by providing a basic underlying spatial mathematics for design compositions. They can be direct, obvious (street grid) or hidden and invisible. When students set out to begin assembling a composition, they often work from a scattered or ambiguous base. The spatial frameworks provide a starting point which are flexible and easily manipulated for novel effects. The block grid in many cities is a visual–spatial framework that assembles and guides the foundation for different forms. Underlying that block grid is a mathematical grid, composed of squares or square derivatives. A curvilinear form may have as a framing structure an underlying grid where the corners, half and quarter points, center, etc. provide intersecting references or anchors for the curved forms, enabling a manageable implementation and assembly process—and it is not (easily) visually perceived in the resulting form.

These frameworks are useful for the designer in that they provide a quantifiable means of making complex form that is plausible, less complicated, and measurable. I refer to them as transparent or ghost structures—invisible. The difference between these and other structures is their hidden role of assembly.

I urge my students when beginning their explorations of composition to use a basic grid for both horizontal and vertical planes—not for regimentation but simply as a flexible guide.

I developed the example illustrated in Figures 4.58 to 4.60 for students to portray an exploratory search for a compositional structure for a complex of buildings. The structure, in this case a resulting triangle, began to emerge as I played with the elements, the site, principles of repetition, and repetition with variety.

Some assumptions: this fictitious complex has an organizational relationship that translates into an initial radial repetition of buildings oriented toward the northwest along a lake edge, not unlike an institutional facility. Phase one is a given, as in the *initial design notion (a)*. The structural relationships are exhibited in this semi-radial first design notion and are deemed suitable for the functioning of the organizational need contained within the buildings.

Based on this first notion, the initial structural composition is interacted with the site context for a starting point. This is important for students: do not try to be "perfect" or final as you bring together the organizational and structural relationships with site context—it is simply a starting point. The *second design notions (b) and (c)* are play efforts to protect the structural relationship *(a)* and expand the concept to the larger site, responding to northwest and southwest orientations along the water's edge. Remember, this is fictitious so use some imagination. These notions also provide emergent design opportunities as they interact with the site in different ways. I began searching for a larger compositional structure that had potential for providing a framework for future development, knowing that many designers will participate in the fulfillment of the master plan over an extended period of time.

The triangle as compositional structure. Based on the water's edge form and the initial semi-radial structure of *(a)*, I tested a triangular compositional structure on the site, making efforts to have corners of buildings coordinate with the triangle edge. Based on some additional play, I decided to apply a more direct geometry to the initial semi-radial structure, maintaining the radial principle and strengthening the composition by using a common center point with radii emanating out to the centers of each building, adjusting them perpendicular to the radius. See *design notions (d and e)*. Both efforts fit into the triangular compositional structure and present new opportunities for site development. As is illustrated in *design notion* (f), building shapes can vary as new phases adapt to changing programs and the compositional structure holds together.

This may seem somewhat complicated but I am interested in the *effort of experimentation* not a predetermined master plan outcome.

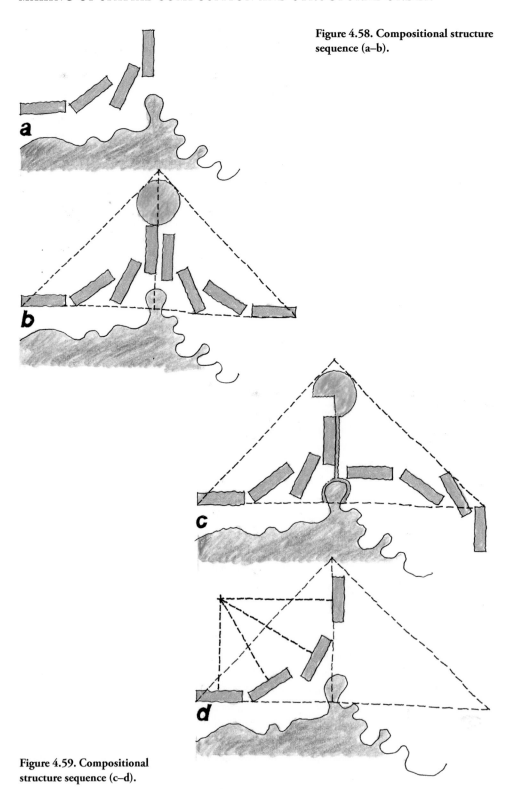

Figure 4.58. Compositional structure sequence (a–b).

Figure 4.59. Compositional structure sequence (c–d).

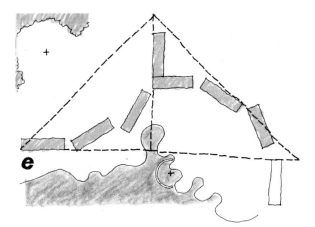

Figure 4.60. Compositional structure sequence (e–f).

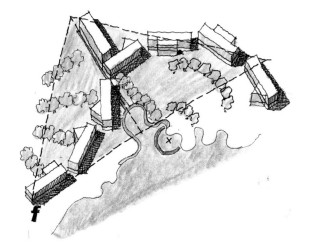

Additional reference frameworks

Continuing with the idea of spatial reference frameworks to aid in design composition, remember that as structures they hold larger complex compositions together, and provide a mathematical or quantifiable basis for design and implementation. They are not necessarily obvious or visual in the final composition—thus this separation from the previous discussions of compositional structures is not the only form of spatial framework although it generates numerous derivatives. As the urban form increases in complexity, the designer can utilize hybrids of the square and circle to establish an underlying order. The use of fractals is an additional basis for spatial frameworks, depending upon the specific context.

These frameworks are useful for emerging designers in that they provide a quantifiable means of making complex form that is plausible, less complicated, and measurable. I refer to these a transparent or ghost structures—invisible. The difference between these and other structures is in their hidden role of assembly.

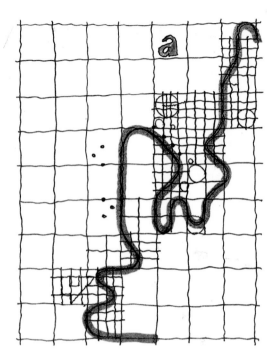

Figure 4.61. Transparent or ghost frameworks with underlying grid. *This playful diagram portrays a curvilinear form being constructed on a variable grid, with squares of different sizes as needed. The curvilinear form is anchored on key intersections of the grid for reference and orientation.*

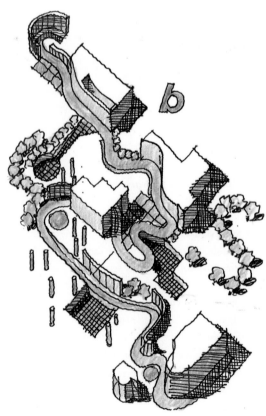

Figure 4.62. Resulting form with invisible grid. *In this illustration, the resulting form is visible without the underlying ghost framework.*

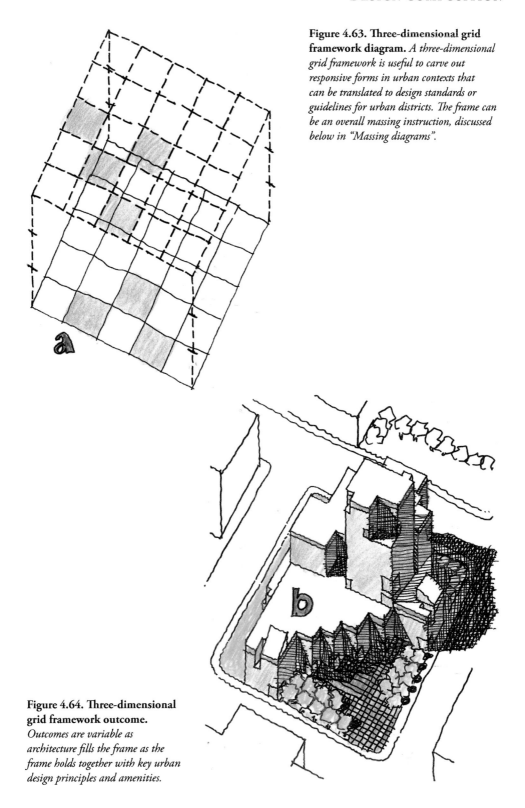

Figure 4.63. Three-dimensional grid framework diagram. *A three-dimensional grid framework is useful to carve out responsive forms in urban contexts that can be translated to design standards or guidelines for urban districts. The frame can be an overall massing instruction, discussed below in "Massing diagrams".*

Figure 4.64. Three-dimensional grid framework outcome. *Outcomes are variable as architecture fills the frame as the frame holds together with key urban design principles and amenities.*

Compositional massing: form-based implementation

Massing diagrams

Compositional massing diagrams are the outer limit of preferred design envelopes in urban (and regional) contexts. They specify use (what), quantity (how much), location (where), and design amenities and/or features related to onsite conditions and off-site relationships. The compositional massing is use dependent in that land and building uses/density influence building typology. Attempting to assemble a form-based design massing diagram without knowledge of potential uses can lead to naïve or problematic implementation of reasonable development within the envelope.

Urban design often serves as a testing procedure for land use, zoning, and planning policy decisions by exploring and visualizing the potential outcomes of development. The testing begins with allowable zoning and proceeds through massing exploration relative to the site, resulting in form that is design-inclusive (as opposed to the conventional economic zoning envelope) and augmented by architectural examples for scale, style and detail. Gordon Cullen used compositional massing in the 1950s and 1960s as a tool in visualizing new built form within an existing and often historic context. His masterful perspective diagrams portray both existing specific built form and the larger massing envelopes, with historic buildings highlighted for reference and orientation (see Cullen, 1961, pp. 107, 214, and 231). They are not new but remain valuable tools in form-based zoning.

Design implementation composition diagrams

Compositional massing plays a critical role in design implementation, particularly when visualizing design standards and guidelines. Interpretation of design guidelines is an ongoing challenge for laypeople and urban planners as they review and assess projects, often leading to unnecessary compromises, vagueness, and mediocrity. Urban design compositional diagrams can clearly portray key design principles both in intent and in specifics. I use the following steps to provide that clear intent, the ability for design flexibility in interpretation of the guidelines, and specific compositional massing:

- *Design intent*: the directed and earnest aspirations of stakeholders represented by specific actions in the guidelines regarding sensitivity to context and design approach to a specific location and/or place.
- *Design principles*: the guiding rules of conduct underlying the intent, specifically related to how the elements and principles of the design composition respond to and fit into the existing and/or emerging context.
- *Design actions*: the specifics regarding design construction re: height, setbacks, access, orientation, connectivity, phasing, etc.
- *Design examples*: architectural, landscape architectural and urban design visualizations of design interpretations that maintain the intent and principle underlying the guidelines. These can describe scale, materials and, in some relative cases, style.
- *Design departures*: this constitutes an argument for departure(s) from established guidelines and standards based on key urban design amenities possible through the departures.

The compositional diagram provides the anchoring mechanism for these five levels of evolving specificity. The following examples use these diagrams during the testing phase when proposals and policy are explored on specific sites and locations, and in the representation of final design guidelines.

"Visions for Sechelt, British Columbia, CA". I include the entire document page for this project to illustrate two examples of design intent, principles and examples for selected sites along the Sechelt waterfront. The vision document went beyond aspirations and future "wish-list" elements, focusing on principles and implementation strategies for this community along the Sunshine Coast of British Columbia, north of Vancouver. Each "vision"—connecting and orienting development to the waterfront, for example—was accompanied by implementation guidelines.

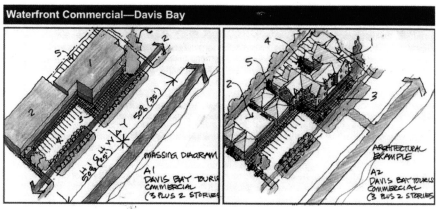

Massing Diagram (B1):

1. Two storey residential over one storey ground level retail on each end of the development.
2. One storey residential or office over ground level retail in centre of development to allow view corridors for adjacent residential areas.
3. Front yard plaza connecting public sidewalk to development.
4. Side yard parking on one or both perimeters of the site.
5. Building mass occupies 55% to 65% of the length of the site to increase view corridors along each end of the site.

Architecture Example (B2):

The sketch represents an architectural translation of the massing diagram, with a mid-complex front yard plaza facing the waterfront and street; and a lower mid-complex building height to afford views from the adjacent residential areas.

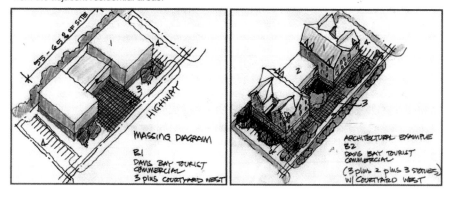

Figure 4.65. Sechelt diagrams. *This type of massing diagram applies at many scales, from small town to urban core.*

"Downtown Design Handbook: Silverdale, WA". This challenging project focused on converting a regional suburban shopping mall into a compact downtown core for an expanding community in Puget Sound, west of Seattle, WA. The "downtown" site consists of the regional mall and surrounding shopping centers and plazas served by a super-block arterial road network with minimal pedestrian amenities and few safe street crossings. Parking lots dominate the landscape and shoppers use their vehicles to travel from one plaza to another with little or no connectivity. This is not unique to North America, although the shopping center has certainly dominated the American landscape.

The challenge was to develop an urban design aspiration or intent for the commercial center: transforming the suburban fragmented pattern into a functioning and meaningful downtown community.

The Silverdale illustrations represent the final compositional massing diagrams approved and adopted by the Board of Commissioners for Kitsap County, WA. They encompass design intent and principles allocated for different design districts within the commercial center area. These districts ranged from a salmon habitat stream watershed corridor and wetland area, to the historic downtown on Dyes Inlet, to the surrounding suburban mall and plaza complex and office parks at the periphery. A local street network is incorporated into the guidelines as a catalytical incremental redevelopment strategy for the older shopping plazas as competition and consumer demands push for change. The compositional massing diagrams are accompanied by architectural visualization examples.

Additional characteristics of design composition

Proportion

Proportion is the amount or part considered in relation to the whole regarding magnitude, quantity or degree; a relationship between quantities or parts such that if one varies then another varies in a manner dependent on the first. Proportions establish a sense of order through the equality of ratios (fixed relationships between two similar elements); a consistent set of visual relationships between the parts and the whole.

Orders

Order is a fixed or definite arrangement of things often described as logical or comprehensive, such that proper functioning or appearance results. Order can also be expanded to complex systems where it is a dynamic force kept in balance by other factors—it is not static.

> healthy economies and healthy societies alike have to keep order and chaos in balance—and not just a wishy-washy, average, middle-of-the road kind of balance . . . Like a living cell, they have to regulate themselves with a dense web of feedbacks and regulation, at the same time that they leave plenty of room for creativity, change, and response to new conditions.
>
> (Waldrop, 1992, p. 294)

SILVERDALE GATEWAY COMPOSITION DIAGRAM

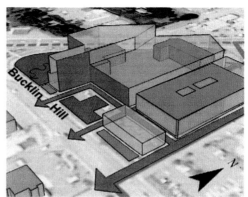

Silverdale Gateway Composition Diagram, 3-33
The Silverdale Gateway Composition Diagram illustrates an intense development pattern (Allowable Buildable Area ABA) complemented by a local street network (LSN—location variable), a daylighted Silverdale Creek open space in the southwest corner of intersection quadrant, and a quadrangle (Q) design feature for new development. Click on image to link to composition movie on page 26, chapter 3.

Figure 4.66. Silverdale Gateway massing. *The overall massing diagram designates the form-based development mass with connections to other sites. This diagram represents the design intent of the gateway area. The underlying text is a part of the images instructions to the observer.*
Source: Kasprisin Pettinari Design.

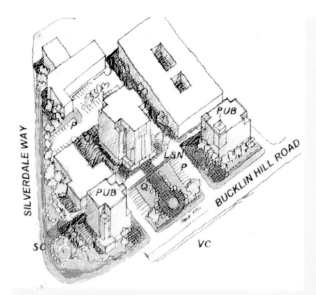

Silverdale Gateway Example Sketch (A), 3-34

The Silverdale Gateway sketch illustrates one example of accomplishing the design intent to intensify the northeast intersection of Silverdale Way and Bucklin Hill Road. The example uses a campus-style development type similar to the Northeast Business Park district. In this example, new buildings are arranged to provide view corridors **(VC)** of Dyes Inlet for existing buildings. Where the Silverdale Creek **(SC)** is day-lighted and incorporated into the open space quadrangles **(Q)**, a building height of eighty-five **(85)** feet is allowed for the participating property owners. A local street network (LSN) and parking lots **(P)** are dispersed throughout developments. Parking-under-buildings (PUB) occurs for new buildings. A pedestrian bridge **(BR)** connects the walkways along Bay Shore Drive with the Dyes Inlet waterfront walkway on the east side of the creek.

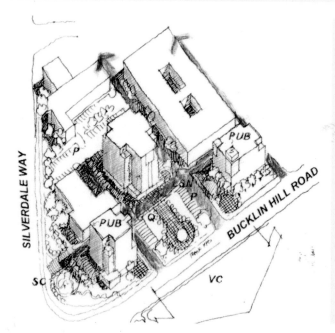

Silverdale Gateway Example Sketch (B), 3-35

Example B focuses on the campus-style quadrangles in a "T" shape oriented toward Bucklin Hill Road. A restaurant-type building **(RS)** is located in the "T" intersection on a plaza facing south towards Dyes Inlet. Silverdale Creek **(SC)** is a part of an open space water feature in a new development at the intersection. Pedestrian plazas or quadrangles connect the interior of the complex.

Figure 4.67. Silverdale Gateway examples. *The intent diagram was followed and augmented by several architectural examples illustrating pedestrian and vehicular circulation, open space/wetland protection and building placement.*

Why is this important for design? Order in design is often perceived as static, unchangeable, when in fact it can be a moving force in design composition, changing and adapting with the dynamic forces of the CST matrix.

- *Architectural orders*
  - a classic column: pedestal four parts, shaft at 12 parts, and capital at three parts
  - a building with a base pedestal of two stories, a main mass or shaft of six stories, and a cap of one story and a cornice.
- *Landscape architecture orders*
  - a main pedestrian concourse 12 feet wide for four people at 3 feet each to walk abreast in either direction
  - a campus master plan ordered around interconnected quadrangle open spaces.
- *Urban design orders*
  - dynamic arrangements or compositional structures in balance for a given time period
  - evolving structures that have the capacity to change and adapt without losing their structural integrity.

Scale

Scale is a reference standard in measurements; a proportion. A progressive classification, of size, amount or importance or rank. Scale is important to the human use of space in that the relationship between humans and their environment is either responsive or sensitive to human scale and perception of space or overpowering, oppressive and out of context to human scale. Buildings and certain master plans can portray power and symbolism, intentionally diminishing the human-scale interaction; and they can be intimate as special "places".

- *Generic scale*
  - lacking specificity, refers to an entire group or class of buildings, for example.
- *Human scale*
  - the built environment that is relative to the human body and includes all aspects of that environment, from building to doorway, from room size to fixtures
  - streets and sidewalks in relation to the grand mall or boulevard (for vehicles, not humans)
  - parks and open space: the small passive park or piazza in comparison to the grand commons and exhibition space.

Scale becomes an important benchmark in urban design compositions, where the human dimension is used to assess the intimacy level of a larger compositional structure. If the human-scale perception (place) is not present, then the structure or order has lost its balance, tilting toward functionality over meaning.

Infrastructure or functional scale

The scale required by the industrialization of our communities: sewers, water systems, transportation modes that are not necessarily human sensitive or in human scale. These can dominate the built environment landscape: for example, the athletic stadium surrounded by acres of car lots.

Bibliography

American Heritage Dictionary of the English Language, 5th edition, 2011: Houghton Mifflin Harcourt, Boston and New York.

Arnheim, Rudolph, 1969: *Visual Thinking*: University of California Press, Berkeley, CA.

Bettisworth, Charles and Kasprisin, Ron, 1982: "Tanana Valley Community College Master Plan": University of Alaska, Fairbanks.

Castells, Manuel, 1983: "The Process of Urban Social Change." Reprinted in Cuthbert, Alexander R. (ed.), 2003, *Designing Cities: Critical Readings in Urban Design*: Blackwell Publishers, Cambridge, MA.

Ching, Francis D.K., 1979: *Architecture: Form, Space and Order*: Van Nostrand Reinhold, New York.

Cullen, Gordon, 1961: *Townscape*: Reinhold Publishing, New York.

Edgewood, City of, 1999: "Town Centre Plan: Community Character and Land Use Study": Kasprisin Pettinari Design, Langley, WA.

Goldstein, Nathan, 1989: *Design and Composition*: Prentice Hall Inc., Englewood Cliffs, NJ.

Johnston, Charles, MD, 1984/1986: *The Creative Imperative*: Celestial Arts, Berkeley, CA.

Johnston, Charles, MD, 1991: *Necessary Wisdom*: Celestial Arts, Berkeley, CA.

Kasprisin, Ron, 2016: *Play in Creative Problem-solving for Planners and Architects:* Routledge, New York.

Kitsap County/Kasprisin Pettinari Design, 2006: *Downtown Design Handbook*: Kitsap County Department of Community Development, Silverdale, WA, and Kasprisin Pettinari Design, Langley, WA.

Sechelt, BC, District of, 2007: *Visions for Sechelt*: John Talbot & Associates, Burnaby, BC, and Kasprisin Pettinari Design, Langley, WA.

Soja, Edward W., 1996: *Thirdspace*: Blackwell Publishers Inc., Cambridge and Oxford, UK.

Soja, Edward W., 2000: *Postmetropolis*: Blackwell Publishers, Oxford, UK.

Waldrop, M. Mitchell, 1992: *Complexity*: Touchstone, Simon & Schuster, NY.

Chapter 5

COMPOSITIONAL TRANSFORMATIONS

SPATIAL ACTIVATORS FOR CREATIVE PROBLEM-SOLVING

We have discussed the major components of design composition, including:

- Understanding the meaning and functionality of human settlements through the CST matrix: addressing complex relationships and needs in human settlements.
- Defining a space program with organizational and structural relationships (meaning, function, component characteristics and assembly).
- Understanding the basic elements and principles (the "nouns" and "verbs" of the spatial language).
- Composing structural order with compositional structures (the assembling actions and mechanisms for composition).

This chapter completes the discussion of the major components with spatial transformations that help change and alter both individual elements and shapes as well as larger compositions. They are discussed within the framework of creative problem-solving, the pursuit of novel and innovative solutions through an open, playful process where outcome is uncertain and discovered through and manifested by the process itself. They include:

- dimensional
- subtractive
- additive
- mingling (formerly merging)
- bridging
- edge energies (connectivity)
- probability trajectories.

Compositional structuring assembles elements with basic rules or principles into meaningful forms and compositions. Based on the CST analysis and understanding of human settlements, the designer/planner is confronted with complex relationships (as both opportunities and problem sets). This requires an ability or capacity to manipulate form and urban patterns into structured urban compositions without losing underlying ordering principles—thus the composition of complexity notion.

Seldom can the primary shapes—planes, volumes, and compositional structures—be used in their pure state in urban design due to the complexity in existing urban form, as well as the new demands of the

CST trialectic (Soja, 1996). There are conditions where cube as house, for example, can be appropriately set in the landscape; or the grid-based residential neighborhood can be set in a greenfield, due to a lack of significant constraints. These are rare, however. In most urban or community situations, urban designers need to grapple with messy, complicated and disjointed urban patterns. Consequently, the compositional structures require playful modifications, manipulations, imagination, hybridization and overall creativity to "fit" into and coherently respond to existing and emerging context, maintaining the intended meaning and functionality of the "story" or program in a wholesome manner. Compositional transformations are key design tools to address this complexity. They build upon conventional transformational actions used in the design fields that also emanate from art.

The first three transformations (dimensional, subtractive, additive) represent those conventions (see Ching, 1979) and have been used for centuries by artists and designers. Merging, bridging, edge energies or connectivity, and probability trajectories are experiments that emanate from applications in practice and teaching inspired by creative systems theory (developed by Fritjof Capra, Edward Soja, Charles Johnston and others—see Chapter 2 of this volume).

Dimensional transformations of change

Dimensional transformations consist of altering one or more measurements of an object, form or composition. The square may become larger or smaller or change shape into a rectangle. If the parent identity is to remain, all relative components are made larger or smaller.

Methods of activating with dimensional change:

- compressing or elongating an axis
- changing a base dimension (as in a triangle or pyramid)
- moving an apex of a triangle off-center
- extending or compressing a radius
- altering dimensions within a grid pattern
- changing height, width, depth of a volume or composition.

Subtractive transformations of change

Subtraction is the act of taking away a portion of an element, volume or composition. At a certain point, the subtraction can cease in order to maintain the parent identity of the original; or it can continue and change the original into an entirely different identity. For example, a cube can have parts subtracted to the point of becoming a pyramid.

Methods of activating with subtractive change:

- Subtract portions of the original element or composition while retaining key characteristics of the original.
- Subtract portions of the original element or composition and alter its original identity into something else.
- Use solid/void activators to alter grade-level elements or compositions.

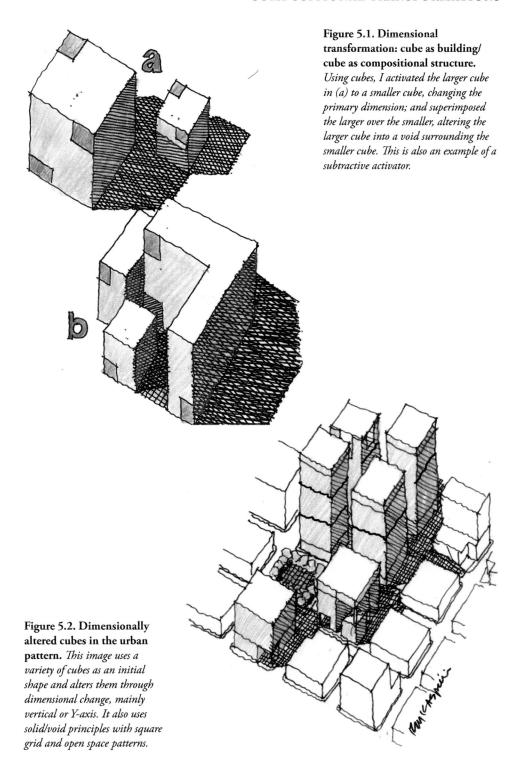

Figure 5.1. Dimensional transformation: cube as building/ cube as compositional structure. *Using cubes, I activated the larger cube in (a) to a smaller cube, changing the primary dimension; and superimposed the larger over the smaller, altering the larger cube into a void surrounding the smaller cube. This is also an example of a subtractive activator.*

Figure 5.2. Dimensionally altered cubes in the urban pattern. *This image uses a variety of cubes as an initial shape and alters them through dimensional change, mainly vertical or Y-axis. It also uses solid/void principles with square grid and open space patterns.*

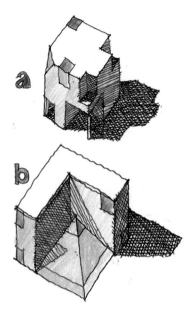

Figure 5.3. Subtractive transformations. *In (a), a cube becomes a house structure with subtracted forms indicating entries, decks, etc.; and in (b), the cube has portions subtracted to form a compositional structure based on the square. This is a fun exercise for beginning design students when asked to retain the original identity characteristics and alter the cube.*

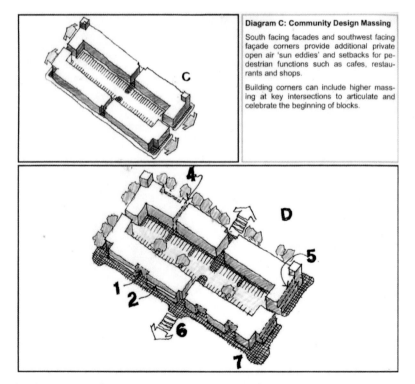

Diagram C: Community Design Massing

South facing facades and southwest facing façade corners provide additional private open air 'sun eddies' and setbacks for pedestrian functions such as cafes, restaurants and shops.

Building corners can include higher massing at key intersections to articulate and celebrate the beginning of blocks.

Figure 5.4. Subtractive transformations in zoning. *As a means of assisting community participants in understanding the use of form-based zoning in a downtown situation (Sechelt, 2007), a sequence of massing diagrams demonstrated with subtractive activators the implementation impacts from the larger original mass. These illustrate only two of the six sequential examples to help stakeholders understand the design implications in zoning.*

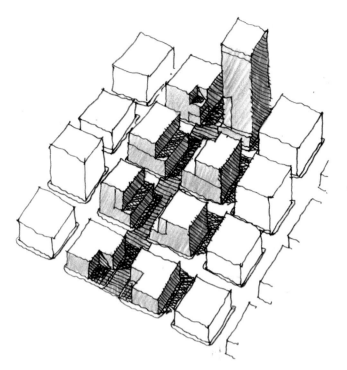

Figure 5.5. Subtractive urban block massing. *In larger urban centers, key streets, open space resources, significant buildings, etc. can be highlighted and supported by form-based design strategies using subtractive activators. In this example, volumes are subtracted from block masses to provide urban design amenities along a particular corridor.*

Additive transformations of change

Additive transformations consist of changing a form by adding another element or composition, keeping the original parent identity or major characteristics (a grid square composition) or changing the original significantly through addition—for example, the grid square to an "L" composition.

Methods of activating with additive changes:

- adding the same form to the original
- replicating the original form in different sizes, attached to the original
- expanding the original form dimensionally and adding complementary elements.

These transformations apply to the larger and more complex compositional structures as well. In certain circumstances, the structural relationships of a larger complex can warrant additive transformations through expansion of previously used forms or same-form additions to the underlying structural composition. As always, site conditions and the overall context require responsive forms.

Mingling as a transformational action

In the first edition of this book, I used the term *merging* to represent the act of combining various elements and compositions into a new whole. However, this term implies that those entities that are absorbed lose their identity—just the opposite of the action's intention. *Mingling* is defined as the act of mixing or bringing together elements and compositions into a combination—a much more appropriate word.

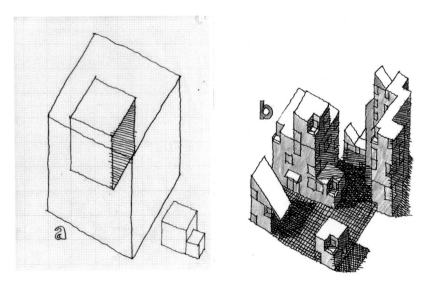

Figure 5.6. Additive transformations. *Illustration (a) displays a simple additive transformation of a small cube changing to a larger cube (also dimensional change), with a dimensional superimposition and a small appendage. Illustration (b) adds multiple cube derivatives to the original cube within the new superimposing cube/square compositional structure. Using repetition with variety, other cube derivatives are playfully added to form a more complex composition.*

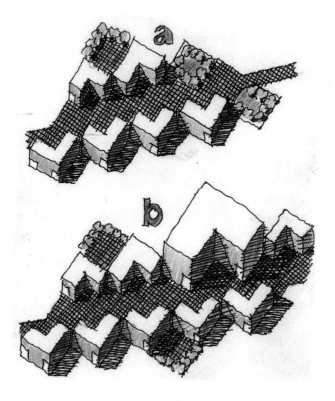

Figure 5.7. Additive transformations of structural compositions. *In this illustration, (a) represents a grid structural composition along an axial structure containing buildings and courtyards. In (b), the structural compositions are changed by adding both a dimensional action and an additive action.*

Mingling in the urban design context is the bringing together of two or more elements or compositions into a combination where the essential characteristics of the original entities are maintained and a third and distinct variation occurs at the transition area. I use an example from watercolor painting: to mix a secondary color such as orange that has variety and interest as opposed to a monochromatic appearance (one color—orange), I bring two colors together, red and yellow, and integrate them in a transition area, but do not paint over and thoroughly mix the two "parent" colors. Thus, I retain characteristics of the parent colors, red and yellow, and achieve a variegated orange effect within the transition area. The color wash now has variety and interest but is still read by the eyes as "orange".

Methods of change with a mingling action:

- colliding, integrating, interspersing two or more elements and compositions in a combination that retains the characteristics of the original entities
- blending transition areas
- merging elements at their edges only.

Figure 5.8. Mingling transformational actions in watercolor. *In this illustration, various strokes of varying blues and orange grays (browns) are mingled but not painted entirely over one another, creating a "blue-ish/black-ish" overall appearance in the ravens with variations in color and stroke combinations—a complex effect rather than one that is monochromatic. The new effect is rich within an overall color made from multiple colors brought together and combined.*

115

Let's experiment with this concept using semi-abstract shapes and compositions and then expand them into urban design applications.

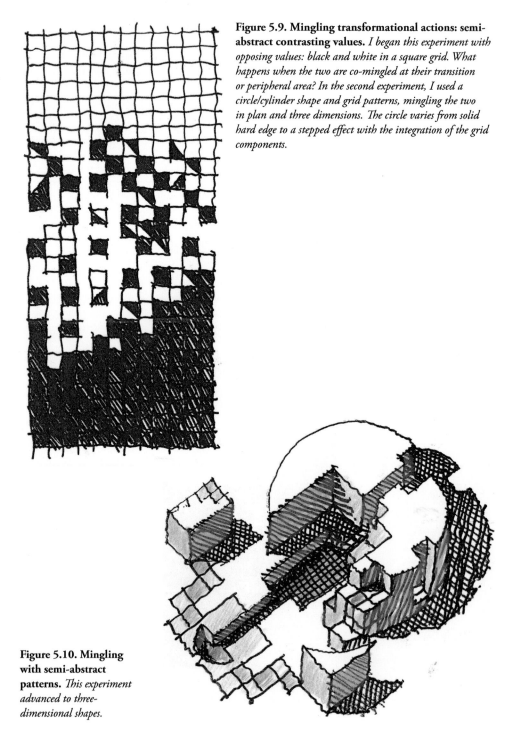

Figure 5.9. Mingling transformational actions: semi-abstract contrasting values. *I began this experiment with opposing values: black and white in a square grid. What happens when the two are co-mingled at their transition or peripheral area? In the second experiment, I used a circle/cylinder shape and grid patterns, mingling the two in plan and three dimensions. The circle varies from solid hard edge to a stepped effect with the integration of the grid components.*

Figure 5.10. Mingling with semi-abstract patterns. *This experiment advanced to three-dimensional shapes.*

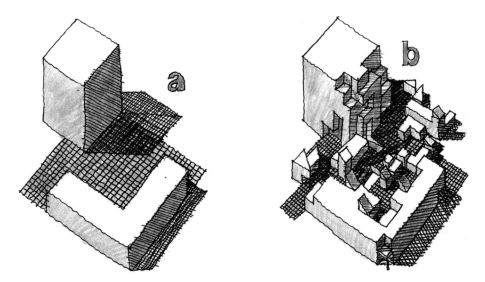

Figure 5.11. Mingling transformational actions: abstract compositions. *In this exercise for my planning students, the intent is to compose a new housing complex with variety, interest and intimacy (b) by mingling two major monolithic housing blocks (a), each representing a different housing typology (medium-rise stacked flats and rowhouses or double-loaded corridor units, with supporting retail uses). The exercise can be further enriched by setting a zero change in mass, with the mingled area absorbing as additive transformation that which is subtracted from the monoliths.*

Now let us experiment with urban design applications, using mingling as a transformative action.

Mingling as mixed-use transitions

Closer to reality, two urban design situations warrant the exploration of mingling transformations: mixed-use and mixed-density developments. Mixed-use is commonly applied as residential and/or office stacked vertically above commercial uses, or residential uses horizontally located behind street-oriented commercial uses.

Other applications can occur when two or more different uses or districts have a transition zone or seam, between residential and commercial and residential and industrial, for example.

Mingling as mixed-density transitions

Mixed-density situations can be found in examples ranging from European hamlet lots (three houses per lot, typically) to the farmsteads of Europe and North America, where varying housing types and support buildings occupy the same lot. As a mingling transformation urban design application, mixed-density brings together a same-use cluster comprised of a variety of housing types. The application can provide a transition between established residential neighborhoods with different physical characteristics and clusters of different building types in rural clusters, mingling the conservation of open space with a tolerable development density and marketing diversity.

The following medium-density example has principles that can apply to higher-density situations as well, exemplified later in book. It can be an effective way to break the suburban/exurban repetitive mode.

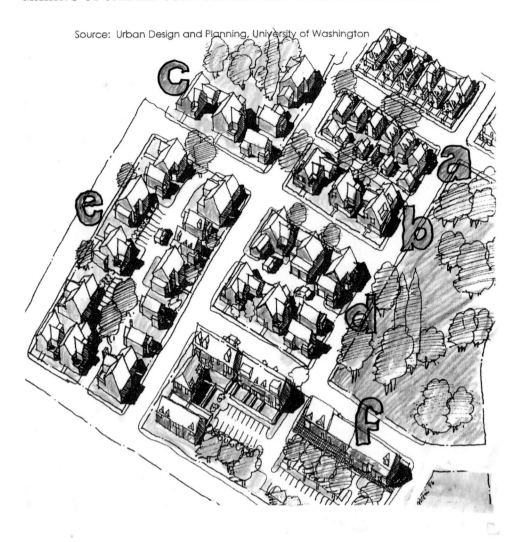

Source: Urban Design and Planning, University of Washington

Figure 5.12. Mingling transformational actions: mixed-use transitions. *This illustration portrays an integration of residential and light industrial live/work uses via interlocking urban blocks of mixed uses (and mixed density), including neighborhood or village retail/residential and single-use residential. Block (a) contains traditional single-family detached residential with fenced yards and rear alley parking. Block (b) contains single-family detached residential buildings with "mother-in-law" rear yard cottages and single-family attached residential with "mother-in-law" units attached to the main house. Multiplex single-entry houses are on corner lots. Block (c) portrays large single-family detached residential on a peripheral block. Block (d) portrays residential/light industrial and general commercial live/work buildings with common interior parking and street frontage orientation for shops. Block (e) portrays a more extensive live/work block with mixed building types ranging from attached larger buildings (residential on second level) plus smaller detached live/work houses. Finally, block (f) portrays a village center with retail commercial and residential uses both vertically and horizontally.*

Bridging transformational actions

Bridging is the act of connecting two distinctly different elements, volumes, or compositions into a new and uncompromised spatial outcome. It is accomplished by maintaining key aspects and principles of the original elements and integrating them into a third, different outcome.

Methods of transformation with bridging:

- between two differing or conflicting compositions, each separate in its function and meaning, maintaining the key principles of each in an integrated new outcome
- between current and anticipated patterns where adjacency and differences in meaning and function may occur; a form of connectivity
- between historic (remnants) and new patterns, where activating or reinvigorating the remnant pattern provides a bridge between past and future.

The act of bridging requires a concerted effort to avoid compromise as characterized by seeking one unifying element or composition (not to be confused with harmony); by separating and disconnecting compositions; or by joining one half of each differing composition wherein key principles of the original compositions are lost or diluted. Compromise in design composition includes clichés, thematic or fanciful or borrowed meanings.

Bridging confrontational or contrasting spatial relationships

Bridging is a form of creative connectivity wherein the design dialogue engages the initial confronting or contrasting relationships, explores their dynamics (CST), and minimizing or eliminating compromise, moves the design resolution process toward a third, distinct outcome that still maintains key principles of the contrasting relationships. Means of achieving this include:

- constructing an ongoing matrix or pattern that results from a multiple and descending scale design dialogue, covering more and more detailed issues, until a third, distinctly different set of relationships emerge within the evolving pattern
- anticipating connecting actions that can bridge differences
- planting catalyst actions that can energize or stimulate existing and evolving spatial patterns.

Within every design problem set, there are dualities that define the current limits of the design dialogue. These are often confrontational in nature. Bridging them is an act of integration without compromise. We explore these bridging actions in the next chapter.

Anticipating connections can be as simple as providing a street connection for future development, or pedestrian trail hook-ups, or a visually and/or physically shared open space. They can be as complex as a major mingling of two spatial relationships; or anticipating edge development probabilities (see "Edge energies" section on p. 125).

Planting catalysts can generate a dynamic ripple effect through an urban precinct or attract energy for future development activity (Attoe and Logan, 1989). More than connections, catalysts have a market and design force to expand their quality in meaning and functionality to other developments. Making design decisions for connective and catalyst devices in current time sets parameters for future and uncertain outcomes.

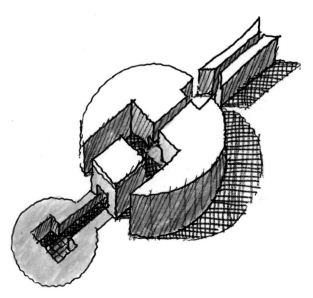

Figure 5.13. Bridging transformational actions: making connections. *Bridging confrontational or contrasting compositions can employ numerous techniques such as mingling and interlocking, as described in this chapter. The challenge is to connect them without losing key aspects of their physical natures. In the illustration, also used in Figure 4.57, bridging works with the experiment of the circle (cylinder) and square (cube) shapes intertwined without losing their original characteristics. The grid helps form the circle and the circle interlocks with the depressed rectangle (a portion of the grid); the axis provides movement and direction, and solidifies the overall assemblage.*

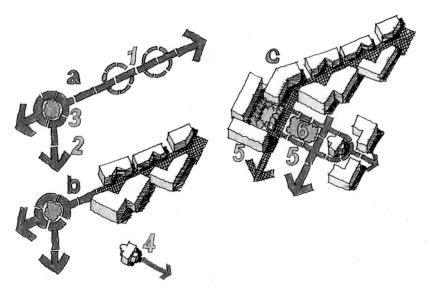

Figure 5.14. Bridging transformational actions: future connections. *Access corridors provide excellent examples of connections or bridges to future uncertain outcomes. TVCC, a community college campus in Alaska with a build-out span of 20 years, is structured around a semi-enclosed pedestrian/service access corridor (1) flanked by the larger assemblage of academic building clusters. The corridor is the compositional structure (axis) and acts as a design policy statement, anticipating future expansion in probable directions (2) around an intersecting open space (3). A later decision earmarks an older building (4) for adaptive reuse rather than removal as part of the larger facility, not anticipated in the original program. The location and orientation of the completed complex, with new building clusters adjusts in response to changing program requirements (5). The axis remains a bridging device in what that the principles of direction, movement, and open space at the intercept are maintained, simply altered based on the new emerging context. The open space intercept is expanded (6) and the adaptively reused (historic) building gains prominence within the larger composition. The principles of the bridging connection held together and adapted to changing conditions.*

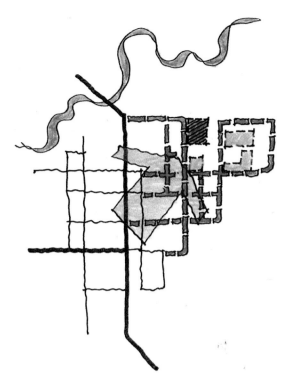

Figure 5.15. Bridging transformational actions: catalyst connections. *This is a hybrid concept diagram of Redmond, Washington's location for a new city hall and civic complex. Constructed over a decade, the new complex altered the direction of development in downtown Redmond and enabled the city to bridge the older commercial center with a new civic and mixed-use district, with improved orientation to the Sammamish River. The initial city hall was constructed with limited supporting infrastructure, awaiting peripheral development to cluster around it. Over time, as the complex and adjacent development matured, a new city hall was constructed, solidifying the new heart of the city.*

Bridging: remnant connections

Remnant: something left over; a surviving trace or vestige of something past.

Aren't remnants merely leftover icons, remainders, derelicts, diluted patterns or outdated monuments from previous periods? Why are they relevant for contemporary urban designers—as bridges to the future?

A remnant is an existing physical pattern (spatial entity as physical element, spatial structure, or spatial relationship) that has exceeded the functions of its original purpose, but its existence may have potential for new functionality and meaning—and become a bridging device from past to future. A remnant can be a defunct church structure; an original street pattern modified and manipulated based on changing uses; a vestige of a forest recharge area eroded by encroaching development; or an historic complex no longer used for its original and intended purpose.

Parent pattern (of the remnant—as system: CST)

The parent pattern of the remnant is the original time–context-specific spatial configuration or composition with cultural signatures (craftmanship, tools, materials, etc.), use and infrastructure technology imprinted in the form. The pattern is a system of connected parts performing a societal need and function. For example, Fort William H. Seward in Haines, Alaska, portrays the original fort constructed by the US Army around 1910–1914 to monitor the Yukon Gold Rush through Haines and Skagway (and possibly serve as Teddy Roosevelt's "big stick" reminder to the Canadians and British). The complex began as a military fort, branded fort "anywhere" architecturally, as it was designed along with numerous others in

Washington, DC. After being auctioned at the end of the Second World War to retired veterans and their families, it assumed many other functions: art community, hotel/restaurants, private residences, native art collective, and tourism attraction. A significant portion of the original fort complex remains as a remnant, both in plan and in building type; and other contemporary buildings and uses have been added, including cruise ship dock. The fort complex has evolved in a sputtering, sometimes destructive manner (major buildings destroyed by fire or disrepair), and provides an opportunity for a significant bridging action for new vigor into the community, with the remnant form as the foundation for a new, significant economic, cultural and physical entity.

Figure 5.16 portrays the remnant fort as it existed in the 1990s with an entirely different "story" or meaning in its current use; an intact parent pattern where the use and heart have changed, but enough of the original form remains as a potential bridge.

Classic remnant pattern

A classic remnant pattern is a historic pattern that has a use and form that transcend culture and time. The Pantheon is one such classic element with context (surrounding piazza) in that its original use, as a religious structure, remains to this day. The style of religion has changed from a temple to various gods to a Christian church (at various times of the year), marking a cultural shift. And pardon the tourists.

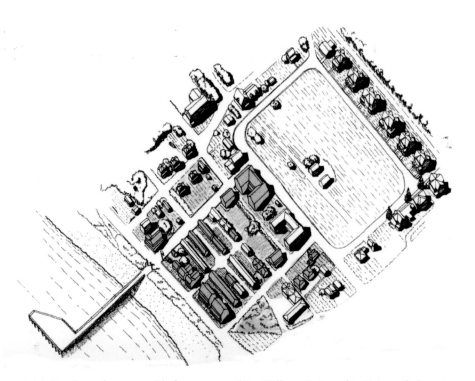

Figure 5.16. Fort Seward remnant. *The basic pattern of Fort William H. Seward in Haines, Alaska, exists to this day. The fort is occupied by artisans, hotels, restaurants, residences, bed-and-breakfasts, and vacant remnant buildings.*

A simple and small-scale example is historic Creek Street in Ketchikan, Alaska—a boardwalk neighborhood overhanging Ketchikan Creek salmon habitat. In the 1800s and early 1900s, Creek Street served as an "entertainment" area for fishermen, loggers, and others working the waters and forests of the Inside Passage of southeast Alaska. Of course, the entertainment ranged from music to taverns to red-light establishments with their ladies of the night. There was also a "married men's walk" discreetly located at the back of the creek. I spent a few fun years on and off living on the creek prior to its redevelopment as a tourist attraction related to cruise ships.

The key design compositional structure is a meandering axis comprised of Ketchikan Creek and the wood-frame boardwalk along the base of a steep bluff. The axis holds together a collection of restored, reclaimed, and reconstructed structures that provide new forms of entertainment, with shops, food services, etc. for thousands of cruise-ship passengers and visitors. During the 1960s and 1980s, the Creek Street complex was dormant, flanked by dilapidated buildings, the creek filled with discarded appliances among the returning king salmon—rescued by changing cultures and their economies.

Remnant context area

This is the adequate area within which key context information and influences exist. It has two components: first, a historical boundary for the time period of the original remnant parent; and second, a current or contemporary boundary for the remnant, which can be significantly different from the parent pattern. Each contributes information for the designer regarding the use of remnants in contemporary design processes. The context area provides a starting point for design analysis and is not considered hard or unchangeable.

Eroded remnant pattern

Over time, parent patterns lose their original use and are affected by emerging changes within the surrounding contexts, eroding the parent and often obscuring the original patterns. The parent is often uncovered through research and accident.

Transitionary remnant pattern

A transitionary remnant exists when the original function still exists in some state and is being eroded or usurped by contextual changes. The parent pattern is dissolving, leaving remnants where original use is no longer dominant in the form; emergent meaning is uncertain.

Enfolded remnant pattern

Enfolded remnants are two distinctly different period patterns folded into one another, superimposed or entwined, retaining characteristics of each original pattern.

Emergent remnant pattern

Emergent remnants are remnants that have incorporated or assumed new developing dynamic uses with new cultures, economies, and spatial adaptations, producing hybrid patterns. Certain alternative communities occupy and flourish in remnants, making adaptations and revitalizing the original remnant.

MAKING OF SPATIAL COMPOSITION AND STRUCTURAL ORDER

Summary

Remnant analysis asks whether a leftover or remaining pattern or element from previous cultures (or previous periods within the same culture) can be useful in design as:

- a hybrid design outcome with new uses compatible with the form characteristics of the remnant
- a bridging device or action between past and the emergent future, where a new use provides a valid and viable function to the historic remnant pattern
- creating a dialogue of urban form analysis for new adjacent or surrounding forms based on the remnant pattern and presenting an opportunity for interconnections between remnant and surrounding emerging forms
- providing a coherence or frame of reference within changing cultures
- providing a basis for comparison between old and new that enables the new to be more clearly identified.

Remnants can be categorized as (but not limited to) the following for discussion:

- natural systems
    - watersheds
    - recharge or discharge areas as forests and wetlands
    - meadows and prairies
    - flood-ways and water courses
    - wildlife habitat and migration patterns/routes
    - land forms as historic events (basalt cliffs, rock outcroppings, etc.)
- human systems
    - settlement patterns, current and historic
    - buildings, monuments
    - open space types
    - districts
    - cultural sites and patterns or routes
    - economic sites (canneries, mills, logging camps, etc.)
    - migration routes
- infrastructure
    - railroads
    - roads and paths
    - boardwalks
    - piers and wharves
    - equipment (gold dredges, ships, trains, etc.)
    - dams and locks
    - waterways
- symbols
    - signage
    - cultural identifying marks, art.

This is a start to identifying remnant patterns in the landscape and human settlements. The important point is to develop an awareness of the remnant pattern in design analysis.

Edge energies

I include "edge energies" as transformational actions because of the dynamics of change inherent in the "edge", as it is not in isolation or a void but always an end and a beginning of difference. They are an inherent aspect or component of every spatial entity or composition. They are also discussed in the section on "Connectivity".

All elements, systems, relationships, and compositions have containers limited by finite physical spatial edge conditions, all with dynamic characteristics. These conditions can be stable due to a dynamic balance of energy or actions, or in constant change through their differences (the wave to the shoreline) as they emerge and reform themselves.

Edges are multi-dimensional spatial entities that can range from remnant patterns to emergent realities. The beach is an example of a transitionary pattern or entity changing due to the wave expending itself on the landscape—sand, grass, cliff, wall, etc. The edge is the resultant effect of the "meeting", grounded in physics and often formed by a dialectic of nature and industry.

An edge is a boundary comprised of at least three elements or energies: A, B and the edge or meeting of the two. Sound basic? Hardly. Edges are transitional membranes: a relatively thin layer of material or energy—the crashing of a wave and the force generated as a result—separating or connecting elements, districts, regions, etc. Think of it as a membrane alive with energy that is a transformational action. There is an external to internal transference of energy, a translation from one spatial entity to another, from one form of spatial language to another. Resources are taken from one and transferred and transformed to another, as interlock, mingling, confrontation and resistance. A resultant effect can be entropic—a breakdown of an existing system—or creative in the formation of new and possibly novel product: the shell on the beach becomes sand; the boulder is dislodged from the cliff and becomes beach; the wharf is reduced to pilings; and creative energy and discovery can occur.

These transitional membranes are sources of creative capacitance: the restored floodplain absorbs the flood waters; the marshes absorb and filter runoff and the incoming tide with nutrient production; the public access facility connects humans to water; and the wharf is the place of exchange for transport mode and goods.

Edges are also barriers, as in the dam and the causeway, or the eight-lane highway traversing the neighborhood or the water's edge. Transportation systems provide access and movement for people and goods and are often planned in isolation from the larger urban reality, creating edge barriers that present future challenges for urban design resolutions.

Edges are always in motion, always emergent, and have both offensive and defensive responses to context. The motion factor is often overlooked in planning and design. Over time, an urban edge sheds structure as uses (economy and culture) change, and can be proactive with additive uses and new structures. The historic riverfronts of mill towns in the Pacific Northwest and the industrial banks of the Thames, blocked from community access for decades, have been revitalized and integrated into the larger urban function—connected.

The dynamics of edge energy are a major force in urban design, from the transition of urban waterfronts from industrial to human-friendly community resources to the protection of the rural edge from suburban encroachment. They offer opportunities for new development and hybrids as the edge energy is integrated into the design process.

Edge conditions are apparent in every aspect of human settlements and urban design—from urban to suburban, neighborhood to freeway, built environment to natural feature, etc.

Components and characteristics of edge

- natural
- manufactured
- solid
- porous
- mingled
- continuous
- intermittent/broken
- length (linearity)
- depth
- dissipative (aspect with the release of energy from one entity to another)
- height
- structure or assemblage
- organization of parts and functions
- portals
- multiplicity of layers
- transparent
- translucent
- opaque
- framed/unframed
- emergent or entropic
- gravity relevant
- culturally influenced: social amity/enmity, defense/privacy, economic, political, religious, etc.
- time-specific.

Urban edge explorations

Let's bring this into the urban design realm with examples and explorations of edge energies—from the human scale to the larger urban scale.

Edges in art play an important role in defining and integrating shapes, one into another. They contain shapes and the content they represent; they separate one shape from another, one content or meaning from another; and they integrate or mingle shapes through contrasts of size, value/tone, intensity, and position.

In urban design, edges define open spaces as courtyards, plazas, meadows, etc. They separate or distinguish one district or use from another, as in the transition from commercial district to residential district, or from single-family detached housing to multiple-family.

Keep in mind the *scale ladder* of edges in the region where you live: from major watersheds, coastal or lake edges to river systems like the Mississippi or the Columbia, to the urban edges of districts, to blocks and individual design elements.

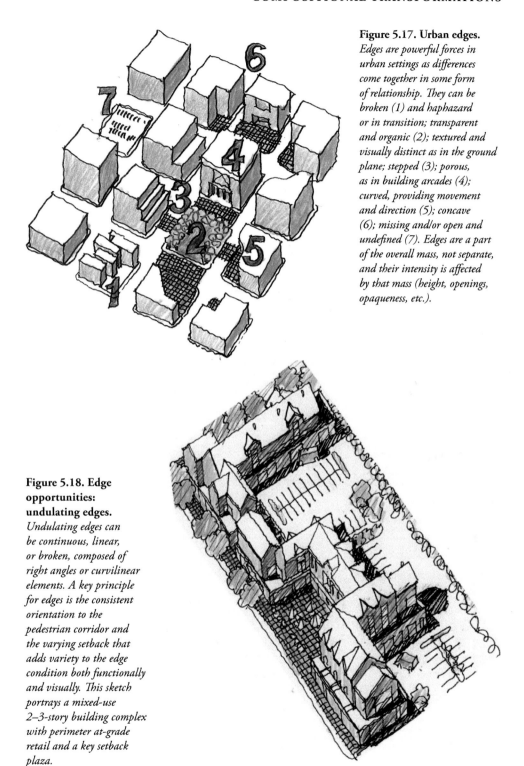

Figure 5.17. Urban edges.
Edges are powerful forces in urban settings as differences come together in some form of relationship. They can be broken (1) and haphazard or in transition; transparent and organic (2); textured and visually distinct as in the ground plane; stepped (3); porous, as in building arcades (4); curved, providing movement and direction (5); concave (6); missing and/or open and undefined (7). Edges are a part of the overall mass, not separate, and their intensity is affected by that mass (height, openings, opaqueness, etc.).

Figure 5.18. Edge opportunities: undulating edges.
Undulating edges can be continuous, linear, or broken, composed of right angles or curvilinear elements. A key principle for edges is the consistent orientation to the pedestrian corridor and the varying setback that adds variety to the edge condition both functionally and visually. This sketch portrays a mixed-use 2–3-story building complex with perimeter at-grade retail and a key setback plaza.

I cannot pass up the moveable or transient edge. The issue is actually quite serious in waterfront communities around the globe regarding view blockage. More and more common in waterfront tourism towns is the modern-day cruise ship, towering over the small-town forms with 8–13-story shops above the waterline. Often, they move in at night or early morning, disgorge thousands of passengers and then slide off into the evening light. I have worked in Ketchikan, Alaska, since 1976 BCS (Before Cruise Ships). The city rises up from the water to foothills and mountains approximately four to eight urban blocks from the waterfront. Many roads are boardwalk structures along the slopes. Views are abundant from the downtown waterfront to the west over Tongass Narrows, Clarence Strait, and the islands of the Inside Passage. The waterfront edge is fixed by docks, piers, and buildings and, every day from early May to late October, it is transformed by transient 13-story-high by three-block-long moveable edges represented by cruise ships. Economic development at what cost?

Edges define space, and space conversely influences edges—particularly with the uses and human activities occurring within the space and points of interaction between two different edges. Formal edges can contain and manage or direct the movements of large groups of people, such as stadiums or the piazza leading into and fronting St Peter's in Rome, where thousands of people flow in, assemble, and flow out. The physical characteristics of such large containers often provide respite within the edges—shade and services—or are hard and smooth to facilitate a quick transmigration of large numbers of people from one space to another, as in stadiums. Other activities may prefer a more playful edge strategy, where people gather, linger, socialize, and play, as in the outdoor edges around the perimeter of the Campo di Fiori in Rome. Activities are influenced by the sun, shade, food, wine, and nightfall along those edges. Edge characteristics respond directly to the CST matrix.

Finally, edges can be an integral part of *capture spaces* where they are designed to encourage lingering, pauses and impulse activities among pedestrians: the contemporary shopping mall complete with entertainment on small and grand scales. Most shopping malls and urban centers are formal structures with key principles of capture: anchor stores as destination attractions; corridors with highly visual and open façade edges facing the passing pedestrians; playful, active and attractive assembly areas, such as courts and food courts; and limited access points to the outside. Conventional commercial centers can have transparent exterior façades/edges to highlight the attractions inside or, opaque façades/edges with grand openings penetrating the façades at key locations.

The edge is a meeting of two or more different spaces, elements, activities, etc. and is a powerful tool in urban design strategies.

Corners

With the exception of the circle and the line or axis, unless broken or bent, most shapes have corners, places of emphasis, turning movements, surprise. They end a vertical plane and may begin another, or break for an opening or passage. Corners can be dynamic or dull, leading to discovery or disappointment.

I can turn a corner into an intimate courtyard or I can end up facing into a parking lot or car park. How corners are treated is a part of the composition methodology. Because they are stopping points or pauses on a journey along a vertical plane, for example, they can elicit drama, suspense, surprise, security or danger, and anticipation. Because they represent a change in a composition, they are a key feature in urban design.

Types of corner include:

- closed
- open
- dramatized or dancing (usually a vertical demarcation shape with movement from art-sculpture, contrasting shapes, etc.)
- corner opening
- curved
- transparent/translucent
- opaque
- connected (as in skyways or physical adjacency)
- soft and hard
- organic and manufactured
- deflecting
- anticipatory.

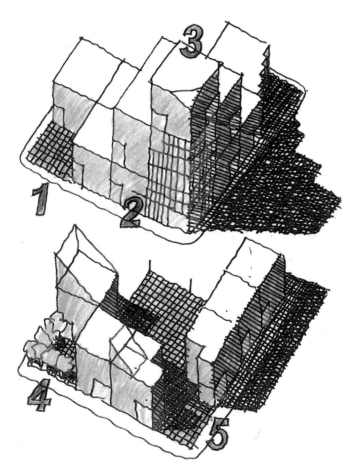

Figure 5.19. Corner opportunities. *This illustrates some of the many physical characteristics of corners, from closed to anticipatory. Corners can be open and inviting with proper climate orientation (1); enclosed and transparent (2); highlighted or dramatized (3); transparent and soft (4); open and penetrating (5); or, of course, closed.*

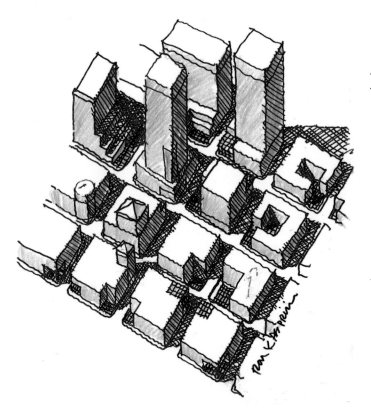

Figure 5.20. Urban corners. *This summarizes the many forms of corner features in urban contexts, from open and transparent to curved, dramatized, and opaque. Corners respond to pedestrian needs, such as outdoor seating areas, safe and clear openings and entries, protected spaces, such as indoor cafes with transparent edges, curved corners providing movement and direction around a corner, deflected corners again providing visual or physical movement, stepped, depressed, etc.*

Surfaces

Surfaces are often overlooked in urban design as compositional features. Gordon Cullen (1961) appreciated and celebrated the textures and decorations of walls and walkways, from cobblestone roughness to walls of color and graphics. Surfaces activate vertical planes with color and stimulate patterns. In central Rome, not only the earthen colors of the walls add to the walking experience: the textures of additions, repairs, and whims of centuries of people add character to the vertical and horizontal planes of the city, enliven the planes, and hint at human stories, from graffiti to protruding classical sculptures along a wall or in a pasture with meandering cows (such as in Sutra, Italy).

Contemporary surfaces can be bland, cold, and stark, offering little respite or interest to the pedestrian. Surface features can go beyond decoration or digital manifestations—providing transparency, direction and orientation, softness in a hard-surfaced urban environment with organic materials, vertical urban agriculture, pleasure and stimulus with arts and crafts, and community information and signatures.

Surface features can include:

- value with light to dark
- texture
- color
- porous to solid
- organic: soft and transparent or translucent

- manufactured: hard
- reflective
- informative
- moving: water features, reader boards, digital imagery
- audible: water cascades, music displays, digital sounds
- temperature-sensitive: warn or cold
- uncertain.

Color is another aspect of urban composition that is overlooked and streamlined into neutral grays and monochromatic applications. *Colour in Townscape* (Duttmann et al., 1981) investigates color typology in townscapes ranging from traditional usage to lively streets to case studies from around the world. Color can emote mood through color temperature (warm or cool) and drama (muted or bright and intense).

An important ingredient accompanying color is value (the varying degrees of light and dark in a composition). The use of value can provide contrast—for example, a light value next to a dark value will create emphasis. Value is discussed as a necessary ingredient in color usage in the arts more than in (urban) design. Placing light next to dark can evoke a strong contrast and draw the eye of the observer: light to mid-light elicits a dispersed light effect; mid-light to dark can evoke a more muted, cooler environment. Two key and favourite references for color and value include Duttmann et al. (1981) noted above, and Lawrence (1994).

Bibliography

Attoe, Wayne and Logan, Donn, 1989: *American Urban Architecture, Catalysts in the Design of Cities*: University of California Press, Berkeley, CA.

Bettisworth, Charles and Kasprisin, Ron, 1982: "Tanana Valley Community College Master Plan": University of Fairbanks, AK.

Capra, Fritjof, 1982: *The Turning Point*: Simon & Schuster, New York.

Ching, Francis D.K., 1979: *Architecture: Form, Space and Order*: Van Nostrand Reinhold, New York.

Cullen, Gordon, 1961: *Townscape*: Reinhold Publishing, New York.

Duttmann, Martina, Schmuck, Friedrich and Uhl, Johannes, 1981: *Colour in Townscape*: W.H. Freeman & Company, San Francisco, CA.

Edgewood, City of, 1999: "Town Centre Plan: Community Character and Land Use Study": Kasprisin Pettinari Design, Langley, WA.

Kasprisin, Ron, 1999: *Design Media*: John Wiley & Sons, Inc., New York.

Kasprisin, Ron, 2016: *Play in Creative Problem-solving for Planners and Architects*: Routledge, New York.

Kasprisin, Ron and Pettinari, James, 1995: *Visual Thinking for Architects and Designers*: John Wiley & Sons, Inc., New York.

Lawrence, William B., 1994: *Painting Light and Shadow in Watercolour*: North Light Books, Cincinnati, OH.

Sechelt, BC, District of, 2007: "Visions for Sechelt": John Talbot and Associates, Burnaby, BC, and Kasprisin Pettinari Design, Langley, WA.

Soja, Edward W., 1996: *Thirdspace*: Blackwell Publishers, Cambridge, MA.

Chapter 6

TYPOLOGIES IN URBAN DESIGN

*T*his chapter is significantly different from the first edition for the following reasons: building and development typologies are changing rapidly in global cities based in part on advances in engineering and manufacturing processes. Having urban planning and design students memorize typologies for many different uses and situations is not as effective as a direct engagement with those changing typologies. Consequently, this chapter focuses on exercises and examples for students of urban design that enable them to engage directly with them and learn by constructing, fashioning and hybridizing various typologies. Students can utilize any materials and tools with which they are comfortable. The key challenge for students is to use their imaginations and fashion typologies in crafted or digital drawings or physical models, without relying on applications of pre-set typologies. Once students become familiar with the various levels and applications of typologies, they can refer more to standard and conventional applications.

Instructors are welcome to use these exercises as a base for their own interpretations and contexts. They are not all-encompassing due to time and space limitations.

As an introduction, I want to set the stage for changes in conventional typologies as well as those that are still valid and current. This chapter deals with both existing and emerging building, landscape and developmental typologies. Numerous texts exist devoted solely to architecture and town form typologies, such as Krier (1988) and others.

Given major proposals for new urban orders, such as city sectors, districts and new cities around the globe, from North America to the Middle East, and the inclusion of new digital technologies in the planning, development and operation of these new urban orders, typologies are changing dramatically. These changes or hybrids can range from employment centers to housing typologies to mobility patterns—and the challenges of global branding and marketing for these new orders. Where and how people meet is a changing pattern, away from established or conventional centers to places of intersection and modal splits—the airport as city, for example.

The urban order

The urban order, the larger structured conglomeration of people, uses, buildings, open space and roads, has many manifestations in form and design, ranging from historic Prague to the hybridized clash of historic and new in Berlin and London after the Second World War, to dispersed and vehicle-dominated Los Angeles, to the "Neom" project in Saudi Arabia, a city based on alternative sources of energy and a hub for technological innovation. They are characterized by centers, districts, neighborhoods, transport corridors, blocks and streets, all imprinted by a certain time period and context. These imprints include cultural specifics that affect(ed) building configurations, construction materials and methods, and transport resources. They reflect history through the confinements of defensive walls and moats and the spreading patterns of outer lands or suburbia (beyond the walls) of North America. They are evident in the curvilinear cul-de-sac street patterns of 1960 "open" America, the New Urban (neo-traditional) grid typologies of the late 1990s, and the gated communities on the fringes of Vancouver, British Columbia.

The new urban order is spawning emergent patterns "post-metropolis"—after the mother city (Soja, 1996)—no longer connected to or dependent upon the *mother*. And this has and is generating new typologies based on innovations (or changes) in transport, engineering and technology. In some cities, a "center" is no longer a focal point for districts and neighborhoods but a place of intersection, a crossing point, a spatial pause in the movement of people and information—an airport, a leisure center or a wi-fi coffee shop. Consequently, can we rely on conventional typologies of the urban order for the emerging "cities" of the world? Less and less, I argue.

Urban order: from planned cities to non-linear evolutions

Urban order is a catch-all phrase for complex urban systems that range from planned cities to serendipitous local discoveries to non-linear evolutions—self-organizing. Students can learn from the typologies utilized in all of these categories, where they range from borrowed or mimicked typologies in foreign classical contexts to corporate modernist and franchised applications to creative hybrids. A word of caution: the desire of many international cities to define or brand themselves in a global economy is characterized by an international sameness in typologies (Marshall, 2003), in many cases designed by architects and urban designers with little or no connection to the region, local contexts and its cultures.

Urban order: emerging contexts

- *Emerging new urbanities*: The new order—new cities or city segments, most still utilizing conventional master plan approaches (Neom, Saudi Arabia) with technological innovations.
- *District scale*: District/neighborhood "revitalization", the techno-master plan approach (Toronto Waterfront Revitalization Initiative, Quayside, Toronto).
- *Super-block*: Super-block development (Chongqing—Jiangbei Area, China).
- *Self-organizing*: The evolving order, piece by piece, small system by small system, the non-linear evolving city.
- *Post-metropolis*: The outer cities (beyond and independent of "mother").

Let's assess key and emerging developments in these contexts for urban design typologies at varying scales. Key questions are: *Do they exhibit differences based on their regions and cultures or do they remain franchised branded applications? Can the techno-master plan strategies produce meaningful typologies beyond efficient data-processing monitored types?*

Emerging urbanity

This term was coined by Professor Dan Abramson, Associate Professor in Urban Design and Planning, College of Built Environments, University of Washington, and represents the new city form of high-tech cities, both in their inception and in their management and monitoring. The term refers to the effects on new urban form of the global economy, dominated by international architecture and international marketing objectives. At the global scale, there is a blurring of regional identity—focused more on global competition and its resulting architecture.

Neom, Saudi Arabia

Neom was still in the initial stages of planning and development at the time of writing, so the urban typologies were in the process of being defined. However, the aspirations for the new city have clear departure points from other new cities and city districts that can significantly alter or produce hybrids in urban order typologies.

Neom is proposed to be sited on 26,500km^2 (10,230 square miles) in Saudi Arabia's northwestern region, including lands from Egypt and Jordan on 468 km^2 (292 square miles) of Red Sea coastline. I include this project as the stated development and economic objectives can significantly produce new urban core typologies, clearly departing from conventions. The ten key development components are as follows:

- A new economic and regulatory zone
  - new tax structure
  - new and independent law structure.
- Energy and water
  - renewable energy
  - green technologies
  - gardens within every neighborhood
  - seawater reclamation
  - desert farming.
- Mobility
  - autonomous vehicles and drones.
- Biotech industries
- Food resources and production
  - aeroponics and hydroponics.
- Advanced manufacturing
  - new materials production (composites and metals)
  - three-dimensional printing
  - robotics.
- Media
  - television and film industries
  - video gaming
  - digital content.
- Entertainment
- Technological and digital sciences
  - artificial intelligence
  - virtual reality
  - augmented reality technologies

- data centers
- e-commerce.
- Living (housing, schools, parks, etc.)

How will each of the development aspirations change the urban order, instigating new typologies? Many of these aspirations have existing physical manifestations, and they may already be obsolete. Integrating them into a cohesive urban core is a laudable and challenging goal—albeit still within a master plan strategy.

How does the urban order change from these aspirations?

Autonomous vehicles: self-driving, computer-directed passenger and service vehicles channeled by what kind of street pattern? A delineated corridor? A conventional street pattern? Or do they have the ability to link up, similar to a Personal Rapid Transit (PRT) system, suggesting designated corridors and link stations?

Drones: at what scale are drones capable of utilization (delivery of small goods or even people)? They are multi-directional and if extensive in use possibly require designated corridors, intercept points, designated access points.

Technological and digital sciences: this is an open book on impacts to the built form. Options include: significant changes in movement patterns regarding employment locations; relationship of residence to those locations; intercept centers where new movement patterns intersect; e-commerce impacts where delivery systems may be more prevalent than shopping movement patterns (from home, digitally).

Living infrastructure: for housing, are typologies conventional drop-ins within super-blocks? How is the nature of housing types affected by digital technologies, including 3-D printing (delivery of food to purchased objects)? Relationship of housing location to supply, entertainment, employment and leisure centers? And what about the change in employment centers themselves? This may be the most significant typology change—dispersed/non-existent/data centers within residential "neighborhoods"?

This is just scratching the surface and there is substance for another book on the subject. The question remains: if these components exist now (and they do), and if they are applied in a comprehensive and coordinated urban master plan, what is the new emergent urbanity, as defined by its new typologies? Does this simply mean larger and taller buildings? Prefabricated housing blocks? How are all of the elements connected in a humane manner and space?

QUAYSIDE AND PORT LANDS (WATERFRONT TORONTO), ONTARIO

Waterfront Toronto was formed in 1999 to spearhead a major revival of the eastern urban waterfront. The Central and Downtown waterfronts, Toronto's "front porch", makes a major recovery of the waterfront for open space from historic industrial uses. The emphasis now is on the eastern waterfront, encompassing 300 hectares (660 acres)—larger than downtown Toronto. Along this waterfront, Quayside (12 acres/5.5 hectares) joins the Distillery District, the Canary District and Villiers Island Neighborhood in major revitalization projects. The new Eastern Waterfront's Phase One Quayside is proposed to be a major departure from the other segments of the revitalized waterfront: a spawning ground for innovation and new prototypes. It is described by the Toronto Planning Department and

Sidewalk Labs (a subsidiary of Alphabet Inc.) as a physical hinge between land and water; a digital hinge as a testbed for innovation in city-making; and a cultural hinge for the waterfront's industrial heritage (Sidewalk Labs, 2018). Sidewalk Labs is focusing on improving infrastructure through technological innovations. The project is billed as a testing ground for new urban infrastructure, urban design and building technologies.

The five planning goals for Quayside are:

- Quayside must differentiate itself as a radical departure from existing developments in Toronto and around the world.
- Quayside must integrate itself as the newest addition to Toronto's existing and diverse quilt of urban neighborhoods.
- Quayside must offer affordability to a diverse set of Torontonians.
- Quayside must start the transition to a public realm planned around pedestrians and not the automobile.
- Quayside must demonstrate the potential implications of the convergence of physical conditions, digital capabilities, and open standards on urban innovation—catalyzing a new urban innovation cluster.

Some of the stated typologies that can emerge from these goals or aspirations are as follows:

- Lightweight, floating bridges.
- Floating parks that can be moved as demand changes.
- Floating civic uses from performance venues to data centers, again capable of being moved.
- Floating communities, increasing housing supply.
- Naturalization of the Don River as an ecological rather than aesthetic action.
- Adaptive reuse of existing historic grain silos, imprints of the Toronto industrial waterfront. (See typology examples in Sidewalk Labs (2018, p. 51), which also portend the dangers of adaptive reuse of historic structures.)
- Public ownership of automobiles, including autonomously driven vehicles.
- Ground-Traffic Control System, including autonomous roving transit shuttle.
- Passive housing via new global standards for building energy efficiency.
- Neighborhoods with bike highways and autonomous ferries and other autonomous transit modes.
- Short blocks (pedestrian-based).
- Flexible pavilions of "radical" mixed use—home, work and play.
- Prefabricated buildings, adaptable for multiple uses.
- Microgrids and thermal grids to balance power usage and manage waste heat and cooling, respectively.
- "Outcome-based" zoning that focuses on pollution and noise reduction rather than specific land uses.
- A "digital layer" of data-harvesting, wi-fi-beaming technologies—a major point of departure for the urban form—that can track movement patterns, usage intensities, waste management and many other functions. (This has raised serious concerns regarding privacy.)
- Ethnically and economically diverse housing opportunities.

Therefore, questions regarding typology innovations based on "innovative" infrastructure systems, including transport, are critical. How will these new infrastructure systems affect building technologies and typologies? By "motorizing" building types, are they automatically more humane and intimate or simply proficient and efficient? Is this new "smart" city a place to live or a new video game to be visited? Disneyland and Disneyworld have been moving toward efficient "smart" cities for decades. Are they cities?

Let's review existing relevant typologies and experiment with the emerging typologies and design compositions that are possible within these new "smart cities" as their path to fruition and a sense of place have many challenges. City as digital-processing machine or as a *place* for living; or a combination of both?

The student is asked to gain insight through exploration of these typologies (developmental, architectural, landscape open space, and connections), including some of the implications of these emerging "smart cities".

Typology

In order to engage complex urban design compositions, students and professionals require a working knowledge of development typologies, beyond land use densities and intensities. In my experience as an educator, typology is overlooked in planning and design programs. Architecture and landscape architecture students are introduced to building and open space typologies in their education as a fundamental component of design, through study and experimentation. In urban planning and urban studies programs, that education can be understated in the larger coursework, viewed as the role of another domain. Some urban design typologies are covered in urban form and site planning courses. As planning and urban design students in planning curricula address density issues, among others, a base knowledge of typologies for development patterns, buildings and open space is critical in that decision-making. For example, students develop development policies for *form-based zoning* without a clear idea of building types that can or cannot work in a given "policy" massing, resulting in ineffective or erroneous policy actions.

One could focus an entire book on typologies for urban design. In the first edition of this book, I attempted to provide basic typologies. In hindsight, given regional and international differences in development regulations and patterns, and changes in building construction, that is a formidable task. Books on typologies, such as Rob Krier's *Architectural Composition* (1988) and *Town Spaces* (2006), are valuable as starting points and references *as long as they are connected to a context*. Taken separately or in isolation, they have, in my opinion, little value and can be misleading and translated into clichés, models devoid of context, or typologies forced into unrelated contexts. In addition, using historic typologies can result in compromised and contrived outcomes—again, devoid of context and derived from historic contexts that are no longer applicable. As Krier states, cities' "architecture could be unmistakably identified as belonging to a specific culture . . . The formerly complex language of architecture with its regional color that produced splendid and surprising variations was reduced to a form of technical expression" based on notions of function, hygiene and structure (Krier, 2006, pp. 8–9). Sound familiar?

Krier points out two main geometrical aspects of urban design: circulation and the city block as the "original cell of every urban design structure" (Krier, 2006, p. 11). And, of course, the city block is again defined by the fractals within it—buildings and open space connected to culture and its related crafting methods—and the evolutionary capability of their structure. Again, CAUTION: the organic and/or dynamics of historic urban patterns are attractive graphics and can lead to compromise and cliché, separated from reality and mired in fanciful nostalgia.

This section takes a different tack in that it recommends a number of exercises for students of urban design that can assist them in developing and exploring the principles behind typologies. This approach can lead to hybrids that are context-based, building upon experience and tested principles.

Typology: in urban design, types are built environment spatial elements and configurations having common traits or characteristics that distinguish them as a class or group. The common traits are usually founded in principles of organization, followed by structure or assembly based on design parameters, program needs, site contexts and cultural orientations.

As we explore typologies in urban design, I find it useful for my students to learn about the spatial aspects of typology through process models. The physical models consist of symbolic object templates that can be manipulated into various experimental compositions, using crafted or digital methods. Investigating and constructing the templates are excellent ways to understand their characteristics and specific application capacities.

Template for design: again, typologies are only as valid as their integral relationship with their proposed physical context and meaning. They are guides, starting points, ingredients in a recipe that form a basis of experimentation, exploration, and hybridization; they are not to be accepted as absolute, nor taken out of context and used as models, copies, or replications (a common practice in development and design worldwide). Many smaller communities "cut and paste" design guidelines from other communities due to staff shortages, budget shortfalls or misguided economic objectives. This proliferation of context-less typologies can lead to clichés, "dormer-ville" and "generic Bavarian", thematic "design"—a mishmash of borrowed and unfounded fantasies. I fondly remember Professor Pat Goeters (University of Notre Dame, 1966) telling us that if we wanted a historic theme, we should copy it exactly or not attempt it at all! Of course, he did not even want it copied, but the point was well made. Historic themes are models, replicas, historic memories not necessarily suited for contemporary use; and they may have compositional principles that can be distilled into hybrid typologies, if appropriate, providing bridges from past form to contemporary patterns.

In design processes, I find templates of typologies to be very useful in exploiting site development potential quickly and accurately, whether by crafting means or digital graphics. I use crafting methods in design concept phases as I find the process flexible, fast, and interactive for multiple participants, and a way of discovering emergent patterns. The digital techniques are useful for processing and evaluating concepts.

Building types are forms and arrangements of organizational relationships, representing use, density, intensity etc. The organizational relationships are key to how the types are formed or assembled. For example, a residential multi-family building can have several types of organizational relationship, as follows:

- Living units on each side of a central corridor, referred to as a double-loaded corridor.
- Living units on one side of a corridor, interior or exterior, referred to as a single-loaded corridor.
- One-story units organized around a central access pod (stair and elevator), stacked vertically, referred to as stacked flats (although terms vary according to region).
- A townhouse or town home is a two-story living unit with adjacent shared walls on one or both sides.
- A rowhouse can be a one-story living unit with adjacent shared wall on one or both sides.
- A townhouse (two stories) stacked atop a one-story ground-level unit (housing or retail/commercial).

The following illustrations provide examples of templates that are useful in design/planning concept generation. They can be set up for crafting methods, as illustrated here, and digital methods or templates. Again, I use the crafting methods because they are flexible and effective for group interactions.

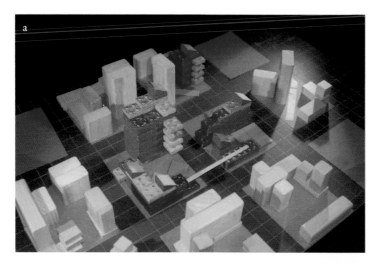

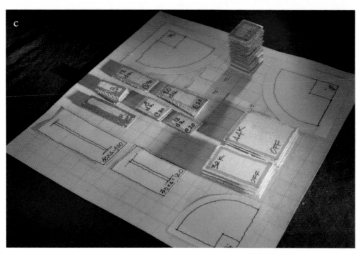

Figure 6.1. (a–d) Typology template examples—medium-to high-density residential uses (center corridor/double-loaded corridor buildings, high-rise structures). *The templates illustrated here are composed of physical symbolic objects formed into shapes that represent various building types. When generating design concepts, it can be useful for an individual designer, team or stakeholder group to "play" with the template pieces as they explore (and gain an understanding of) various design compositions. Included here are cardboard cut-outs for residential buildings, retail uses, etc. In addition, other "toys" and symbolic objects can be effectively used at the appropriate scale such as wood blocks of all sorts.*

In built environment configurations, similar principles can apply:

- A classic retail street evident in many smaller communities, pre-shopping mall, is a double-loaded corridor, with contiguous retail shops with common walls, lining both sides of a roadway.
- In shopping malls, a common concourse assembles contiguous shops along both sides, augmented by "capture" spaces such as food courts, and major department stores at the ends of key concourses or axes.

I expand on these typologies later in this chapter, but they all represent a set of functioning principles rather than how they are assembled and structured. Without an understanding of these typologies (and they are only starting points), the planner/designer cannot address shapes and elements within a composition.

The exercises in this section are designed to assist the student in understanding the importance and utilization of urban design and building/open space typologies in specific contexts. Their organizational requirements have an *appropriateness of application* factor, and are context-scale-sensitive. Simply put, they may not be applied everywhere, in any physical situation. For example, if a site in a low-density residential area is allocated for 30 housing units, the typology based on urban design concerns selected for implementation in many cases is driven by both allowable zoning (what and how much) and surrounding context. A one-story medium-rise building that accommodates 30 units may be buildable on the site but inappropriate, given the context.

I have observed planning students arrange land-use "blobs" or "bubbles" of housing units in situations that are not appropriate for either function or quality of life because they did not understand the type characteristics and requirements of certain buildings based on density, site conditions, etc.

Residential typologies

The following examples range in scale from low-density clusters suitable for outlying, suburban and "rurban" (Kasprisin Pettinari Design, 2004) areas, especially where the protection of open space is critical, to high-rise residential buildings for high-density urban core applications. Also discussed with respect to these typologies are the changes in technology that have ramifications for conventional typologies. The physical characteristics of building types determine their relationship to site and context. For example, a double-loaded or center corridor building layout has units on both sides of the corridor, requiring light, "view" etc. on two sides of a building, affecting orientation and location of such buildings. Based on these characteristics, each external elongated façade requires some form of open space (light, view, air) adjacent to the building, requiring minimal setbacks between buildings and/or property lines and adjacent uses. Placing this building next to a bluff, for example, does not work for an array of units. The typology has within its characteristics an emerging and implied contextual relationship. This may sound overly simple for architects but I have witnessed others in urban studies misuse building types through a lack of understanding of these built-in relational factors.

Housing can stand alone on large parcels, along waterways and beaches, or be tucked away in verdant forests. Most housing occurs in groups, with levels of relationship forged by their placement. Below, I list the types used in urban design applications.

- Single-family detached house (one- to two-story, one-story ranch)
    - attached garage (front, side, rear)
    - detached garage (side, rear)
    - carport
    - alley or street parking.
- Single-family attached house
    - at garage walls
    - with arbors/shared-entry walks
    - at habitable walls usually one side (zero lot line).
- Cottage
    - small one- to one-and-a-half stories
    - detached and attached
    - usually with shared parking.
- Shotgun house
    - one-story rectangular structure, one room wide
    - usually 12ft (4m) to 15ft (5m) wide
    - three or four rooms deep
    - straight central openings though all rooms
    - camelback variation has one second-story bedroom over kitchen.
- Small cabin
    - one room plus sleeping loft or attic
    - front porch
    - storage shed.

Note: Lester Walker's Tiny Houses *(1987) provides a fascinating range of small houses, both contemporary and historic, in North America. They are suitable for infill in compact urban and rurban applications.*

- Prefabricated house
    - Many variations from stick-built to recycled shipping containers to modular panel structures.
- Guest house or studio outbuilding
    - one room with work space (studio)
    - semi-enclosed extensions optional.
- Accessory/"mother-in-law" unit/"granny annexe"
    - separate or attached to main structure
    - component of other structures such as garage/studio.
- Multiplex buildings with separate entry per unit
    - one or two stories
    - attached garage or shared parking/carports.

- Multiplex houses ("Captain's House")
  - two or three stories
  - three to five residential units
  - common shared entry/lobby/foyer
  - shared open space (porch, yard)
  - private open space per unit (optional)
  - shared parking (one garage, carport, shared lot)
  - suitable for corner-lot developments with access from two streets.
- Contemporary boarding house
  - individual small units with minimum kitchen/bath facilities
  - common shared entry/lobby/foyer
  - shared spaces (living room, study areas, shared work spaces, kitchen, dining area)
  - shared open space
  - shared parking.
- Rowhouse
  - one or two stories, attached common wall on one or both sides
  - individual entry
  - private open space in rear.
- Court or atrium house
  - attached linear around central open space spine
  - attached/stacked with interior or u-shaped open space
  - shared entry atrium.
- Townhouse/town home
  - two- to three-story units
  - common wall on one or both sides
  - individual entry
  - private open space in rear
  - two-story unit above garage option
  - two-story unit above one-story flat option
  - two-story unit above retail and/or shared work space, i.e. including live/work.
- Stacked flats: garden homes
  - one-story units stacked vertically
  - shared entry to lobby/foyer
  - shared parking
  - shared open space
  - two to four stories, no elevator/lift
  - courtyard arrangements optional.
- Center corridor/double-loaded corridor building
  - units on both sides of central corridor
  - two to four stories without elevator/lift
  - unit entry from corridor
  - width depending on unit size/market and underground parking option.
- Single-loaded corridor building
  - front or rear shared exterior access corridor

- – unit entry from corridor
- – two to four stories without elevator/lift.
- Live/work mixed-use housing
  - – residential use above or behind commercial, office, service uses; same tenant
  - – larger upper deck to compensate for residence-oriented open space
  - – central parking, dispersed small lot parking, common service vehicle storage and parking
  - – landscaped front yard setbacks (option)
  - – suitable for transition areas from residential to other uses
  - – suitable for non-residential areas such as light industrial, warehouse, etc.
- Mixed-density housing
  - – two or more different housing types combined into the same development pod
  - – shared and private open space
  - – shared parking
  - – shared accessory buildings such as studio, garden sheds, greenhouses, work space, community use
  - – suitable for urban compounds and rural clusters such as farmsteads and hamlets.
- High-rise central corridor for elevator/lift
  - – square, rectangular, circular, expanded towers floor plans, stepped
  - – form varies on unit/market type, local codes
  - – mixed density with other typologies integrated into main structure
  - – mixed use with retail, service shops and shared work space opportunities (service shops can include gyms, civic uses, live/work units, etc.).
- High-rise central corridor multi-center for elevator/lifts

The variations and hybrids are many but the above list should provide the emerging designer and student with a place to start. How these types are manipulated to respond to context is the challenge of the composing process.

Low- to medium-density housing types/examples

We begin with the low- to medium-density housing examples and work toward high-density urban core typologies later in the chapter. As I have expressed before, urban design is in action at all levels and scales of development, not just in the high-density urban core. The following diagrams are semi-abstract and do not reflect an architectural style; rather, they illustrate principles of organization and assembly of housing types. Many of these are suitable for infill development in changing neighborhoods and districts, particularly in areas where increases in density are desired along with a protection or conservation of the existing scale of the neighborhood or district. Do not dismiss small-scale design improvements as they are the incremental building blocks of urban/local/regional design.

Exercise 6.1 Low-density and mixed-density residential development

Intent

As a means of engaging students in an investigation of diverse low-density typologies, I am using the concept of mixed density: different building typologies incorporated into the same development cluster, phase or pod. This can promote a variety and diversity of users through building typologies, from empty nesters to families.

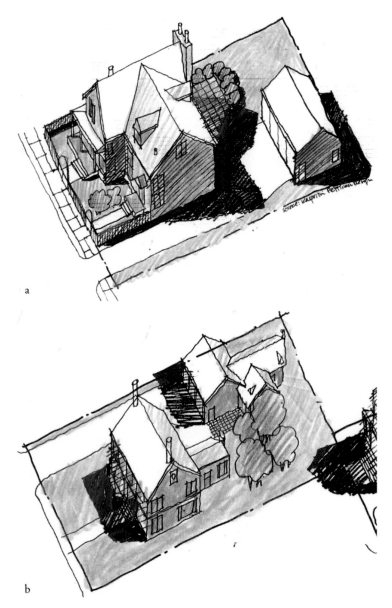

Figure 6.2. (a–r) Typology template examples—low- to medium-density residential types. *The following illustrations provide a sampling of the many variations of housing types and configurations available for low- to medium-density context-sensitive applications. The principles of organization and structure for these types are key: connections to surrounding context; building to open space and parking requirements/relationships. The first group, infill/mixed density, is suitable for infill and smaller-lot developments. Mixed density refers to a group of residential buildings consisting of different building types (bungalow, cottage, townhouse, etc.). The second group, conservation design, is suitable for larger-lot developments with significant open space features and is density-neutral (no loss of density with increased open space requirements). The third group, medium- to high-density, illustrates basic building type as stand-alone or in cluster or courtyard configurations.*
Infill/mixed-density types:
a) Attached duplex with individual entries, with one unit larger and/or set back from second unit
b) "In-law" accessory unit above or attached to accessory building with small private yard

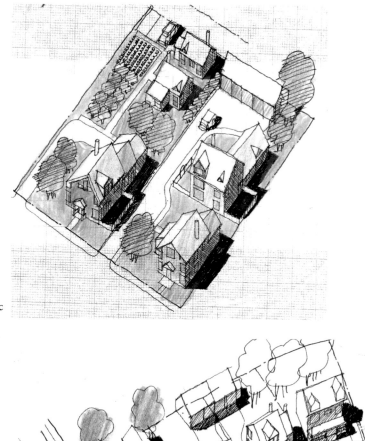

c

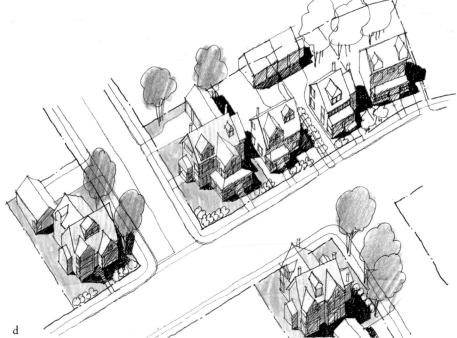

d

c) Hamlet lot (three units) with mix of detached and attached units with shared driveway and individual entries and private yards

d) Multiplex homes (single-entry foyer, three to five units—two + two + one) suitable for corner lots with two frontages, with shared parking/garage and shared open space; can also be developed as contemporary boarding house

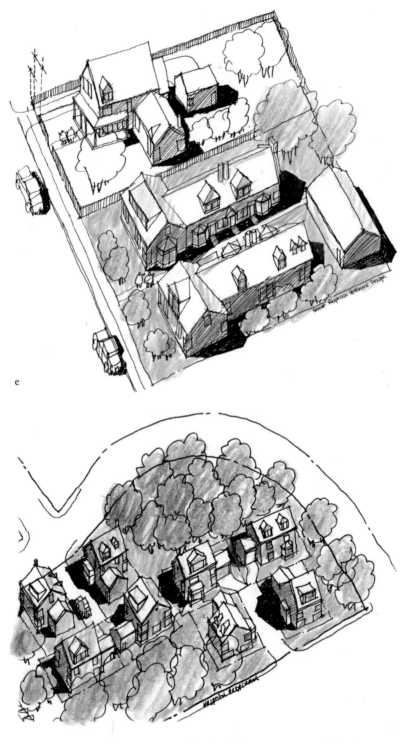

e) Courtyard housing with key units facing street, with individual entries, private and shared open space
f) Panhandle cluster with shared driveways, small lots and conserved open space

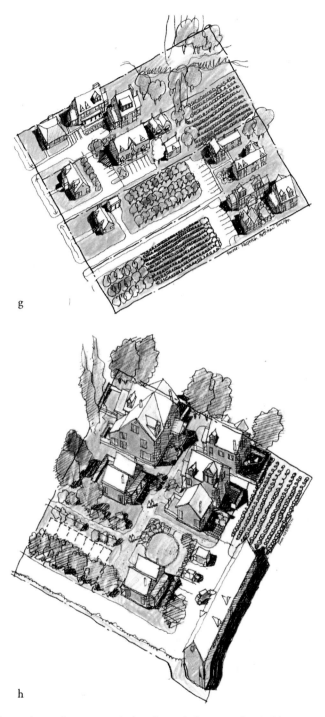

g

h

g) Mixed-density linear clusters (long, narrow lots) with attached cottages, detached bungalows, multiplex homes with private and shared open space
h) Mixed-density farmsteads with detached bungalows, attached and detached cottages, duplexes, shared accessory buildings, private and shared yards

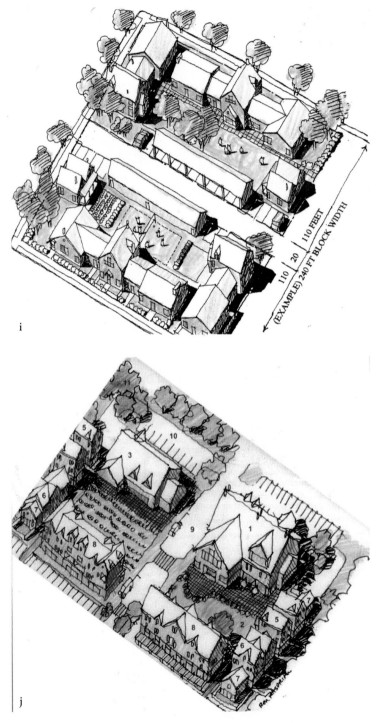

i) Small-scale urban infill complex with alley, private and shared yards, attached bungalows
Conservation design:
j) Conservation hamlet with multiplex home, detached and attached bungalows clustered around common green

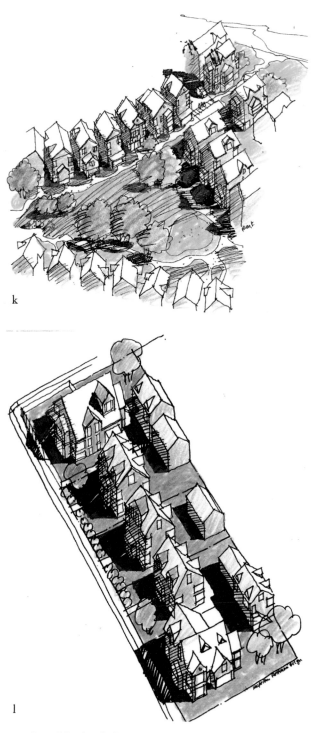

k

l

k) Conservation design with small-lot detached units with garage
l) Repetition with variety, single-family detached home and varying front yard setbacks

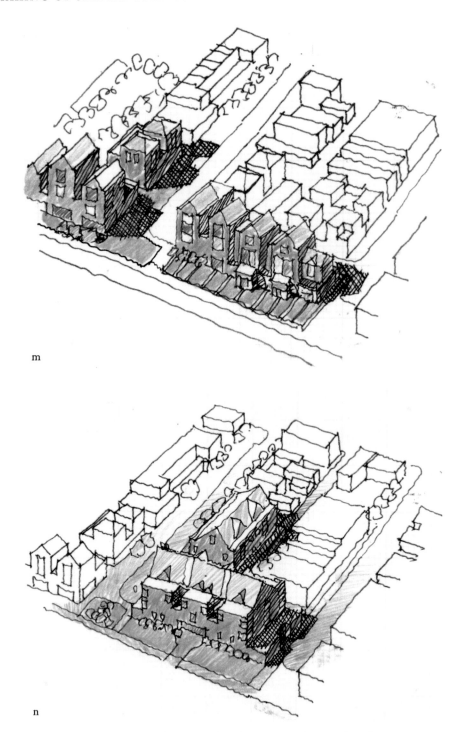

m

n

m) Townhouse complex with diminished repetition through compositional variety along the streetscape
n) Double-loaded/central corridor stacked flats above commercial with optional underground parking one- or
two-way direction, depending upon building width

o

p

o) Townhouse boxes composite; under-building parking at grade, one-half level and full level below grade
p) Civic center and conservation design with residential live/work units with central green area

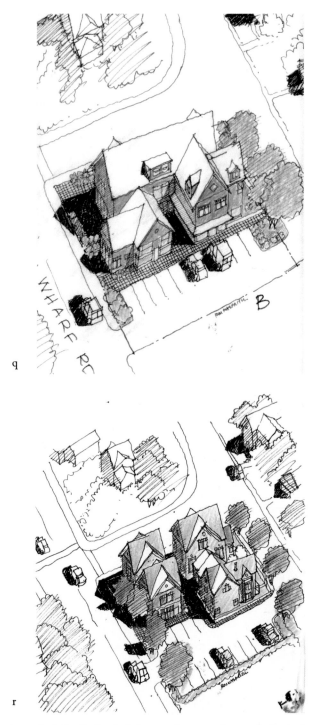

q) Live/work housing as single-family detached above work space and as attached units (row/townhouses, etc.)
r) Other mixed-use residential and commercial types designed to fit into urban neighborhoods and districts with side and/or rear yard parking, front yard landscaping, and residential-scale massing

Principle

Use at least three different building and open space typologies to construct a coherent development pod. For example: multiple-unit "house" with single entry and shared open space; cottages (attached and detached); and variations of town home boxes.

Tools

Axonometric drawings with felt tip pens, color optional.

Exercise 6.2 Mixed-density/mixed-use development block

Intent

Given the development objectives for age/gender/cultural/economic diversity, this exercise asks students to investigate two aspects of typology, assuming a larger-scale phased development of the neighborhood: a) mixed-(higher-)density housing which by the nature of a diversity of housing types can include a diversity of residents; and b) mixed uses within the neighborhood pod or cell that reflect the technological underpinning of the development.

Principles

Principles include a) incorporate housing that encourages a diversity in the population from age and gender to culture and economics; b) assume a higher-density population for the overall pod or cell with a diversity in intensity of development.

Tools

Choose your "fractal" materials:

*   preferably interlocking blocks (wood or plastic), or
*   construction paper
*   color pencils
*   paper glue and tape
*   scissors
*   cutting knives
*   cutting surfaces.

Halsam American Building Bricks, as examples of wood blocks, date back to the 1940s and are a toy offshoot of the lumber industry. They are the forerunners of interlocking wood and plastic symbolic object toys.

Tasks

1   Investigate the various typologies for higher-density housing, from single access core to stacked flats, single- and double-loaded corridors, town homes and town homes stacked on flats, etc. Review the various types available for medium to higher densities. Always be aware of possible hybrids for specific contexts.

2   Construct graphic or process model templates of selected typologies as templates for play.

3   Play with various compositions and explore how what works and what can be changed to improve the composition.

4   Numerous iterations are required to progress to a comprehensive design.

Hybrid uses for changing low-density residential areas

Before leaving the low-density housing infill discussion, I include this section on the transitioning of single-family typologies to other uses. In many North American cities and towns, housing areas within or on the edge of commercial cores are impacted by the growth of those core areas, often deteriorating in physical condition. As their value for housing decreases, they can become quality transition buildings for small-scale general commercial, live/work, and office uses for smaller companies such as surveyors, designers, etc. I refer to these transition areas as "incubator zones", where the housing stock and key open space features are maintained with the addition of off-street parking or car parks.

Figure 6.3. Incubator zones with housing typologies. *Lynden Village sketch illustrates the reclamation of a single-family structure with infill addition between the main structure and the garage, all converted to professional office space; but retaining key elements of the surrounding landscaped yard.*

154

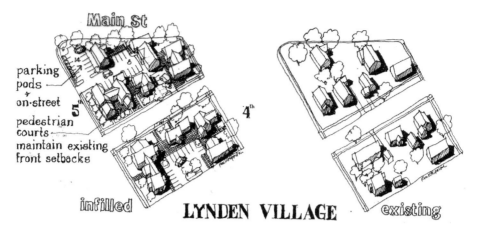

Figure 6.4. Incubator typology overview. *Two former housing blocks are transformed into incubator clusters but retain key physical features of the housing patterns (setbacks, landscaped yards, human scale).*

Hybrid medium-density typologies: the "maze" and the distorted grid

Hybrid typologies build on conventional types and offer a number of characteristics that benefit the human scale. Keeping in mind the need for an order to accommodate infrastructure and a reasonable orientation to surroundings, these hybrids utilize standard principles and add an intimate and sensual atmosphere through a manipulation of spatial elements.

The Maze. The Maze is an urban design typology useful for district or neighborhood applications with medium densities. *Maze: an intricate, usually confusing network of interconnecting pathways . . . a labyrinth* (American Heritage Dictionary of the English Language). The confusion aspect can be removed with an underlying order that maintains orientation and way-finding in an intricate pattern of building placement and circulation routes. Key principles at work in these examples include the following:

- A sense of anticipation through deflected and probable but less specific movement patterns.
- A human scale achieved through building heights and street widths.
- Pausing or "breathing" spaces achieved through small courtyards and plazas also contributing to way-finding.
- An implied access "spine" (implied through materials, width and continuity yet meandering).
- Opportunities for small-scale retail at key intersections and gathering places.
- Edge energy: the ability to interlock, merge, or reflect adjacent and differing districts or neighborhood patterns.

The maze is a mixed-density order that utilizes a variety of housing types and support components, including:

- Townhouse/town home boxes (two-story residential units).
- Townhouse/town home boxes stacked above one-story flats or retail.

- Courtyard housing with one- to three-story residential units.
- Stacked flats with two- to four-story residential units.
- Central core elevator/lift buildings ranging from six to 12 stories, with potential street-level retail and/or shared work space.
- Small retail/service shops/shared work space facilities interspersed within the maze at key intersection locations.

These principles, types and components are a starting point and not absolute ingredients. Context drives the specific determinants. There follows a suggested exercise for students and designers that can be tailored to specific regions and cultures.

Exercise 6.3 The Maze

Intent

Construct a neighborhood district (one large urban block or four or more moderate-scale urban blocks as a starting point) that is assumed to be a part of a larger and denser urban district. Within the principle of intimacy and intricacy, maintain an "order" that is flexible, human-scaled, and coherent.

Principles

Utilize the principles listed above, then add others that relate to the specific context (location, region, culture) as guides for the larger composition.

Tools

Utilize tools that are fast and flexible. In the examples that follow, I use color construction paper for its ease of manipulation and color coding. The results can subsequently be digitized for further processing options and evaluations. Obviously, the choice is the participant's, and keep in mind the idea of "plurality of methodology" in these exercises.

Tasks

- Create a base scale and spatial extent that is neither micro-scale nor excessive in size, making for "busy work" as opposed to quality explorations.
- Experiment with a section of the maze as a larger mass that is composed internally of reasonable building type. I suggest doing a quick diagram over a mass shape and experimenting with the types and sizes of various residential buildings, for example, that can be accommodated within the mass. This leads to adjustments and discoveries on where open space can be located and interconnected within the maze.
- Do as many as you can until a coherent pattern and order emerge. This will not necessarily happen during the first experiment.

Figure 6.5. The "Maze" A. *Maze A contains medium-density housing (orange) using townhouses, courtyard housing, with central core elevator/lift buildings (yellow) on the perimeter. Small retail and shared work spaces (red) are dispersed along the main edge as a connecting device and in the central plaza or gathering place. The movement pattern is a hierarchy of a shared street spine (service vehicles, bicycles, pedestrians) and smaller pedestrian connecting corridors through and connecting sub-areas of the maze. Parking is limited and distributed along the maze edge in small lots.*

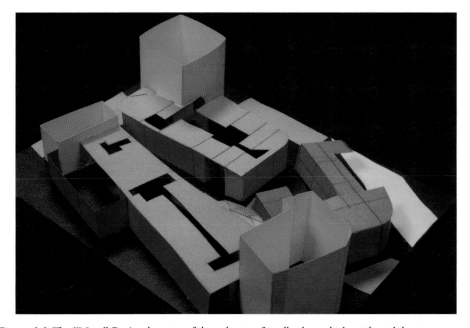

Figure 6.6. The "Maze" B. *Another view of the pedestrian-friendly, slow-vehicle residential district.*

The distorted grid. The distorted grid is another form of intricate hybrid pattern that utilizes a standard street grid and distorts that grid to add anticipation, deflected vistas/views, and intimacy yet retains an orderly infrastructure pattern within the district development. Key principles include the following:

- A continuous grid pattern, distorted or bent at various angles to slow vehicle speeds and add anticipation and a bit of suspense to each intersection; creates additional interest and stimulation.
- Mixed-density housing typologies including townhouses, rowhouses, courtyard housing, stacked flats, and medium-rise central core elevator/lift buildings.
- Mixed use with shared work spaces incorporated into the base of medium-rise buildings and/or in a central retail/service shop/shared work space with associated open space.

Exercise 6.4 The distorted grid

Intent

Construct an urban composition using a base grid that is distorted in various ways. Utilize a street hierarchy for small vehicles, service vehicles as well as smaller, slower shared streets in a continuous pattern. Use mixed-density building types to infill the district blocks.

Principles

Incorporate the principles cited above as guides for a coherent yet flexible and intricate district composition that emphasizes human interaction with the surroundings.

Tools

Same as Exercise 6.3.

Tasks

- Select a grid pattern that has a hierarchy of streets (square, rectangular, etc.).
- Manipulate or distort the grid without destroying its continuity and connectedness.
- Articulate building masses to match the distorted block shapes.
- Incorporate retail/service facilities/shared work space(s) into the distorted grid.

Medium- to high-rise residential typologies

Changes in high-rise residential typologies are occurring at a rapid pace on a global scale as lucrative economies compete in the global market, creating a new urban order as discussed previously. The design of individual buildings has entered a bold, and in many cases fanciful, phase of architectural design, for both residential and office structures. Flexibility and the ability to hybridize conventional types are key to meeting changing contexts in differing cultures around the globe. The major challenge for designers is, in my opinion, less the novelty of the individual building (complex) and more how the artifact is connected and integrated into the built form, adjacent and surrounding contexts. And how can these larger-scale, novel and fanciful artifacts relate to and configure a human scale—a sense of place?

Figure 6.7. The distorted grid A. *The example contains medium-density housing types (orange), ranging from rowhouses to townhouses to stacked flats as well as, medium-rise central core buildings (yellow) that are oriented along the original non-distorted grid for variety and visual orientation. Repetition with variety is always a useful compositional principle superimposed on to a distorted non-orthographic pattern.*

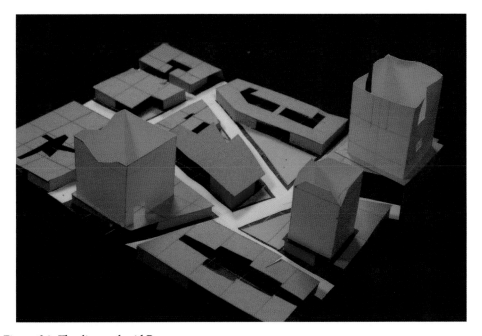

Figure 6.8. The distorted grid B.

For students, experimenting with various typologies and potential hybrids can be the most effective learning process—in addition to reviewing case studies. Consequently, this section exemplifies various typologies suitable for residential high-rise living as a starting point for experimentation. It by no means deals with all potentials of form. At the end of this section, I focus on the various means and methods or types of *meeting the ground*—reconnecting with human space.

Explorations in medium- to high-rise residential constructs

I use the word "constructs" instead of buildings as some of the world's new architecture can challenge the imagination. The technologies of medium- to high-rise construction have changed to the point that architects are pushing the envelope on what is a building. Two critical factors are important for urban design, beyond the architecture: the essential underlying principles of the typology (not style); and the connectivity of that new architecture to the ground plane, human scale, and local and larger contexts. To describe all of the variations of high-rise typologies is beyond the scope of this chapter. I will begin my exploration of them with an initial list and examples, but, as with in other typologies, students can best learn about them by constructing examples using basic principles—and searching for hybrids. First, though, let's look at some typologies to build upon, as a basis for exercises.

- Central vertical circulation typologies
    - central vertical access core elements
    - limits on horizontal extension
    - square, circle, cross, rectangle, triangle, pinwheel variations (and other circle/square derivations) configurations with a central core
    - hybrids: pyramidal, tree-shape, etc.
- Multiple vertical circulation typologies
    - two or more vertical circulation access cores
    - expanded horizontal and cross extensions
    - linear, curvilinear, extended.
- Stepped tower typologies
    - one or more vertical circulation elements
    - inclined elevator options
    - stepped levels
    - tower/stepped combinations
    - expanded roof surface utilization
    - various plan configurations ("L", cross, linear, etc.).
- Stacked tower typologies
    - one or more vertical circulation elements
    - components appear to be stacked as separate elements.
- Tower(s) with pedestal base typologies
    - standard base (two to six stories)
    - stepped base/mound base
    - floating base

- – solid/void base
- – vegetative/agricultural base
- – fragmented base
- – merged base
- – undulating base.
- Courtyard typologies
  - – enclosed courtyard
  - – semi-enclosed courtyard
  - – galleria courtyard.
- Other variations
  - – undulating
  - – scalloped
  - – splayed
  - – spiral
  - – work space housing.

Many of these typologies apply to both high-rise residential and commercial building types. The significant differences are in the principles associated with habitat (light, air, view) versus work place space that affect building configurations.

Central vertical circulation core typology explorations

Exercise 6.5 Central vertical core explorations

Intent

Understand the nature and characteristics of basic medium- to high-rise residential buildings by constructing various configurations, evaluating them, and experimenting with hybrids and playful adaptations.

Principles

- One central vertical circulation core (lifts, elevator core) emanating from central lobby/entry space(s).
- Light, air and potential view access are critical determinants.
- Horizontal extension options and extents based on local/regional codes.
- Adaptations based on one central vertical access core: multiple wings, pinwheels, etc.

Tasks

- Review case study examples of the many variations of residential towers, evaluating the base floor plates based on types and sizes of residential units per floor.
- Tower footprints and heights vary according to local/regional codes and regulations.
- Construct basic tower constructs and evaluate.

- Explore hybrid variations.
- Experiment with a composition made up of the various typology constructs.

Exercise 6.6 Multiple vertical core explorations

Intent

Understand the nature and characteristics of multiple vertical access core residential buildings by constructing various configurations, evaluating them, and experimenting with hybrids and playful adaptations.

Principles

- Two or more vertical access circulation cores (elevator cores) emanating from multiple lobby/entry space(s).
- Horizontal extension options and extents are increased with multiple circulation cores and based on local/regional codes.
- Vary the configurations in different ways to reduce length impacts.

Tasks

- Review case study examples of the many variations of residential towers, evaluating the base floor plates based on types and sizes of residential units per floor.
- Tower footprints and heights vary according to local/regional codes and regulations.
- Construct basic tower constructs and evaluate.
- Explore hybrid variations.
- Experiment with a composition made up of the various typology constructs.

Examples

Obviously, there are many possible building configurations, and practicing and crafting variations are excellent ways to understand what does and doesn't work. Again, the key is not how novel the building construct is but how it connects and integrates with the larger context, including the human scale and environs.

High-rise residential complexes with urban agriculture

Urban agriculture typologies are an emerging additive to both residential and commercial complexes. In these examples, urban agriculture is explored as a catalyst for dense residential development as it can serve as both open space/recreation and food production purposes. These are illustrated in both vertical formats,

Figure 6.9. Single central vertical access core over retail pedestal. *The first example includes medium-rise central vertical access buildings ranging in height from eight to 18 stories over retail or work spaces. The overall composition is a basic typology.*

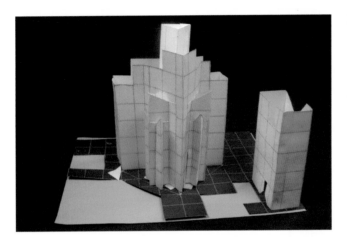

Figure 6.10. Fractal tower cluster. *This tower is constructed of a basic fractal formula, working from the larger form down to smaller components, in a cluster of two towers.*

Figure 6.11. High-rise with two vertical access cores. *Multiple towers are connected to each other with two vertical access cores.*

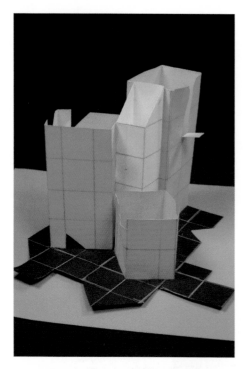

Figure 6.12. Single access core with three towers in a pinwheel. *Multiple towers can be attached to a single access core.*

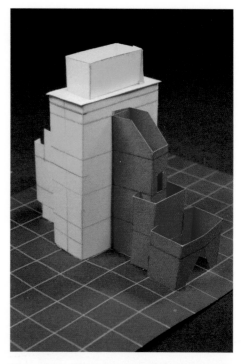

Figure 6.13. High-rise tower with major retail commercial component. *This example includes a multiple-storied retail/commercial component attached to the residential tower.*

Figure 6.14. Expanded single access core with shared work space. *Multiple towers are attached to an expanded vertical core with shared work spaces as a part of the core.*

reaching four to six stories in height to horizontal ground plane elements as part of the overall development, and as structuring compositions.

The agriculture structures can offer covered spaces for outdoor passive recreational areas, as entry artifacts, as edges, and can have interior work spaces for maintenance and harvesting purposes.

These concepts and typologies are revisited in the next chapter with larger-scale experiments.

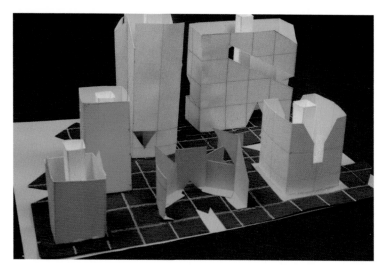

Figure 6.15. Mixed residential cluster with urban agriculture. *A variety of residential medium- to high-rise towers are clustered around a vertical urban agriculture facility that serves as a major landscape and entry element.*

Figure 6.16. Mixed-use, medium-density complex with an urban agriculture linear spine. *The spine has multiple uses from pea patches to surface water filtration to recreational areas. The commercial center is connected directly to the agriculture spine as well as walkways, bicycle paths and other pedestrian amenities.*

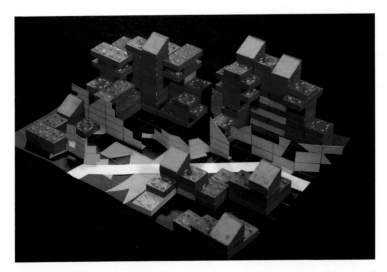

Figure 6.17. Mixed-density residential complex with urban agriculture. *The urban agriculture component acts as a vertical axial structure incorporated with an access road and the main open space component of the residential complex, serving the entire district or neighborhood.*

Commercial building typologies

Commercial building typologies are continually changing in form and function as a result of competition, market share, and consumer preferences. As online purchasing gains momentum, many are challenged to redefine themselves, morphing from shopping center to mixed-use city district. In the US, in some instances, the traditional double-loaded contiguous corridor typology that dates from the early 1900s has come full circle, with numerous malls removing their roofs and "going natural" again, similar to their predecessors. Some information on the categories listed below comes from the International Council of Shopping Centers (ICSC). Below, I list some of the more common types of commercial center.

Historic downtown/neighborhood centers

- North American typologies
  - compact grid pattern, downtown, pedestrian-oriented retail with office/housing above
  - dispersed small "corner" retail shops in neighborhood grids.
- European typologies
  - compact, non-orthographic, downtown, pedestrian-oriented retail with office/housing above
  - single-use/product shops associated with square, plaza, assembly space
  - village centers
  - open-air markets.
- Asian typologies
  - shop houses with housing above single-use/product shops.

Shopping plazas/strip malls

- Single, linear, contiguous shops with front or side onsite parking.
- Under 30,000ft²/3,300m².

General purpose centers

- Neighborhood center
    - convenience oriented for day-to-day consumer needs
    - single, linear, contiguous shops with front or side onsite parking
    - not enclosed
    - 30,000–125,000ft^2/3,300–14,000m^2
    - anchor store: supermarket
    - 5–20 tenants.
- Community center
    - general merchandise, convenience
    - straight line, "L" or "U" configurations
    - not enclosed
    - in addition to food needs: apparel
    - 125,000–400,000ft^2/14,000–45,000m^2
    - anchor stores: discount department store, supermarket, drug store, home improvement, large specialty discount, apparel
    - 15–40 tenants.
- Regional center
    - general merchandise, fashion
    - enclosed mall type (double-loaded corridor/concourse with one or two department stores)
    - full-line department store, junior department store, mass merchant, discount department store, fashion apparel
    - 400,000–800,000ft^2/45,000–89,000m^2
    - anchor stores: department stores
    - 40–80 tenants.
- Super-regional center
    - larger regional center with more anchors and merchandise variety
    - enclosed mall with multiple levels
    - 800,000+ft^2/89,000m^2
    - anchor stores: full-line department store, junior department store, mass merchant, fashion apparel
    - tenants: variable.
- Town/city center
    - large regional center with diverse uses that comprise a small city including broad-based retail, department stores, offices, hotel, housing, entertainment, other civic uses (concert halls, public offices), and major transit links
    - enclosed and unenclosed with multiple levels
    - some reduced retail square feet/meters to accommodate new uses (500,000–750,000ft^2/ 56,000–84,000m^2 for both retail and office uses)
    - parking structures
    - open space and parks
    - specialized-purpose centers
    - town centers on sites of existing shopping malls, recycled spaces such as golf courses, athletic facilities, depending on market location factors.

- Lifestyle
    - upscale stores with dining and entertainment
    - not usually enclosed
    - referred to as "comfort centers"
    - attention to design
    - can be thematic in identity
    - 150,000–500,000ft^2/16,500–56,000m^2
    - may have no anchors, or one or two.
- Power center
    - category-dominant anchors
    - home improvement, discount department stores, warehouse club, discount stores
    - 250,000–600,000ft^2/28,000–67,000m^2.
- Thematic/festival center/leisure center
    - leisure, tourist, retail and service-oriented offerings
    - not enclosed
    - 80,000–250,000ft^2/8,900–28,000m^2
    - no anchors.
- Outlet center
    - manufacturers' and retailers' outlet stores for brand-name goods at a discount
    - enclosed and unenclosed, village cluster, strip configuration are options
    - 50,000–400,000ft^2/5,600–45,000m^2
    - no anchors.

Limited purpose centers

- Aerotropolis component: airport retail
    - shopping center incorporated into airports or new so-called "smart cities" (Songdo, South Korea, for example)
    - some with department stores
    - restaurants, entertainment, specialty stores, apparel
    - 75,000–300,000ft^2/8,300–33,000m^2.

Before engaging the various typologies of commercial developments, it is worth discussing the issues of "authenticity" as a manufactured brand or authentic identity in communities as new large-scale commercial centers spread across the globe. Urban design can play an important role in fostering both authentic and creative design in the development of these large urban centers.

Manufactured "authenticity" versus authentic commercial centers

The competition among the various shopping center typologies generates market approaches that appeal to consumers in various ways: as town centers that replace older historic downtowns; as thematic or nostalgic architectural treatments (thus the term "manufactured authenticity"); as civic centers with operatic, concert and museum facilities, and, in some instances, civic uses (city/town halls, for example). Market branding is a challenge for architects and urban designers when a theme approach is preferred by developers. The basis for an argument for authenticity may come from regional environmental characteristics re: materials, style, building configurations responding to weather and climate, etc.

Another part of the challenge for designers is the fact that most tenants of these new centers—from lifestyle/leisure to regional and town centers—are national/international brands, often accompanied with architectural packaging.

There are a number of descriptions of European and North American commercial centers (downtowns) that specify various approaches for urban design. They provide a starting point for students, particularly as we all explore hybrids as part of a creative problem-solving process.

I begin with a summary from Attoe and Logan's *American Urban Architecture: Catalysts in the Design of Cities* (1989) and add to it as a starting point for a review of urban commercial centers. They distinguish North American city cores from European cores by highlighting major differences in their physical characteristics. North American cities have an "orderliness" or new town appearance, differing from the European "circumstantial" patterns, which reflect their origins in medieval agriculture and trade activities. The layering of centuries in Europe has altered and obscured even the early Roman grids and forms of the Middle Ages, resulting in a more organic, non-orthographic urban pattern. American urban cores can be viewed as functionalist with the monotony that can accompany that critique. Many small towns even along the West Coast were laid out in grids by surveyors on the East Coast (for railroads) with little or no knowledge of local terrain or context. American cities "grew up" with the automobile as the major catalyst after the Second World War, impacting and altering the European influences in cities like Milwaukee, Cleveland and St Louis.

> The *architectural character* of American cities is as characteristic as the grid plan itself. A photograph of nearly any downtown [post-colonial] or Main Street scene can readily be identified as American, for American cities *look* like American cities, not like Italian, English, or French cities. Our cities look as they do for several reasons: streets are straight and wide; antiquarian monuments are infrequent; buildings date from the nineteenth century or later; signs—literal and figurative—of commerce abound, and, most important, there is a grain and pattern to building development different from that of European cities. . . . In the United States, unlike Europe, individuated buildings usually make up the grain of towns and cities. Whereas freestanding buildings in Europe tend to be royal or religious institutions, in the United States [and Canada] *most* public buildings have been deemed worthy of such monumental treatment. *Monuments to the market economy, too—bank, department store, office building—have asserted their own importance by standing out and standing tall.*
>
> (Attoe and Logan, 1989, pp. 129–130; final emphasis added)

And the automobile and expansion or escape to the suburbs, the outer areas, "post-metropolis", has fashioned new competitive patterns. Moreover, along with a global market economy, new cities and city districts are being fashioned under terms such as "smart cities", "creative cities", "AI cities", "digital cities".

Historically, commercial centers were integral parts of downtowns and urban cores, from Cleveland to Manchester. The mall, the new kid on the block and major competitor, began as an island on the edge of the core, redefining the entire concept of the commercial center. Neither the conventional downtown/urban core nor the mall remain static; they are constantly responding to market and consumer pressures and preferences. The mall as island is changing into the mall as town center, a new urban center hybrid. Many downtowns are investing in large-scale developments to compete on national and international scales.

Categories that help define various commercial centers:

- functionalist
- humanist
- systemic
- formalist
- catalytic
- digital/technological
- circumstantial
- creative (as in process, not label or branding).

These terms refer to a broader planning process and also influence and guide urban design practices, particularly as they relate to city sectors and districts such as commercial centers of all types.

Functionalist approach

The urban core or commercial center is a thoroughly defined and planned entity with "intelligent" forecasts for foreseen extensions, goal-driven, and limiting any excesses in advance. The mall concept fits into this category in that it is highly structured and planned; with a tight control on activities, marketing, operation etc. This is a highly structured approach to planning, design and marketing, based on the concepts of workability, competence, and accommodation (residence, work, leisure, and traffic systems organized as in a machine)—cartesian, as goals as set forth by the Athens Charter of the Congrès Internationaux d'Architecture Moderne (CIAM), 1933.

Humanist approach

Both the functionalist and the humanist approaches address community needs regarding marketing and services. The humanist approach differs by examining the impact of small-scale elements on day-to-day operations—attention to small scale, people activities at street level—and seeks to realize and enhance existing and underlying social structures, while also enhancing the visual sensuality of space (Attoe and Logan, 1989). Within the humanist viewpoint lies the idea of "place-making": to forge a positive and meaningful bond between the participant and the place, at the scale of that place.

Systemic approach

An overriding value of the systemic approach is "comprehensibility"—accepting the growth of urbanization and its increased social complexity as inevitable. Essentially, this is defined as organizing and establishing the relationships within the underlying systems, not just individual buildings. The systemic approach also began to integrate basic systems such as transport and infrastructure, addressing connections in a complex web of interacting systems. In the older historic European approach, in urban design the decision-making process is centralized and guided by professionals, mainly architects, developing an underlying order that directs and influences later decisions. Unlike functionalism, this approach embraces "obsolescence" as a natural part of a growing and changing system, an organism.

The systemic approach has evolved over time to incorporate critical aspects of creative problem-solving, with more attention given to the quality and creativity of the product as well as the process.

The formalist stance

The formalist stance places emphasis on particular archetypal or universal configurations of space and form: Beaux-Arts planners focused on axial organizations and structures and static spaces emanating from elementary geometries—formal ordering systems (Attoe and Logan, 1989). New Urbanists fit into this approach in their use of archetypal configurations—the grid etc. The formalist reliance on timeless forms places more emphasis on accommodating changing patterns than addressing specific needs. And yet, as Attoe and Logan point out in their summary of European-based urban design theories, the formalist also values the urban center, the place where the energy of cities is brought together—grand, noble, ordered with harmony.

Catalytic stimulation

Catalytic architecture refers to the positive impact an individual project (building, open space, infrastructure component) can exert on subsequent projects and the form of a city center or commercial center. The catalyst approach can be both sensitive to context and strong enough to restructure a center. The concept is simple and powerful: insert catalysts within the existing context as stimulants for change without destroying or reconstructing the entire area. This generates a controlled catalytic chain reaction that stimulates and guides future development. The catalyst can be an integration of use and form that shape other forms. These catalysts also appear to have a descending impact the farther away from the original catalyst(s), which makes perfect sense given the complexity of the urban center, which implies a network or strategy of catalysts.

Digital cities/smart cities approach

There is no one definition of "smart cities". However, two main camps or directions can be identified in the literature: technological sustainability and ecological sustainability. They are significantly different in definition and applications.

Technological sustainability essentially assumes or asserts that there is a technological or market solution to every urban challenge and that expert interventions are needed to address these challenges. Technological sustainability relies on an approach to "smart cities" where three principles guide smart city design: people, process and technology. Here "smart" is defined as the use of technological resources (electronic data collection through various means in infrastructure) to manage a city's assets efficiently. This convergent approach—the processing and analysis of information from people, devices and other tools—purportedly enables city officials to interact with citizens and the infrastructure in the planning and implementation of the city's operations (waste, security, etc.). Literature references to "people" and "process" reflect current planning terminology such as the preservation of history, culture, heritage, etc. There are aspects of the technological sustainability approach to smart cities that can significantly alter building and development typologies: impacts on online services from shopping to entertainment to work locations. The Quayside neighborhood in Waterfront Toronto is an emerging example (see earlier discussion).

Ecological sustainability essentially engages a creative problem-solving process where the interactive dynamics of a city determine (in a non-linear evolution) the nature, characteristics and probabilities of the city. It is similar to the creative urbanism approach that I advocate in this work, without the use of the term "sustainability", which is overused, politicized and misused (as is evidenced by the divergence in "smart city" definitions). More on this later in the book.

Circumstantial recognition

"Circumstantial: the sum of determining factors beyond wilful control; incidental." I use the word "recognition" in the subheading as circumstantial city form happens *incidentally* due to particular occurrences that interrupt normal functions (and subsequently alter the norm or expected). In North American cities, this may be viewed as the normative approach—planning by accident or expediency.

Creative (urbanism) approach

Not to be confused with "creative cities" branding, the creative approach is a direct application of creative problem-solving in design, a dynamic process that seeks novel outcomes that can lead to innovation—a creative urbanism. This creative approach, founded in ecological principles, is an open process, with uncertain outcomes dealing with probability trajectories not predictions or predetermined outcomes in a goal-driven process. And it is not limited to a "process" or way of thinking because it requires a spatial product or outcome, an emergent pattern, as part of a non-linear evolutionary process. This dynamic process also brings to the forefront the concept or approach of "connectivity" or connected incrementalism. As portions or areas of a city exhibit creative characteristics and capacitance, how are they connected to adjacent and nearby districts that may be substantially different for various reasons? Connectivity is a powerful force in that it forms the relationship between two or more entities . . . and it is this design challenge that can have far-reaching effects on the quality of city form.

Part of the challenge of the creative approach is in the resultant form from a dynamic process. If the approach is genuinely and dynamically creative, the outcome may also be creative. What does this mean for an emerging city district, neighborhood, waterfront area, or new city? What does this mean for master planning?

All these approaches (and derivations of them) have value for the urban design process and practice in part because they represent design approaches and theories from Europe and North America. They have also been reflected upon by urbanists, with an array of critiques depending upon the specifics of cultures, time-frames, and spatial locations. Each in its own way offers an approach that can be integrated into a larger creative dynamic, away from set typologies, branding (creative city, smart city), and models.

Critics will most likely accuse this work of endorsing a hodge-podge of approaches by selectively applying particular aspects. I counter by saying that in a dynamic creative process, context-specific, various aspects have value in the larger urban design process. For example, understanding elementary geometry and its principles provides a base spatial language for exploration. And that exploration subsequently can lead to hybrids and innovations that originate and depart from that geometry.

Let's explore a few of these typologies and then experiment with related hybrids.

Urban core commercial districts/centers

In North American cities, devoid of centuries of historic town pattern evolution (with the exception of some colonial influences), urban core patterns followed a structured grid pattern, often set forth by government surveyors. Most still have distinct and compact commercial centers. Grid patterns vary based on terrain, orientation to waterfront areas, railroad networks etc.

Example urban block sizes: North America

- Seattle urban blocks vary from the smaller 236ft/73m by 240ft/74m in the historic Pioneer Square area to the larger financial downtown area of 320ft/98m by 420ft/129m, most with service alleys.
- Portland, OR, blocks are 200ft/62m square with no service alleys.
- Vancouver, BC, blocks range in size from 224ft/69m by 376ft/116m to 284ft/87m by 528ft/163m.
- San Francisco has three variations: 340ft/105m by 470ft/145m, 400ft/123m by 250ft/77m, and 500ft/154m by 900ft/277m.
- Toronto blocks are 390ft/120m by 812ft/250m.
- Chicago and Minneapolis block sizes are 660ft/200m by 330ft/100m.
- Calgary block sizes are 330ft/100m by 650ft/170m.
- Edmonton block sizes are 197ft/60m by 560ft/171m.

Therefore, there is quite a variation across the continent, and quite a variation from European cities. Engineers often use 100,000ft^2/11,120m^2 to estimate block size areas, about 16–17 blocks per mile (New York has 20 blocks per mile).

Common block characteristics include:

- zero setback
- common side walls
- front entry
- entry hybrids: atrium, arcade
- double-loaded or central corridor street pattern
- service to rear alley and/or front within designated time periods
- parking in street (historically) and in shared lots/structures; also under building
- transparent street façades for pedestrian view/impulse shopping
- open space setbacks or plazas for higher-density structures
- alley access where feasible
- marquee/weather-protection overhangs.

Scale and configuration of downtown urban core blocks are key determinants for commercial building types. The orthographic block configuration determines most building types and is considered a more economical construction configuration. Downtown blocks function well in compact, continuous arrangements with strong pedestrian orientation along the street (the Portland, OR, block). Historic North American block configurations are characterized by many of the conditions listed above. Contemporary downtown developments have evolved to expanded lobbies, atriums, pedestrian mixing areas and courtyards that contain multiple retail entry points. These can contain eating and entertainment facilities in one- to two-story or higher balconies within the atrium (IDS Tower, Minneapolis, MN).

Numerous North American cities have had disruptions to the functioning of the downtown block grid pattern with the insertion of one-way street patterns that create two competing commercial streets, urban renewal (US) that instigated large-scale block demolition, and the inception of the super-block, often resulting in a dispersal of retail and financial (bank) facilities based on parking and automobile circulation impacts.

Smaller block sizes facilitate improved pedestrian flow throughout a downtown district. Larger block sizes are best served by mid-block pedestrian penetrations at grade and above and below, depending on contextual conditions. Arcades through the blocks can provide protected pedestrian flows along retail corridors connecting one street to another (Cleveland Superior–Euclid Arcade, Cleveland, OH) and many European arcade typologies. These are characteristics adapted by shopping malls, both urban and suburban. And remember, downtown commercial centers are in competition with outlying malls and town centers. Consequently, both contain key ingredients for consumer marketing: comfort, security, variety—enclosed atriums, restaurants and bars, upscale shops and services.

Many cold-climate cities incorporate above-grade enclosed skyways (public and private) through key downtown blocks. These are pedestrian-friendly and can also degrade ground-level retail function by drawing consumers away from street-level activities.

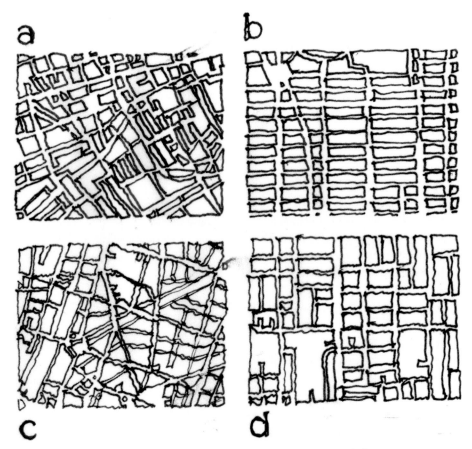

Figure 6.18. Urban core block characteristics. *Block patterns differ significantly from major city to city. This diagram illustrates block patterns for London (a), New York (b), Paris (c), and Toronto (d) (redrawn by author from resource material presented by Spacing Toronto, 2008, by Robin Chubb).*

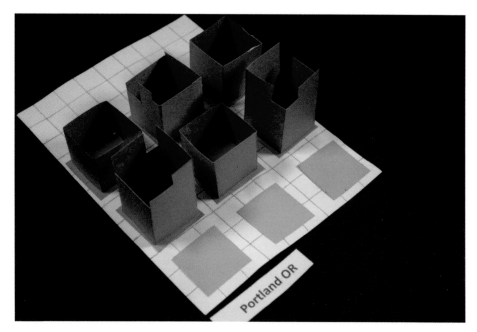

Figure 6.19a. Urban core block manifestations—Portland, OR, base. *This model series portrays block comparisons between (b) Portland, OR, and Vancouver, BC; (c) Portland, OR, and Seattle, WA; (d) Portland, OR, and Edmonton Alberta; (e) Portland, OR. and London (e). Portland is used as the base due to its 200ft/ 62m square configuration (no alleys)—an example of efficient pedestrian walkability.*

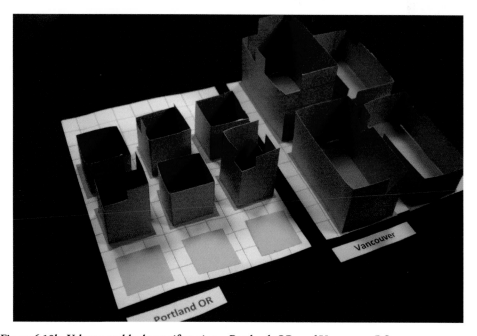

Figure 6.19b. Urban core block manifestation—Portland, OR, and Vancouver, BC.

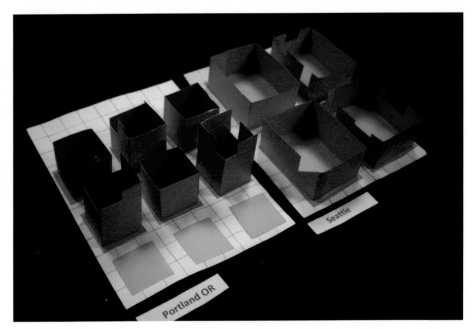

Figure 6.19c. Urban core block manifestation—Portland, OR, and Seattle, WA.

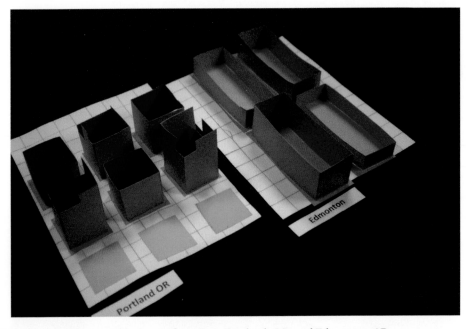

Figure 6.19d. Urban core block manifestation—Portland, OR, and Edmonton, AB.

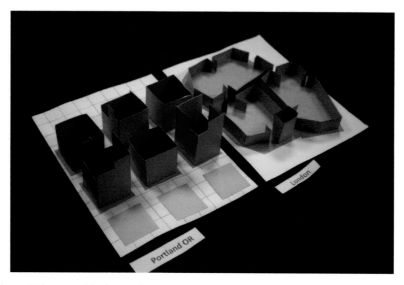

Figure 6.19e. Urban core block manifestation—Portland, OR, and London.

Block dimensions and massing affect the overall urban design of the area, adjacent and nearby forms, as well as the architecture and open space within the block. Given that these patterns occur in many North American and European cities, the typology discussion includes means and methods to alter or manipulate the overall compositions of compact urban commercial center blocks.

Historically the street frontage of the blocks as well as large formal lobbies and arcades provided access and penetration into these urban blocks. Competition with outlying commercial centers, consumer preferences, and changing trends in retail and entertainment functions have added to the list of urban design block manipulations. Prior to describing an exercise on urban block manipulations, a few examples can provide the student with starting points for understanding urban core commercial center typologies.

Urban core commercial center manipulations and examples

1   Free-standing building with open space, with or without pedestal.

2   Building as open space (enclosed and semi-enclosed).

3   Open or semi-enclosed plazas and entryways.

4   Interior arcades, courtyards and concourses.

5   Atriums, galleries and lobbies.

6   Enclosed public (event/work space) floors (upper).

7   Enclosed or semi-enclosed markets.

8   Urban gardens/farms.

9   Event spaces.

10   Roof gardens.

11   Corner celebrations.

12   Weather protection features.

13   Civic and/or cultural activities/facilities.

14   Water features as space-defining elements (as opposed to space-occupying "fountains").

15   Art as building element.

16   Building as art.

17   Block as "new-town/in-town".

This list is not exhaustive and students are urged to explore various city block manipulations for other typology examples.

As I mentioned in the Introduction, I use semi-abstract/semi-real symbolic objects to explore and visualize various principles of composition. There are two reasons for this: I enjoy playing with symbolic objects—it is fun; and I don't want to be drawn into visualizing architectural styles, etc. With steel framing, architecture can be quite "plastic", meaning that shape and form are varied, diverse and certainly not limited to orthographic shapes. You should let your imagination take you wherever.

For most of these examples, as preludes to suggested exercises, I use two block types: a grid block pattern (Seattle); and a circumstantial non-orthographic block pattern (similar to London, UK). On average, North American city blocks are 264ft/75m by 352ft/100m.

Free-standing building with open space

The principles at play regarding urban design include the location and relationship of the high-rise building to the ground plane, the pedestrian zone, and the surrounding context of adjacent and nearby buildings forms. Urban design has a responsibility to influence the architecture regarding these factors. Architects can do wonders with high-rise office buildings (and mixed-use complexes) and, again, the key challenge is to relate that architecture to the larger context—and hopefully have the architecture influenced by the context.

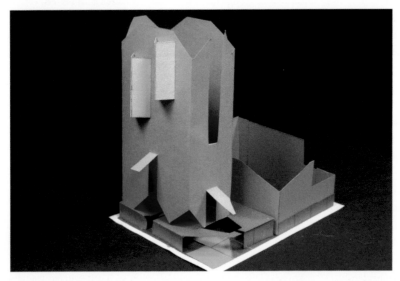

Figure 6.20. Free-standing high-rise office complex with pedestal. *The high-rise office tower occupies 50% of an urban block. The building has a four-story pedestal base with retail and entertainment uses (red), with an atrium/galleria oriented toward an unenclosed open space plaza on the southwest corner. Residential or hotel uses occupy the upper floors (yellow), and the base of the tower is articulated with major transparent planes to reduce the mass of the tower structure.*

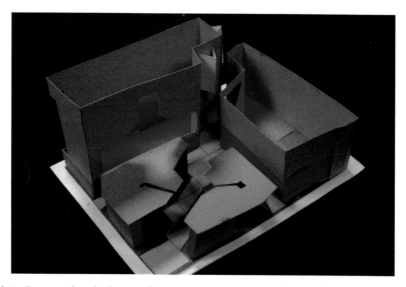

Figure 6.21. Free-standing high-rise office complex, no pedestal. *This example has two medium-rise office buildings with retail at ground floor, no pedestal, with a separate retail facility at its southwest corner with an outdoor plaza.*

Exercise 6.7 Free-standing high-rise office complexes

Intent

Explore the typologies of high-rise office buildings, including mixed use (housing, hotel, commercial, civic) with at least two variants. Do not hesitate to explore hybrids as they emerge in your explorations. The overall intent is to understand office tower typologies through a hands-on experimentation process—so play!

Principles

• Assume an existing onsite context of existing buildings and use varieties.

• Be aware of the orientation of the tower to surrounding contexts and its relationship to the ground plane or primary pedestrian plane.

• In at least two examples, experiment with various vertical circulation principles (central versus multiple or separated).

Tools

Use what you are comfortable with, but I feel that using crafting methods initially is faster and can lead to more hybrid discoveries than beginning with digital technologies. The examples here use construction and poster paper with glue and scissors as they are fast, semi-abstract, and color-coded, enabling numerous constructs within a short period of time. The results can then be digitized and processed further in sophistication.

Tasks

- Investigate the many variations of high-rise office building typologies on an international viewpoint. Assess their vertical access systems, mixed-use integrations and the relationship to surrounding context and pedestrian planes. Once these principles and typologies are assessed, begin exploring various compositions, always looking for hybrids—and have fun!
- Select a block scale as in the previous exercise with surrounding physical/use context.

Arcades and interior block pedestrian concourses

Interior arcades and concourses require thoughtful insertion as they can negatively impact the vitality of the street frontage retail activities. In dense, compact cores, with a dense pedestrian population (residents, office workers, shoppers), the interior arcade can serve to expand the pedestrian/retail/dining/entertainment experience and remain connected to the exterior block frontage.

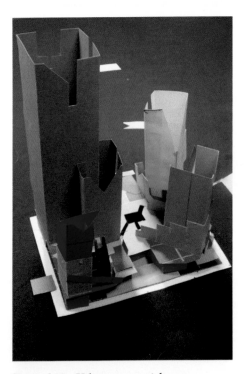
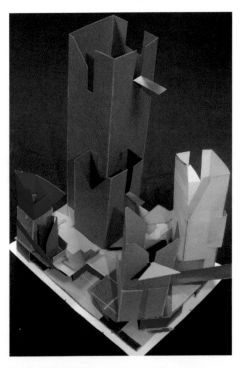

Figure 6.22a. Urban commercial center composed around interior arcade network. *This arcade can be enclosed, partially enclosed or open to the weather, depending upon regional circumstances. Retail and entertainment (red) can stand alone at the high-density corner—here six stories with theaters, restaurants, and shops in glass-enclosed transparency along the arcade—and be incorporated into the base of office blocks (purple).*

Figure 6.22b. Urban commercial center composed around interior arcade/open space network. *This view highlights ground plane and upper landscape elements that can range from hard surface areas to pea patches to urban agriculture facilities connecting office structures to residential high-rise structure (yellow).*

Exercise 6.8 Arcades and interior block pedestrian elements

Intent

Explore design compositions, at least two, for an urban high-density mixed-use block—urban core intensity.

Principles

- Use the arcade, interior concourse element as a catalyst in defining the mixed-use intensities on the urban block.
- Assume and describe in general terms an existing physical/use context adjacent and near the test block. (I have students assign at least a half-block context surrounding the site with historic or architecturally significant buildings, building heights and setbacks, street widths, etc., as this can assist design decisions in the absence of marketing and demographic data.)
- The design composition responds to onsite relationships and offsite contexts.

Tools

Same as Exercise 6.7.

Tasks

- Establish an adjacent and surrounding context.
- Begin with the arcade/concourse element and relate it to surrounding context and onsite elements.
- After a number of experiments with the pedestrian system as catalyst, begin integrating other high-intensity uses and building types into the urban core block.

Urban centers with urban farming/water recycling catalysts

In many new town/city and city district visions, the concepts of farming and urban agriculture are featured as key ingredients in the new communities. We explored their use in residential developments in earlier sections. Urban farming in commercial centers has advanced to a degree that it now goes beyond the horizontal garden integrated into the master plan. Vertical, titled planes, domes, and cylinders all are becoming part of the urban design (architecture and landscape architecture elements). The key principle for these compositions is the use of the urban farming/agricultural element as a catalyst of the entire development, where it can become a key open space feature or architectural feature. This section asks the student to experiment and explore urban farming features as catalysts in large-scale intense urban center developments. Given the intensity of buildings and hard space in an urban core commercial center, the urban farming concept can be a softening compositional ingredient as well as an economic component for downtown areas. It may be possible for developments of this type to gain financial incentives from local governments for this type of "green" insertion into the physical downtown structure.

In the early 2000s, artist Lorna Jordan undertook a project for the City of Seattle regarding Westlake Avenue, which runs from downtown Seattle to South Lake Union, wherein gray and surface runoff water was cleaned as it ran through new high-rise office buildings and into a street pedestrian concourse before eventually trickling into Lake Union to the north, providing clean water for a street art structure as well as urban farming structures.

The technology is well founded with proposed developments occurring around the globe: Indonesia, Shanghai, Toronto, Brooklyn, Paris, Copenhagen, Detroit and Pittsburgh—catalysts for major urban core commercial and residential centers.

Key features of urban farming in commercial centers

Obviously, light, sun, warmth and water/soil are the key ingredients of urban farming. Vertical farming, also referred to as "in-steading", "farmscrapers", etc., can occur in many types of structure, including, but not limited to:

- geodesic domes
- tilted stepped planes, free-standing or as building components
- vertical greenhouses
- "A"-frame structures with mechanized interiors
- "green" arcades and concourses
- "green" lobbies and atriums
- "green" walls
- "green" façade components
- building components (corner elements, rooftops)
- abandoned buildings and complexes
- water features (hydroponics)
- and many others.

Urban commercial center free-standing farm component and building component

Again, there are so many variations that the student should investigate and catalogue the applications and then seek hybrids that relate to any given project and context. The following examples are my attempt to help the student start the exploration process.

Exercise 6.9 Urban farming in urban core commercial centers

Intent

Compose an urban core block with the urban farming component as the catalyst structure. Explore various types of urban farming on a large scale to incorporate into the urban block.

Principles

The urban farming typology is a major compositional structure. Explore the vertical potential of the farming structures as a part of the building design.

Figure 6.23. Urban commercial center free-standing farm features. *OK, this was fun! Here, I integrated a number of vertical agricultural features into the block composition with a high-rise office building (30 stories; purple) and an adjacent high-rise residential tower (yellow). The urban farming components include a series of ascending vertical triangular frames delineating the pedestrian entry to the main commercial center (red). The vertical frames are along an axis, highlighting the diagonal compositional structure for the block, from southwest to northeast. On each major entry to the site, northwest and mid-southeast, vertical greenhouses rise above the four-story commercial pedestal and the residential tower, respectively. At the base of the main office tower is a green façade attachment that provides open space for office workers and a commercial venture.*

Urban centers with building configurations as art (as opposed to art in the configuration)

A debate that engages urban design composition directly is: what is the meaning of experimental architecture in an urban design context? London is an excellent example: given a Dark Ages/Middle Ages circumstantial growth to cities, compacting within fortified walls and subsequently spilling out into "suburban" lands (below the castle) outside of the fortresses, a pattern of "plastic", non-orthographic urban core blocks dominated the landscape. Not by choice; by circumstance.

And the insertion of architecture and urban form that is a conflict at least and a polarity at best into that historic context can be dramatic and successful. Or, if overdone, disastrous.

So, let us play with urban core commercial centers that are just that—playful—and functioning architecture that is at the same time an artwork in and of itself, with its own harmony and playful irritation with the surrounding historic context. Many argue that civic buildings can be the anomaly, the departure from the established context. And yet, architecture wants to explore and experiment, and we ask: how does it integrate into the context, strengthen it and yet highlight it and emphasize it with difference and variety?

A disclaimer: art is in the eye of the beholder, so if you do not like my version of urban design art form—DO YOUR OWN!

Figure 6.24a. Urban center as art configuration. *I had fun with this, and if you are in Lancaster (UK), Toronto or Cleveland, you may laugh at my artistic stretch. Do your own and have fun. This is my meager effort: a tumbled grouping of blocks (office buildings), oriented on a diagonal compositional structure, with a strong axis composed of a horizontal building extracting from a high-rise office tower, carrying surface runoff water under and through office spaces down into the pedestrian space/courtyard. The diagonal forms are tilted elevators/escalators providing access between retail centers (red) and office uses above (purple). Grade-level space is protected from the weather and contains eating courts, arcade, and an active human environment. The building complex serves as a departure from the surrounding context.*

Exercise 6.10 Urban center as art

Intent

Assemble a block composition where the urban commercial center is comprised of building and open space forms that constitute an art piece, such as sculpture, three-dimensional collage, etc., with commercial center functions and activities. Remain mindful of connections to adjacent and nearby spatial context.

Principles

- Construct an eidetic vision: the integration of meaning and form into a semi-abstract composition that still functions as an urban center.
- Express the block composition as a spatial metaphor, for example.
- View the composition as sculpture, using architecture and landscape architecture as vehicles for a larger "image".

Tasks

- Investigate block and building design compositions that are anomalies or significant and intentional departures from the prevailing physical context.
- Identify the key principles as opposed to style features that distinguish the composition as comprising an artful statement.

Figure 6.24b. Urban center as art configuration.

Figure 6.24c. Urban center as art configuration.

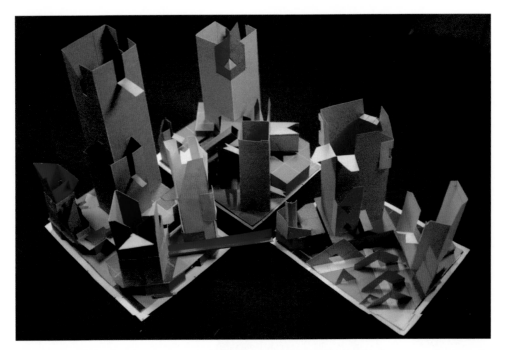

Figure 6.25a. Urban block composites. *I had some fun playing with the four blocks constructed as examples above. I looked for ways to connect the blocks in various compositions.*

Figure 6.25b. Urban block composites. *Another view and composition experiment.*

Shopping center typologies

Shopping center typologies are constantly changing due to competition, consumer preferences, and marketing factors. They can range from one-building, multi-level structures to sprawling complexes mostly on one level. They are usually self-contained, "capturing" consumers with entertainment, food and beverages plus accessory facilities ranging from gyms to children's play areas. In most cases, they are "islands" in the built form with minimal meaningful connections to surrounding areas. This section focuses on the shopping center as town center, wherein the historic shopping center is evolving into a multi-use community facility and activity place. The pattern of ownership in shopping centers varies from one major investment holder to multiple ownerships; and they are in private ownership, thus controlling the use of common areas such as concourses, food and entertainment areas.

Common characteristics of shopping centers include:

- Enclosed and semi-enclosed spaces.
- Major anchor retailers (department and apparel stores) serving as anchors at strategic locations within the complex.
- Controlled concourses usually with double-loaded retail facilities and stacked retail facilities around courtyards and arcades.
- Parking in parking structures and at grade level.
- Food and entertainment uses at key locations (intersections, "capture" areas).
- Recreational facilities.
- In North America, free-standing shopping center buildings may occupy no more than 25–30% of a given site, with the remainder used for parking, delivery etc.; as the centers evolve, other uses such as housing and civic facilities develop, supported by mass transit additions and connections.

The list goes on as shopping centers compete with large warehouse "big box" facilities, outlet centers, intercept centers, and large-scale specialty markets. How are they evolving and in what form? How can they be better connected to surrounding built form? Because of this evolution, I do not devote significant space to the shopping center typology as current examples are largely obsolete. However, I do experiment with the evolution and manipulation of standard shopping centers for the benefit of students who want to engage the exercises.

Shopping centers and malls come in many varieties, from a single enclosed "building", to redeveloped athletics stadiums, to meandering "village" configurations, to formal multi-level concourse/courtyard configurations. In this initial semi-abstract example, the principles are basic: a "capture" space, a double-loaded "street" corridor, intersection points, major destination uses at key termini. They are physical islands in the urban landscape, requiring additional design strategies to connect them to the urban context.

NOTE: this book does not promote the development of shopping centers and malls. They have a significant international consumer base and are constantly evolving. Understanding the typology of these centers can enable urban designers to explore hybrids of this phenomenon and improve the manner in which they are integrated into the larger urban fabric.

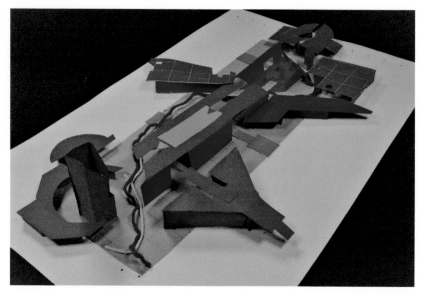

Figure 6.26a. Shopping center/mall typologies. *This initial example illustrates basic relationships of the shopping center/mall, including circulation, concourse principles, anchor stores, parking, etc. They are characterized by one or more linear concourses, lined with shops on both sides (double-loaded), with two or more major anchors such as department stores, major apparel, stores, sport stores, etc. This example includes open, semi-enclosed, and enclosed linear arcade and concourse, natural features such as a green corridor stream system, water features (blue), major event facilities (circle forms), entertainment retail, and major dramatized entry points with surrounding parking areas.*

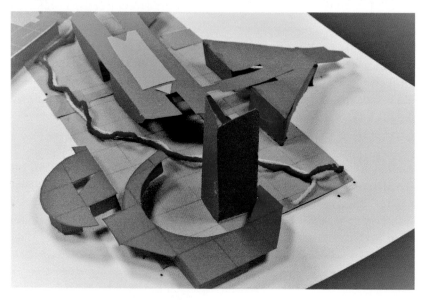

Figure 6.26b. Shopping center/mall typologies. *Alternate view.*

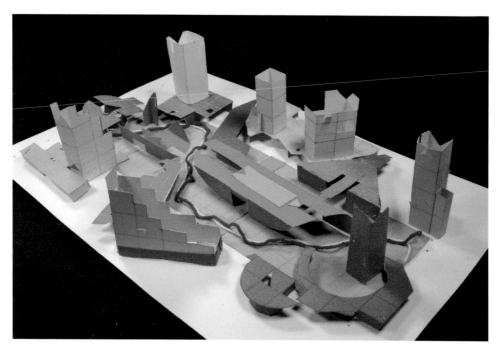

Figure 6.27a. Shopping center/mall typology modifications. *Let us begin manipulations: here, I have added a transit hub with new housing elements and car park structures.*

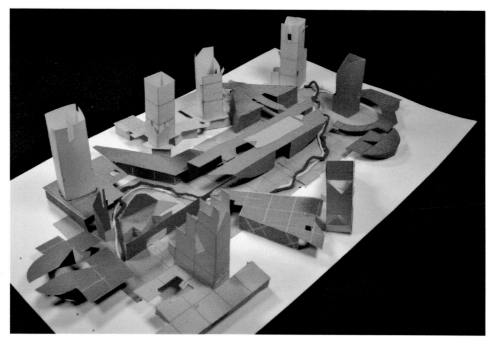

Figure 6.27b. Shopping center/mall typology modifications. *Add more housing and open space recreation on space previously occupied by surface parking.*

Exercise 6.11 Shopping center evolutions

Intent

Transform a regional shopping center/mall into a neighborhood or multi-use district.

Principles and tasks

- Begin with an existing shopping center/mall, preferably a regional facility.
- Use compositional structures to assign an underlying order to the manipulated forms: cross, axial, diagonal structures, repetition with variety.
- Focus on places within the composition that have potential for human connections and interactions, highlight and dramatize them.
- Assess the scale of housing in relation to the commercial center and its "street".
- Do not be obsessed with architectural style; focus on compositional structures.

Compact shopping center manipulation

In this example, the regional center is a compact urban structure built in association with a high-rise residential tower. The intent is to increase the density and intensity of the site, evolving toward a neighborhood or district community. The existing site is maintained in area without expansion.

The example series is not contextually influenced, assuming a vacant, large, flat-site super-block surrounded by major street arterials.

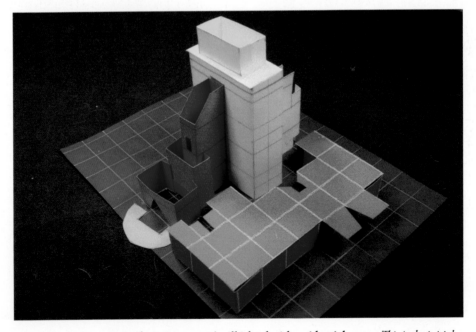

Figure 6.28a. Basic compact shopping center/mall island with residential tower. *This is the initial development program: a high-rise residential tower with multiple-story retail/commercial compact urban center.*

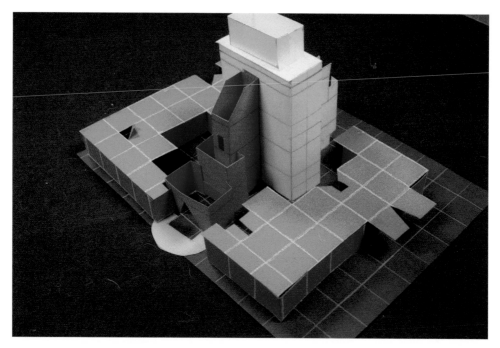

Figure 6.28b. Center/mall expanded with retail. *The complex is doubled in retail/commercial uses and form.*

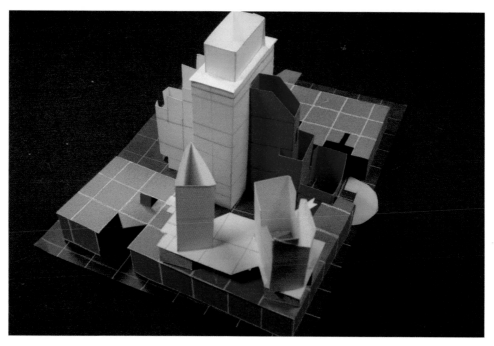

Figure 6.28c. Center/mall expanded with housing/employment centers. *Residential towers and employment centers as shared work space and a medium-rise office tower are added.*

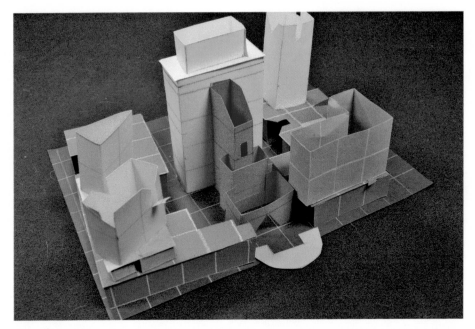

Figure 6.28d. Additional housing tower added. *A final residential tower is added to complete the compact center, which now approximates a neighborhood district. Further additions are possible.*

Making connections offsite

Shopping malls and centers globally tend to be isolated islands within the built-form landscape. Connecting them to the rest of the community and form is a challenge, given property ownership, parking issues, etc., but it is a critical responsibility of urban design to make those connections.

The following examples begin with a basic shopping mall organization and structure, three anchor stores and a double-loaded corridor of shops along a pedestrian concourse (open, semi-enclosed and enclosed). Parking lots surround the complex, with sufficient distance between it and the primary street. The sequence illustrates the initial mall, the introduction of mass transit and housing, and finally a physical and activity connection to the primary street.

Exercise 6.12 Shopping center connections

Intent

Explore design methods and tactics that can effect a meaningful integration of a shopping center/mall complex into the surrounding or emerging urban fabric.

Principles and tasks

- Select a shopping center within your region.
- Assess the surrounding context (form, uses, circulation, etc.).

Figure 6.29a. Shopping center/mall typology modifications II. *These centers are land banks with major parking surface areas, sometimes encompassing 70% of a given site. This is a basic center/mall with three anchors and a double-loaded corridor concourse with adjacent office buildings, an island in a sea of parking.*

Figure 6.29b. Shopping center/mall typology modifications II and connections. *The modifications include medium-density housing elements (orange), transit hub (asterisk), perimeter retail/commercial on the primary street within housing frontage, an open space connection between the existing mall and the new housing, softening the transition and providing leisure space; and a major connection with housing to that (pedestrian) street. The mall becomes a town center with a town square (semi-enclosed), with dispersed surface parking lots and car park structures. Civic and cultural uses are also possible.*

- Explore design methods or actions that can effect a spatial connection (visual as well as physical) between the center and surrounding area.
- Consider new use activities, open space features, circulation network, building forms etc.
- How can building typologies make those connections and function properly, i.e. housing and its amenities and quality of living.

Town centers

We essentially engaged the evolution of a shopping center/mall into a town center in the preceding work. When housing, office and employment centers and even civic and cultural uses are incorporated into the composition, it develops into a town center. Let us explore the characteristics and potentials.

Common characteristics for town centers (as opposed to regional or major shopping centers) include the following:

- major anchors, including department stores, furniture and hardware stores, theaters (motion picture and live), and major food markets
- hotels
- banks
- car rental
- food and drink
- entertainment
- health and fitness
- health clinics
- arts and specialty
- pet stores
- fashion (clothes, shoes etc.)
- sports and fitness
- toys and hobbies
- travel and hospitality
- office space for both private and public entities as tenants
- civic uses (concert halls, live theater)
- housing in various typologies
- mass transit access
- library and other semi-public uses
- pedestrian amenities (parks, special landscape features, restored habitat areas)
- dispersed parking (smaller lots with strong pedestrian-separated connections) and parking structures.

A major distinction between historic small downtown/village commercial centers and planned town centers is the dominance in the planned centers of national and international shops and services: corporate franchise ownership and management. And shopping centers and town centers are privately owned, with set hours of operation.

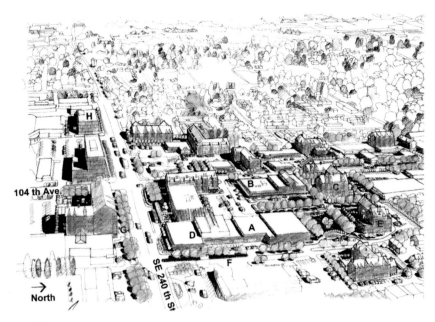

Figure 6.30. Shopping mall evolving into town center. *Shopping malls are typically islands of enclosed commercial space arranged around a captive pedestrian-oriented core within a field of parking and hard surfaces. As they mature and evolve, key compositional relationships and uses can be added to the existing complex to make the mall compact and provide improved connections to adjacent and nearby elements of the urban area. In the illustration, these include: the introduction of a local slow street network that can connect incrementally to adjacent redevelopment parcels and to the main thoroughfare; the development of peripheral development that is oriented to the main thoroughfare, the new street network, and adjacent development; a green open space that connects the modified mall to the main thoroughfare and acts as a centerpiece for pedestrian activities, providing a visual corridor to the interior of the complex; reducing the mass of the mall with breakouts of transparent vertical planes oriented toward the new local street network; small dispersed landscaped parking lots with strong pedestrian connecting paths; and combined or shared service roads and alleys. The sketch illustrates an older shopping mall with infill residential, office, transit, entertainment, and open space elements, transforming the older center into a new neighborhood/town center—connected to the surrounding city.*

The town center concept applies aptly to historic medium- and small-sized downtowns and village centers that have been negatively impacted by outlying shopping and intercept centers. The addition of housing within historic town centers amplifies the social and market energies, often acting as a catalyst for new commercial and office uses. Historic town centers can provide an authenticity that is not possible with new centers where franchised thematic branding often occurs as part of the marketing strategy.

Exercise 6.13 Town center typologies

Intent

Begin with an established urban/suburban shopping mall or regional center. Expand development onsite to transform the existing center into a multi-use town center that serves as a new urban district or neighborhood and is connected to the surrounding context, or at least provides opportunities for future connectivity.

Principles and tasks

- Investigate current town center developments in a number of different regions to identify various components and configuration typologies. Study a number of typologies: new town center, redeveloped mall/town center, and historic downtown/village center modified into town center. Each has features and components that can contribute to the exercise.
- Incorporate regional transit facilities, new housing typologies integrated with open space amenities, new office, shared work space and other employment center typologies into the redevelopment strategy.
- A major strategy for transformation from shopping mall/center to town center relates to how the new expanded complex is integrated and connected to adjacent and nearby context, using circulation systems, transit, open space patterns, and building types and uses to make various connections.

Leisure and village centers

Leisure and village centers are small multi-use complexes that are programmed and designed to attract customers as destinations for social activities as well as shopping and other commercial services. They are often located close to larger commercial centers and are in contrast to the latter's larger scale and intensity. Uses include but are not limited to specialty retail shops, coffee shops, cafes, bookstores, shared work spaces, health and fitness services, meeting rooms, office space for local or neighborhood associations and groups, and smaller-scale housing facilities.

Numerous leisure and village centers take advantage of existing buildings such as defunct schools, churches, and office buildings, which are used as bases. For example, a former school building can be transformed into a community center with attached or nearby housing and limited specialty retail uses, as mentioned above. They are set in a park like setting, imitating a landscaped "main" street or village square formation.

NOTE: why spend time on the smaller commercial centers? Aren't they suburban and therefore irrelevant to "urban design"? The argument here is that all the pieces, large and small, are incremental additions or modifications to the urban landscape. Making improvements in the human experience through design at all scales contributes to the larger creative process.

Small mixed-use typologies

Smaller-scale mixed-use typologies often contain residential or office uses. The types vary in configuration from housing units above or adjacent to retail uses, to stacked flats above commercial units, to townhouses above flats. They serve an important function in maintaining activity on streets, as transition types between residential neighborhoods and retail centers, and provide transparency on the ground level. They can be stand-alone buildings, attached or in semi-attached clusters. Parking is either to the rear or side yards of the building or in an interior compound. Emphasis is placed on the pedestrian relationship to the building with direct sidewalk access and visibility and pedestrian amenities (seating, landscaping, cafes, etc.). The "shop-house" typology is found worldwide and dates back to antiquity.

Built-form typologies exist in most cultures that have transferability to larger-scale development patterns. They can have unusual or novel characteristics in their compositions that can add strength and personal or local identity to new configurations. I have experimented with a number of hybrids in professional practice, particularly in rurban or edge communities where people want growth and services without using suburban or franchised typologies (thus the term *rurban*). Two examples are illustrated here.

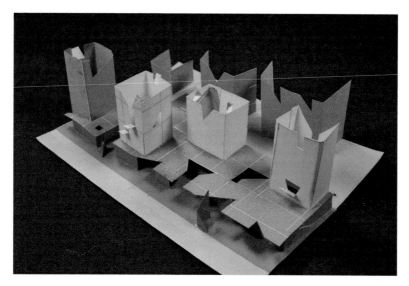

Figure 6.31. *Leisure center typologies. There are many variations of leisure centers around the globe, most mimicking in some way the historic small downtowns and village centers of North America and the hamlets of Europe. This example is a linear construct along a major arterial in a linear axial composition, not uncommon in North America. Key characteristics include a continuous landscaped spine or axis that unites the store fronts and small-scale retail commercial uses such as book stores, cafes, dry cleaning etc. The relationship of the building to the open space, linear in this example, is designed to encourage people to linger. Select setbacks in the retail frontage enhance and expand the linear green space. Housing and small shared work spaces or offices are included in the complex. Connections to other retail and office developments are critical to their survival. They are most often in close relationship to major malls.*

Figure 6.32. Leisure center: hamlet type. *This example portrays a more compact center that incorporates a historic building (former church building) into the development with a major open space "green" within the retail commercial area. The hamlet is supported by shared work space and offices.*

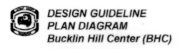

DESIGN GUIDELINE
PLAN DIAGRAM
Bucklin Hill Center (BHC)

SV Silverdale Village

Source: KPD

Plan Diagram, 3-23
Forty (45) feet building heights from entry grade (45)
to top of parapet or one half height of gable
Allowable Buildable Area (ABA)
Village squares (VS)
"Main Street" (MS)
Local street network (LSN)
Landscaped front yard setback of twelve (12) feet minimum in depth (LFY)
Potential local street connection to Bay Shore Drive (CON)
Potential local street connection to Bucklin Hill Road and Randall Way (RW)
Two pedestrian activated crossings of Silverdale Way (PC)

Silverdale Village Example Sketch (A), 3-24
The Silverdale Village sketch illustrates two mixed-use developments, one on each side of Silverdale Way, with retail commercial, office and residential uses. Each has a town or village square visually related across Silverdale Way and physically connected with pedestrian-activated signals and raised crosswalks.

Figure 6.33. Village center: Silverdale. *This example illustrates the expansion of two small shopping plazas, on opposite sides of a major entry arterial, into a combined leisure center. Additions to the existing shops include housing (stacked flats and townhouses) to the rear of the complexes and new small retail and café facilities on a small open space square or green. In this case, the two open space additions, one on each side of the arterial, provide a visual connecting device. Parking lots are small and dispersed with designated and separated pedestrian paths and walkways connecting them to shops and services. Source: Kasprisin Pettinari Design.*

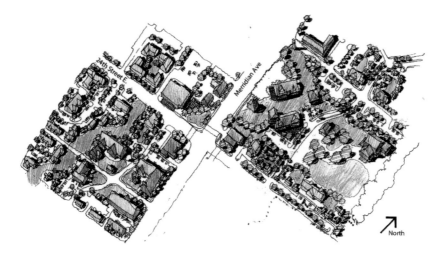

Figure 6.34. Village center: Edgewood. *A cluster of smaller village centers are connected by a wetland/ meadow network to form part of a larger town center.*

Figure 6.35. Mixed-use single-site typologies. *In smaller cities and towns, mixed-use infill on single sites, both corner and block interior lots, can re-energize older downtowns with new residential uses that support older retail/commercial buildings.*

Hybrid mixed-use typologies

Both examples of hybrid typologies are derived from local conditions or typologies. As development expands and intensifies at the edge of metropolitan areas, it often consumes and eradicates unique or specialty uses and forms. Utilizing these forms as the basis for connections between new growth and local identity can strengthen and enrich community identity. Three examples found in North America and Europe are the *crossroads mixed-use cluster, the nursery/market compound,* and *recycled housing blocks.*

Crossroads mixed-use cluster

Crossroads are generally places or locations of intersection of circulation paths (streets, concourses, sidewalks, etc.). They represent a pause in flow, gathering places, and basic services for local communities. Characteristics include:

- intersecting circulation paths (crossing streets, T-intersects, roundabouts, etc.)
- compact building configurations often containing old mill or agriculture supply facilities, churches, cafes, etc. that are suitable for adaptive reuse
- a "main street" orientation along the crossroads center
- often an open space focal area (small park, cluster of vegetation, etc.)
- parking to side and/or rear of buildings
- pedestrian connectivity via paths and block penetrations
- varying street patterns that can increase the special nature of the place (deflected streets, oblique intersections).

The crossroads typology is a rural and semi-rural built form that is recognizable as small scale and local. Many developed around local feed and agricultural supply stores, grocery stores, meeting halls such as granges, guild halls and churches, all located within close proximity to the key intersection(s). A significant negative impact for these typologies is the street widening that often accompanies new growth. Existing crossroads developments can be economically enhanced with residential and commercial infill, with both existing and new hybrids serving as new centers for larger-scale developments.

Nursery/market mixed-use compound

The nursery compound was inspired by urban design work in a semi-rural community experiencing significant new growth pressures. The community aspired to a new civic/town center in close proximity to an existing nursery compound, an historic part of the community and in transition due to growth pressures. The nursery was to be phased out and the land sold for new development. The nursery form provided a basis for a new town center development that incorporated existing and new civic, commercial and housing components. Key characteristics include the following:

- recycled, adaptive or new nursery compounds as the basis or core of new development
- mixed building types: nursery buildings such as greenhouses, retail stores, cafes, accessory buildings (barns, sheds, etc.), a hierarchy of residential buildings integrated within the compound (not as a separate attached entity)

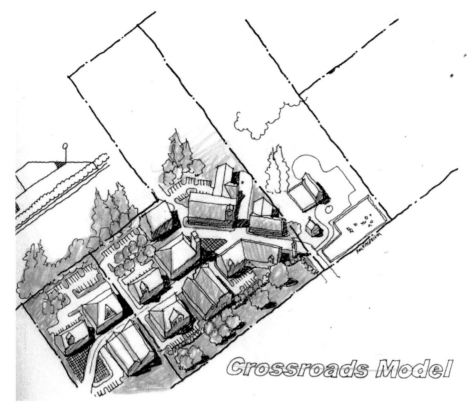

Figure 6.36. Crossroads mixed-use cluster. *Key features of the crossroads hybrid include slow-moving streets parallel and connected to a main thoroughfare with variations in the street axis (deflected, curvilinear, T-intersects). Pedestrians are a top priority with larger sidewalks, small intimate open space features (parks and/or setbacks) and dramatized corner elements on intersection buildings.*

- mixed-use civic buildings if appropriate (including athletics facilities, meeting facilities, bookstores etc.)
- small dispersed clustered parking green lots
- enclosed and semi-enclosed pedestrian concourses (greenhouses)
- mixed-density residential buildings for added diversity in scale and population characteristics.

Recycled residential blocks

Many residential blocks adjacent to existing downtowns undergo a process of transition that can include changes from owner-occupied tenancy to rental units to marginal commercial uses. These changing block dynamics can provide a positive repository for small-scale non-residential uses such as professional offices, printing and computer technology services, wine shops etc. Key features remaining from their former residential uses such as landscaping, front and side yards, and a small "residential" scale can be expanded.

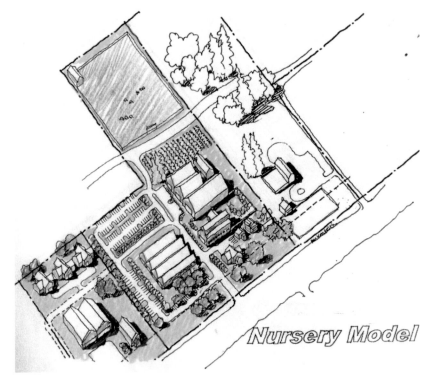

Figure 6.37. Nursery/market compound typology. *This hybrid contains elements of the existing nursery with a new city hall building (blue) located at a key entry access drive. Retail uses are located in arcade-type buildings—long and narrow with interconnecting openings not unlike many market buildings. Residential buildings of mixed types are distributed throughout the compound, with private open space and a strong connectivity to the overall compound. Gardens and pea patches intersperse the compound in the manner of a nursery, buffering dispersed parking lots. This typology provided the basis for an expanded town center.*

Bibliography

American Heritage Dictionary of the English Language, 5th edition, 2011: Houghton Mifflin Harcourt, Boston, MA, and New York.

Attoe, Wayne and Logan, Donn, 1989: *American Urban Architecture: Catalysts in the Design of Cities*: University of California Press, Berkeley/Los Angeles/London.

Kasprisin Pettinari Design, 2004: *City of Edgewood: Town Center and Meridian Avenue Corridor Master Plans*: Kasprisin Pettinari Design, Seattle.

Krier, Rob, 1988: *Architectural Composition*: Rizzoli International Publications, Inc., New York.

Krier, Rob, 2006: *Town Spaces*: Birkhauser—Publishers for Architecture, Basel/Berlin/Boston.

Marshall, Stephen, 2012: "Planning, Design and the Complexity of Cities." In Portugali, Juval, Meyer, Han, Stolk, Egbert and Tan, Ekim (eds): *Complexity Theories of Cities Have Come of Age*: Springer, Heidelberg, Dordrecht/London/New York.

Sidewalk Labs, 2018: *Quayside Site Plan*: Sidewalk Labs, Toronto.

Soja, Edward, 1996: *Postmetropolis*: Blackwell Publishing, Oxford.

Walker, Lester, 1987: *Tiny Houses*: The Overlook Press, Woodstock, NY.

Chapter 7

URBAN DESIGN EXPLORATIONS

Urban design applications

The technological advances in structural assembly of buildings has opened wide the door to almost unlimited form in architecture. From vertical circular office buildings such as the BBVA Headquarters Building (Madrid, Spain) to the building as frame in the Abu Dhabi National Oil Headquarters Building to "the Gherkin", 30 St Mary Axe (London, UK) and on and on, architecture is reaching new levels of form-expression. One only needs to view the architecture in Abu Dhabi to absorb the variety and extent of contemporary architecture. How does this variety and diversity affect urban design? Is this architectural expression distinctly separate, a departure from the influence of urban design—the preference of architects without input from the planning community? Do cities comprise a conglomeration of buildings without cohesiveness or harmony?

Urban design can influence contemporary architecture through guidelines and regulations regarding height, massing, setbacks, responses to historically significant features, etc. But is that its full extent and role in the making of urban form?

In this book, I define urban design as a process of creating variations of *order* for cities—a structural composition driven by organizational relationships (people and related functions) made up of the elements and principles of urban form—the buildings and other objects of cities *activated* by compositional structures or structuring devices. Consequently, I am focusing on the following key aspects of this interpretation of urban design.

- Composition as a structuring order for urban form and urban meaning.
- Composition as a connecting device within the urban form.
- Compositional transitions in urban form over time.
- Compositional probabilities as trajectories in time.
- Compositional order as fertile ground for creative design expression: the composition of complexity.

I make the argument again that all designers and planners are agents of change in urban form and involved in various ways in the making of urban form—thus the need to recognize and understand the elements and principles of design composition, and their application within the complex reality of cities, seeking responsive and creative order.

Let's play and explore these key aspects using a variety of real contexts. To establish a number of varied contextual study areas, I selected three sites to experiment with:

- Villiers Island, Toronto Waterfront, Ontario, Canada—a high-density new town in-town.
- St Paul's Precinct, London, UK—high-intensity development in an historic context.
- Lake City, Seattle, WA—transitions from suburban to new town in-town.

The following exercises and experiments introduce urban context and conditions to the previous semi-abstract exercises. The exercises represent projects similar to those that I incorporated into my Urban Design Composition course (UW) over many years. They range in duration from one to two weeks and are considered "sketch problems". Their purpose is to engage students in compositional challenges without immersing them in the longer and more involved studio challenge. They focus on the elements and principles of design composition; on the need for hybridity and novel solutions versus a master plan "typology plug-in" process; and on the role and function of technology in city-making. None of the resulting schemes is assumed to be a full solution. Their value is in the act of experimentation with composition.

Villiers Island Precinct, Toronto, Canada

The Villiers Island compositional exercise encompasses an area of 35.5 hectares (88 acres) along the Toronto Waterfront area at the intersection of the Don River with the Inner Harbour. The project area will be a newly constructed island surrounded by a new course of the Don River to the east and south, the existing Keating Channel to the north and the Inner Harbour to the west. The project is in essence a new town/in-town with a projected population of 8,000 to 10,000 residents, 4,800 housing units, employment and retail centers, civic uses, and park space, particularly at the western and eastern portions of the new island. Waterfront Toronto (a collaboration between the City of Toronto and the Region Conservation Authority) anticipates that 22 hectares (54 acres) of the site will be developed, with the remaining area allocated to waterfront parks and public spaces. The island will afford views of Toronto's Inner Harbour and the downtown skyline, and will form a gateway to the West Don Lands and East Bayfront neighborhoods to the west of the Port Lands.

This exercise builds on the current precinct development plan and alters aspects of it to accommodate the educational intent of the exercise—large-scale compositional design.

Guiding principles of the current precinct development plan (Waterfront Toronto):

1   Animate and activate the water's edge to provide a variety of memorable experiences along the river, harbour and channel edges.
2   Plan for a diversity of great open spaces and waterside parks to serve the local precinct community, city and region.
3   Provide for a catalytic opportunity—a facility, experience, use or activity that reinforces the island as a regional and transformative destination.
4   Reinforce the island as a key gateway and access point to the main Waterfront, Lower Don Lands, and Port Lands districts.
5   Celebrate the area's industrial heritage, character and legacy through appropriate conservation.
6   Prioritize transportation choices to, from and on the island by providing connected pedestrian and cycling networks and optimizing planned transit infrastructure.
7   Plan for a diverse, mixed-use and inclusive community.
8   Provide a variety of building forms to create a comfortable and inviting public realm, and establish a distinct skyline.
9   Develop an innovative model for a sustainable urban community and demonstrate excellence in community design.
10 Ensure that the precinct plan is viable and implementable and maximizes place-making opportunities in the initial phases of redevelopment.

Major structuring moves for the island (Waterfront Toronto):

- *A green and blue loop*: the green and blue loop consists of a combination of water's edge parks and open space with water bodies consisting of the historic Keating Channel, the Inner Harbour, and the naturalized valley lands (new water course) along the east and south edges of the new island.

- *A central living room*: the existing proposal calls for the creation of a "living room" using the Keating Channel as a central spine to integrate the Keating Precinct to the north with the new Villiers Island to the south.

- *A connected island*: a fine-grain street network and block pattern will provide a balanced movement within the island with a north–south arterial and an east–west arterial, both connecting to off-island street networks.

- *A complete island*: a sustainable and complete community serving between 8,000 and 10,000 people.

- *A destination place*: a place defined by waterfront parks and open space, heritage attractions and an as-yet undetermined catalyst use.

- *An island precinct with history*: highlighting the industrial history of the island as a core attraction and feature.

Exercise 7.1 Villiers Island compositional exercise

Intent

Building large-scale districts, neighborhoods or city sectors on the land is a major challenge; building on a shoreline is another. Why? *Edge energies!* This exercise asks students to step out of the "box" and

Figure 7.1. Villiers Island location. *Villiers Island is located a 30-minute walk from downtown Toronto along the Keating Channel, south of the Gardiner Expressway and west of the Don Valley Parkway. It is bordered to the west by the Toronto Inner Harbour and the Toronto Islands; and to the south and southeast by Lake Ontario. The proposed site is accessed north–south via Cherry Street and from the east via Commissioner Street.*

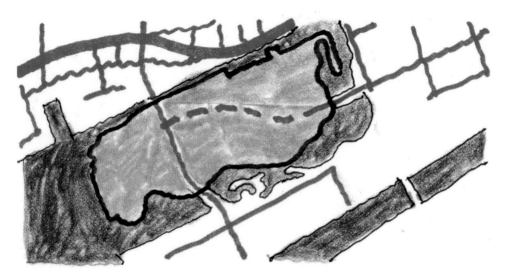

Figure 7.2. Villiers Island. *Villiers Island is proposed to be 88 acres (35.5 hectares) in total size, with approximately 54 acres (22 hectares; 61%) of developable area. The island is bounded by the reconfigured Keating Channel to the north, Toronto's Inner Harbour to the west, and a new course for the Don River to the east and south, incorporating Polson Slip on the south. Cherry and Commissioner streets transect the area of the proposed island. The reconfigured Don River is the eastern boundary of the island. Keating Channel is to the north and Toronto's Inner Harbour to the west. Lake Ontario is to the south and southeast.*

first of all ask how the Lake Ontario/Toronto water's edge was formed? What forces and factors were at work and how can they influence or impact new water's edge development besides or in addition to the norm: buildings with water views, marinas, promenades, floating homes, etc.? The industrial history of the Toronto Waterfront is contemporary relative to the forces that shaped the landscape. Think beyond that recent history.

Principles

Are there forces and historic dynamics in the formation of the waterfront that can be translated into design principles? You will notice that I have not stated any principles here as I think they should be discovered through experimentation.

Tools

Digital imagery is available regarding the geologic history of Lake Ontario and its water's edge, connected to the formation of the Great Lakes and the St Lawrence River. I used a combination of paper models and wood blocks to experiment with compositions. Use what ever tools you prefer.

Tasks

- Using the basic island configuration as defined in the Villiers Island Precinct Plan as a starting point, explore compositional strategies, elements and principles that encompass the plan's guidelines:
  - 4,800 housing units
  - 8,000 to 10,000 people
  - employment center(s) for approximately 3,000 people
  - waterfront access
  - 11.2 hectares (25 acres) of parkland
  - recognize and utilize the proposed bridge access points to and from the island.
- Explore various compositional structures as a basis for the development strategies.

Geologic history and background of the Toronto Waterfront

Catalysts for urban design can be found in the geologic formation of a region's land forms. Toronto, on Lake Ontario, is no exception, and reviewing some of the major events from both long ago and recent history can provide a wider perspective for design explorations. So let's step back a bit in time.

Quayside is on the north coast of Lake Ontario, just south of the Canadian Shield, with a geological heritage that involves the formation of the Great Lakes. This is not merely about a freshwater lake frontage. It is about the forces of nature that transformed the foundation of the Toronto area, which at one point in history was located south of the equator, with southern Ontario covered by the Iapetus Ocean. About 150 million years ago, as the super-continent of Pangea was breaking up, North America assumed its present shape.

About 3 million years ago, water cut channels into the bedrock, forming axes or channels that were the foundation of the four lower Great Lakes: Ontario, Huron, Erie and Michigan. Toronto's location emerged from the first manifestation of the ancient St Lawrence River system, with one portion called the Laurentian Channel. This flowed south from present Georgian Bay between the Niagara Escarpment and Lake Simcoe, into the Toronto area and consisted of multiple rivers or flowages. The last Ice Age buried the Laurentian Channel. Glacial meltwater flowed into the "Lake Ontario" system, or rather Lake Coleman, the precursor to Lake Ontario. One kilometer of ice covered what is now Toronto.

About 13,000 years ago, the ice retreated from the basin and Lake Coleman became Lake Iroquois: 35 meters deeper and 60 meters higher than the present lake. Subsequently, the shoreline of Lake Ontario underwent many shape manifestations, including marsh lands and ponds.

The Laurentian Channel and the ancestral St Lawrence River system are major determinants in the shoreline of Lake Ontario in the vicinity of contemporary Toronto.

This is a brief history of the Toronto shoreline along Lake Ontario—a dynamic edge energy that we can use in waterfront development experiments.

The historic water's edge of Lake Ontario and its predecessors comprised wetlands, marshes and streams. These wetlands and marshes can play a vital role in flood management when the Don River is reconfigured—beyond containment.

Marshland along the waterfront in the 1880s consisted of a marshland estuary known as Ashbridge's Bay at the mouth of the Don River, an historic activity and subsistence area of Indigenous Peoples. In 1890, the Keating Channel was constructed by filling in portions of the lake frontage. In 1911 and 1912, the Harbour Commission Plan transformed Ashbridge's Bay into the Toronto Industrial District and dredged 260 hectares (572 acres) of marshland. In 1916, the Keating Channel was completed at the mouth of the Don River when the river was diverted to its current alignment.

The new configuration of the Don River was planned with flood protection features coordinated by the Don Mouth Naturalization and Port Lands Flood Protection Environmental Assessment (DMNP EA), the Lower Don Lands Master Plan Environmental Assessment (LDL EA), and the Port Lands Planning Framework.

In the first compositional exercise, the current proposed alignments are maintained as they define the new island. In the second compositional exercise, I experiment with the island's water's edge definition using marshlands.

Villiers Island compositional exercise: Example 1

I am using Villiers Island as a base project for student exercises in large-scale development compositions, but I vary significantly from the current proposed plan as part of a larger educational and experimental process—my apologies to Waterfront Toronto. Students should keep in mind the key objectives of the exercises: the elements (objects/shapes) and principles (spatial activators) that along with compositional structures are at the heart of this exercise intent. The proposed island provides an excellent compositional experiment base as an urban enclave or district within the larger metropolitan Toronto area.

Example 1: major catalysts

1   The creation of the island is the primary catalyst for the overall composition and it provides four major waterfront features.
2   The second catalyst is a greenway of marshes and ponds, connected by a streamway from northeast to southwest on the island—from the Keating Channel to Polson Slip/Don River.
3   A heritage area of historic buildings and industrial structures is located on the north central portion of the island, along the Keating Channel.
4   East and west end parklands.
5   Floodway.

Example 1: compositional structure(s) and activators

I initially constructed a variety of residential building typologies to use in the composition: yellow for the high-rise structures; orange for the medium-rise structures; red for retail/commercial; and purple for office and other employment centers, including shared work spaces.

Compositional structures, activators and connectors used in the composition include:

1   Diagonality: an open space corridor running from the northeast to the southwest through the site to act as a linear spine; the corridor contains water features, rain gardens, community gardens and an irrigation channel in stream form; and a portion of the green corridor collects and processes surface water runoff.

2   Four clusters of a "maze" typology for new neighborhoods wherein a diversity of two- to six-story residential buildings in compact configurations is served by a slow-street, continuous network for pedestrians, bicycles, small cars and service vehicles. Each cluster serves also as a pedestal for high-rise residential towers using a repetition with variety activating principle.

3   A diagonal compositional orientation for numerous high-rise towers in a northeast to southwest orientation.

4   A "cross" compositional structure that connects the Keating Channel with the interior of the site and the diagonal open space green corridor, wherein the cross comprises a precinct retail commercial center and employment center.

5   A major focus area encompassing a community assembly area with outdoor theater, music tent area, open air markets, and passive recreation open space that serves as a connector among three key features: the Keating Channel commercial center, the open space green corridor, and the Pilson Slip portion of the new Don River.

6   An entertainment retail/events facility complex is located on the western edge of the western neighborhood oriented toward the Inner Harbour and western waterfront park.

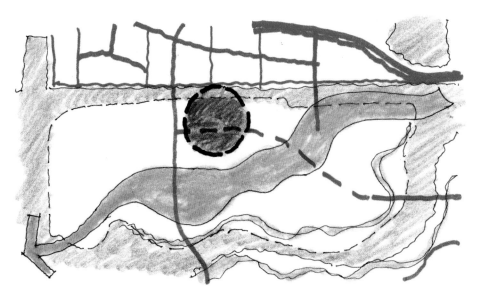

Figure 7.3. Major compositional structure diagram, Example 1. *The diagram illustrates the overall compositional structure approach: a diagonal open space corridor from northeast to southwest. This open space organic axis provides the spine and catalyst form for the major village residential neighborhoods on the island with a heritage area to the north. Waterfront parks and floodways are undulating along the south edge, with a hard edge on the Keating Channel and Inner Harbour sides (north and west, respectively).*

Figure 7.4. Areal view from the west. *The view from the west highlights two of the four major residential neighborhoods west of New Cherry Street, and connected to the diagonal open space corridor from the northeast.*

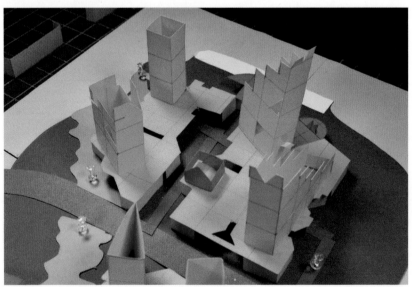

Figure 7.5. Western neighborhood cluster A. *Slow streets serve the four primary residential towers and the "maze" residential base with open courtyards and small parks. A community center (red) terminates the pedestrian slow-street network on the western waterfront. Small retail cafés and shops are embedded into the maze as part of the close-knit pedestrian network.*

Figure 7.6. Western neighborhood cluster B. *The four residential towers are repeated with variety in orientation and stepped versus non-stepped typologies.*

Figure 7.7. Eastern neighborhood cluster from the east A. *The view from the east highlights two of the four major residential neighborhoods facing the Keating Channel to the north, the Don River to the east and Pilson Slip to the south. Each neighborhood abuts Villiers Street, the main east–west arterial through the island. Both are oriented in a diagonal southwest direction.*

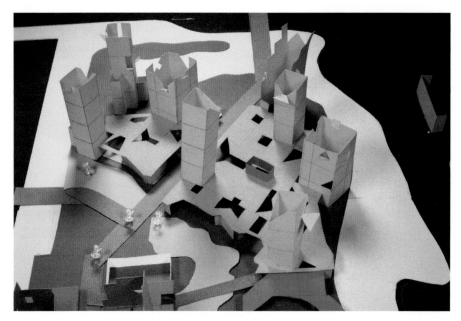

Figure 7.8. Eastern neighborhood cluster from the east B. *Three residential towers, varying in size and mass, comprise a cluster to the northeast; five residential towers, also varying in size and orientation, comprise the southeastern cluster. Small-scale retail commercial/cafes are interspersed throughout the residential maze.*

Figure 7.9. Overall view from the south. *The view from the south highlights all four neighborhoods and the southern portion of the "living room" or heart of Villiers Island, and the termination of the diagonal open space corridor.*

Figure 7.10. Areal view from the north. *The view from the north highlights all four neighborhoods and the central island "living room" that connects the north and south edges along the open space axis. The major employment (purple) and commercial (red) centers are oriented toward the Keating Channel.*

Figure 7.11. Open space green corridor A. *The open space corridor traverses the island from the northeast to the southwest as a catalytic diagonal axis compositional structure, connecting all neighborhoods and the island's "living room" vision components. Its functions include passive visual and physical recreation, surface water filtration, and irrigation system for associated urban gardens, public and private.*

Figure 7.12. Open space green corridor B. *The green space component forms part of a larger "living room" for Villiers Island.*

Figure 7.13. Commercial/employment center and community "living room" to the southwest. *The center of the island community contains retail/commercial (red), entertainment/retail, office (purple), shared work space and civic uses and activities. The circular area symbolizes and focuses on an open music venue area with outdoor market arcades and space for small and large community gatherings. The center connects and unites both the north and south edges of the island, highlighted by an arcade interlock extending into the green corridor. Villiers Street is the main circulation arterial that serves as a main street through the heritage area.*

Figure 7.14. Commercial center with shared work space. *Shared work spaces and an employment center (purple) integrated with retail/commercial and entertainment/retail (red) highlight the "living room" area. The composition incorporates a semi-enclosed arcade system from the Keating Channel to the green corridor and across to the event/market area, providing a key connecting element from north to south.*

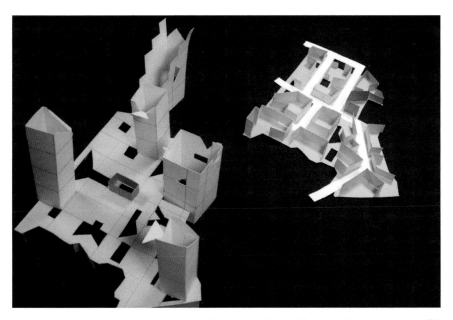

Figure 7.15. Maze typology example A. *In this illustration, the overall two- to four-story massing of the eastern neighborhood is compared to a detail at the same scale of the maze typology, wherein a small-scale, continuous local street network serves the interior of the maze complex for small vehicles, bicycles, pedestrians and service vehicles.*

Figure 7.16. Maze enlargement B. *The maze has many variation potentials and exemplifies a compact medium-density neighborhood component that is intended to be intimate and human scale, providing access to the green corridor, "living room" and water edges. Note: smaller service streets and lanes are not shown in the model at this scale.*

Villiers Island compositional exercise: Example 2

Example 2 focuses on key principles and activators to assemble a composition for Villiers Island as a means of highlighting and illustrating their use in large-scale development patterns.

Example 2: Major catalysts

1   The creation of the island is again the primary catalyst for the overall composition.
2   A significant difference between Example 1 and Example 2 is the treatment of the southern perimeter of the island: a network of wetlands and streams, reminiscent of the geologic formation of Lake Ontario.
3   Each "stream" is in effect a large rain garden and surface water runoff filter system, complete with appropriate vegetation, water retention areas and controlled cascades; surface runoff is also captured from the surfaces of building structures channeled into the filtration streams.

Example 2: Compositional structure(s) and activators

1   An overall use of polarity in the formation of the island mass itself (see Figure 7.17): the western and northern edges along the Keating Channel are characterized by hard edges; the southern and eastern edges along Pilson Slip and the Don River are organic, comprising wetlands, ponds, and filtration streams that shape the essential form approach of the larger composition.

2   Using the filtration streams, with repetition with variety activators, the composition comprises repeated high-density village clusters, each with mixed building typologies for a mixed-density outcome, all oriented toward the southern island edge.

3   Each village cluster has the same footprint and a variety of mixed-density typologies: repetition with variety. Each cluster, as it is phased, can respond to specific market and space programming needs over time.

4   Development along the northern hard edge is immediately adjacent to that manufactured or human-made edge as opposed to the southern edge, with setbacks for wetlands, filtration streams and floodway.

5   The "living room" is centered on the heritage area on the northern edge, with commercial, civic and employment facilities connected to the waterfront and a hardscape promenade along the north edge.

6   The internal road network is again located to the northern portion of the island so as not to dissect it with a major arterial.

7   The western component of the island, west of New Cherry Street, contains smaller repeated versions of the larger village clusters to the east in conjunction with an urban farm complex as part of the west open space.

Example 2: Connectivity elements

1   Major roadways connecting island components to off-island precincts are limited and located to the northern portion of the site to reduce a "splitting" effect by non-local traffic; the internal road network comprises smaller, slow-moving rights-of-way for local vehicles, bicycles and pedestrians.

2   The entry road from the northeast, New Munitions Street, is aligned with an open space corridor that connects the commercial center of the island to the Pilson Slip/Don River extension to the south.

3   Vegetated open spaces are repeated along New Cherry Street and are used to visually connect the "view from the road" to the hamlet clusters west of New Cherry Street.

4   Each village and hamlet cluster is connected to the next via open space elements used for passive and moderate activity recreational activities.

5   A defined pedestrian concourse, both vegetated and hard space, connects the commercial center to adjacent employment complexes and residential clusters.

6   The commercial/employment center contains shops, offices, retail, entertainment activities, shared work spaces and civic activities, and provides a major connecting element to the Keating Channel and future north channel neighborhoods.

7   The filtration streams in each of the village and hamlet clusters connect the residential neighborhoods to the water's edge and provide visual and physical open space features at the human scale.

8   An urban farm agriculture project provides a connection between the hamlet clusters and the Inner Harbour waterfront. The farm consists of horizontal and vertical grow-structures with south and west exposures. These structures are incorporated into the western park area.

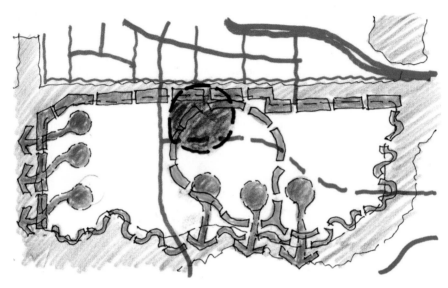

Figure 7.17. Major compositional structure diagram, Example 2. *The diagram illustrates the intentional polarities assigned to the island as a whole: a hard edge along the west (Inner Harbour) and the north (Keating Channel), complete with industrial dockage, pedestrian promenades, and lookout areas to downtown; a soft or organic edge along the east (Don River extension) and the south (Pilson Slip/Don River extension), comprising reconstructed wetlands, ponds and artificial filtration streams connected to each of the village clusters, highlighted by a southwest orientation for village and hamlet.*

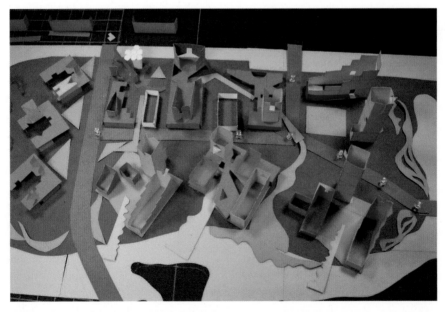

Figure 7.18. Areal view from the south. *The view to the north highlights the village clusters, with artificial filtration streams oriented toward the southwest, Pilson Slip, and the Don River extension, with associated wetlands and ponds.*

Figure 7.19. Areal view from the west. *The western edge park oriented to Inner Harbour, with the urban farm complex in the foreground.*

Figure 7.20. Areal view from the east. *New reconstructed wetlands and a high-density residential cluster are in the foreground, with walking paths, wildlife areas and water access points.*

Figure 7.21. Western neighborhood hamlet/agriculture clusters. *The view from the southwest highlights the three neighborhood clusters of mixed-density housing with small-scale retail. Integrated with the clusters is an urban agriculture facility with vertical structures serving both an economic agricultural function and a visual open space function with limited access.*

Figure 7.22. Southern residential cluster A. *This is a view of the three southern residential mixed-density clusters, each connected to the Pilson Slip via a water filtration/green corridor system.*

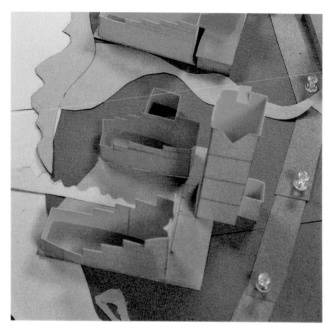

Figure 7.23. Village cluster A. *This village cluster is a high-density mixed typology configuration of buildings around an open court oriented to the southwest and the new river. Spatial activators at play include: diagonality, repetition with variety, solid/void spaces, and visual and physical connectors to the water's edge.*

Figure 7.24. Village cluster B. *Both similar to and different from Village A. Due its proximity to roadway, the typology includes more of a retail/commercial mix and uses repetition with variety, mixed density through typology variations; water connection to the waterfront from common courtyards and small retail areas.*

221

Figure 7.25. Village cluster C. *Both similar to and different from Villages A and B, using repetition with variety and mixed typology building arrangements with a high-rise structure and separate retail/commercial/ shared work space building. This cluster is connected to the green space loop that connects to the northern "living room" complex. Again, the water filtration/irrigation/gardening facility is used to connect the cluster to the waterfront (Pilson Slip).*

Figure 7.26. Commercial center on the Keating Channel. *The Keating Channel center is a key component of the Villiers Island "living room" that provides an activity center for the island and forms a connective link to the north shore neighborhoods. The center is oriented toward the Keating Channel and is connected to island neighborhood clusters via key pedestrian walkways, concourses and plazas. Employment centers and residential uses are also incorporated into the center.*

Figure 7.27. Commercial center closeup. *The interior green space loop threads through the "living room" on the Keating Channel, connecting the "room" to the southern portions of the village.*

The Precincts of St Paul's Cathedral

Some context regarding this study project: in my urban design composition course, I assign a number of one- to two-week design problems. The early assignments usually involve urban projects in North American cities, mostly set in downtown grid patterns. At the end of the project sequence, I assign a project area that breaks from that grid pattern and challenges the students with a more organic or plastic and historic context—thus the St Paul's Precinct selection.

I was introduced to St Paul's Precinct on a trip to London in 1967, at a time when the Barbican project was emerging out of the ground, and concrete elevator towers dotted the London skyline. Urban blocks of five- and six-story buildings were being razed for new development. St Paul's Precinct fascinated me because of the post-war reconstruction challenge of the area, given the bomb damage to adjacent and nearby blocks. That damage opened up areas surrounding the cathedral for special development opportunities.

Consequently, St Paul's Precinct, prior to reconstruction, provided a challenging project for students to address historic structures and contexts with contemporary design compositions.

Background and context

The following diagrams chronicle the St Paul's Churchyard and surrounding area from 1677 to post-war damage in 1949 (Holford, 1956). Bomb damage occurred essentially to the north, east, southeast and south of the Churchyard.

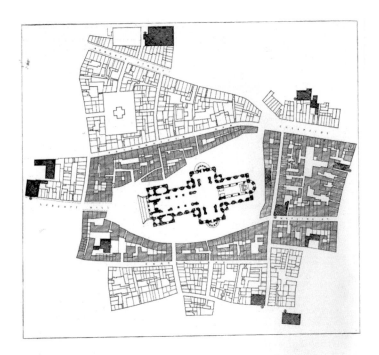

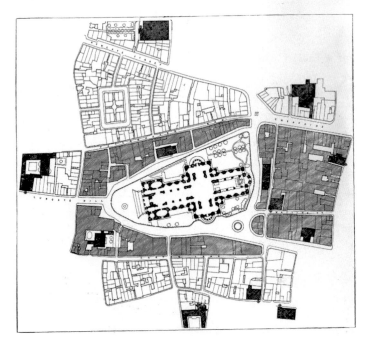

Figure 7.28. The Churchyard in 1677 (top) and 1875 (bottom). *St Paul's Cathedral as designed by Christopher Wren, with Paternoster Row to the north, Ludgate Hill to the east, Carter Lane to the south, and St Paul's Churchyard (Lane) to the east. By 1875, streets were delineated within the churchyard area, altering somewhat the surrounding built form and adding detail to the pedestrian areas surrounding the cathedral. Source: Holford, 1956.*

Figure 7.29. The Churchyard in 1949. *War damage occurred to all areas surrounding the cathedral with extensive damage to the north, east, southeast and south. Contrary to popular belief, the cathedral and grounds were bombed, with one device failing to detonate within the boundaries of the cathedral itself. The diagram generalizes damaged areas surrounding the cathedral and churchyard.*

Following the bombardments, St Paul's Cathedral appeared like a ship

at anchor in a devastated harbour. From Cheapside down to Queen Victoria Street, the whole of the ground to the east and south-east of St. Paul's (was) cleared of standing buildings, with the exception of one of the textile warehouses and the shells of two of the City churches—St. Augustine, Watling Street, and St. Nicholas Cole Abbey. The damaged area (extended) eastwards below Cheapside, up to and including the famous church of St. Mary-le-Bow, whose tower and steeple, slightly leaning, remain(ed) as one of the great sculpturesque monuments of London.

(Holden and Holford, 1951, pp. 197–198)

Figure 7.30 outlines the major redevelopment areas revealed by the bombardment damage; and constitutes the area of this exercise sketch problem. As the cathedral was "revealed" due to bomb damage, with open areas primarily to the north, east and south, a "view management framework" was established with emphasis on the dome of the cathedral. The Millennium Bridge crossing the Thames east of Blackfriars Bridge is an example of design strategies to focus on the dome, in this case via EC4 Street (Millennium Bridge Approach).

Students are asked not to review contemporary developments until after they complete the compositional assignments. To repeat, this is about practicing compositional elements and principles, not arriving at the *perfect* solution, as there are too many variables not addressed in the exercise.

Overall intent

The overall intent of the exercise is to use the context of 1950 Precinct of St Paul's Cathedral, London, following the Second World War and the bombardments suffered by the precinct for a series of urban design

Figure 7.30. Major redevelopment areas circa 1950. *I generalized the redevelopment areas from the 1956 proposed Precincts of St Paul's Plan (Holford, 1956) as the target areas for urban design composition exercises. This is the base for all examples in this section. Area 1 is referred to as "Paternoster Square"; Areas 2 and 3 are combined into "Old Change".*

composition studies. The studies are considered "sketch problems"—short-term exercises dealing with the elements and principles of urban design composition without engaging in architectural detail or style.

Major damage occurred to the north, east and southeast of St Paul's Cathedral, as shown on the initial reference model, Figure 7.29. Each of the three primary study areas is experimented with activators regarding certain design principles, all related to the cathedral itself. Compositional studies are applied to each area using specific elements and principles, including compositional structures and spatial activators.

For the student, remember: this is a learning exercise accomplished through experimentation and explorations, not a quest for the perfect solution for each site, as there are many complexities associated with the precinct, design guidelines etc. that are not addressed in these exercises.

Overall principles

- For each site, respond to a general stated program and design aspirations.
- Develop urban design compositions that respond to and respect the physical/spatial characteristics and relationships of the cathedral, churchyard and surrounds.
- Focus on connectivity between the study area and St Paul's.
- Experiment with building/open space typologies, variations and hybrids.
- Be playful and not reticent about experimenting with design elements.
- The following general design guidelines are set forth for the assignment, with any "departures" thoroughly vetted.
- St Paul's Cathedral and dome are the focus of a "view framework" policy for all surrounding developments and their architecture—it is the heart of design determinants.
- Height limits for this study, generalized from the City of London's height limits, are as follows:
  - North of cathedral   50m (162ft)
  - East of cathedral   45m (146ft)

- – West of cathedral   43m (140ft)
- – South of cathedral   40m (130ft)
- Respond to and respect the cathedral and its spatial characteristics.
- Assume architecture to be contemporary, not historically thematic.
- Focus on connectivity, catalysts, and the larger context.
- This is a major office, festival, retail and visitor destination, with limited housing.
- Assume the 1949–1950 damage footprint as the focus area.

Overall tasks

- Prepare design composition studies in physical model form, using the elements and principles discussed in the book.
- This is a process of learning through experimentation, not a search for a definitive final outcome.
- Explore suitable building typologies.
- Make the use of compositional structures, elements and principles clear in experiments.
- If a "departure" is desired, justify its role in responding to and respecting the cathedral's spatial characteristics.
- Prepare an urban design composition of each area component and relate those components to the churchyard and each other—they need to have "connectivity".

Figure 7.31. Model of study areas. *The author crafted the base model for the students to reduce their time commitment for a two-week sketch problem. The brown areas indicate the extent of the project area, generalized, and represent a substantial portion of the bombardment damage. The model is constructed of chipboard cardboard and illustration board set on a base map of the area from the Holford's 1956 report. Heights are generalized, too.*

Exercise 7.3 The Precincts of St Paul's Cathedral: Paternoster Square, London

Paternoster Square is immediately north of the cathedral and churchyard. It was redeveloped in 2001 to 2003 as an office/open space development with market area. Included are Wren's relocated Temple Bar gateway (1672), offices, stock exchange, shops, market area and formal open space square.

Contemporary development is excluded from this series of exercises.

Design aspirations

- Given the formal and classical context of surrounding areas, insert a level of intimacy and human scale into the square development and its connectivity to the cathedral.
- Include housing options within the office-dominated uses.
- Provide open space that serves both as formal event/festival space and intimate/personal environment.
- Explore polarity in design compositions: formal/informal, classic/artistic, context-driven/departure.

Exploration 1: Paternoster Square warm-up exercise

There are many places to begin a design composition process—not one. In this exercise, I chose to begin with one or more compositional structures to set the foundational order for buildings and open space. The structure responds to contextual factors, plan/program requirements (including CST matrix relationships), historical/heritage issues and many other considerations. Obviously, in this learning exercise, not all of these factors are addressed due to time constraints and available information; consequently, the focus is on physical context and design composition.

Figure 7.32. *Paternoster Square study area.* *The area encompasses over 4 hectares (8–9 acres), without a major arterial between the square area and the churchyard on the northside.*

As in all cases, and it bears repeating, the human dimension is considered in any compositional structure selected. At the scale of these exercises, it is not expressed in intimate detail and exists as a future layer to be specified and detailed.

Design aspirations:

- Office development with supplementary residential uses and a commercial market area.
- Orientation and focus on the cathedral and churchyard, specifically the dome and western towers.
- Connections to surrounding streets and key building features.
- View corridors to the cathedral and dome.

In this warm-up exercise, I began with two compositional structures: a bent axis aligned from southeast—diagonally, centered on the dome, to the north-central area on Newgate Street; and a radial burst centered on the open-air market structure radiating to the west, southwest, south and southeast to the cathedral and churchyard, and north to Newgate Street. The axis serves a series of open space plazas including an entry plaza that focuses on the north nave and dome of the cathedral, with vegetated open space and retail uses focused on the churchyard, and an interior formal open space plaza related to the office buildings and market area. The radial burst connects to outlying streets and provides view corridors into the interior of the area and its open space plazas.

Uses within this exercise include major office uses, including the stock exchange, a semi-open market arcade that activates the interior of the "block", providing human scale and activities at the ground plane. The retail structure in the southwest corner is four stories with larger retail stores. Residential uses are provided in consort with the market retail area to activate and support those uses during the day and evening. The Temple Bar gateway highlights the southwest entrance to the plazas.

The model massing is a bit high for the base model but conforms to around 50m.

Major compositional structures:

- radial burst
- axes supported
- solid/void as enclosed and semi-enclosed open space areas
- diagonality.

Endeavor

The first endeavor (1) began with two compositional structures and variations: a cross of two axes and an axis with a graded (gradation) termination focused on the cathedral dome. At work here is a principle of intersection: where two or more linear elements intersect, generating a dynamic of intersecting movement patterns. The axial movement corridors connect the site and churchyard to nearby contextual features (churches, main streets) both physically and visually.

I limited the model in this endeavor as another modification began to emerge. In the truncated model, I placed a commercial market facility at the intersection and realized it was in the interior of the block without a strong connection to the churchyard. In the second variation (Endeavor 2), I moved the commercial market area between the two axial corridors (2) but as a result reduced the idea of a formal "square".

Figure 7.33. Warm-up Endeavor (1) diagram. *As a prelude to compositional experiments, I established a plan diagram that highlighted various view corridors and pedestrian courses to and from the cathedral to major streets and intersections with an open space component at the south edge adjacent to the cathedral. The diagram sets the overall structure for the composition.*

Figure 7.34. Warm-up diagram with commercial center A. *This diagram variation explores the placement of a commercial center focus in relation to the various corridors and pedestrian courses.*

Figure 7.35. Warm-up diagram with commercial center B. *Another variation of the commercial center at key intersections.*

Figure 7.36. Warm-up view north from the cathedral. *This view focuses on the main visual corridor from the northwest toward the cathedral and transitional open space. The commercial center is split along both sides of the main pedestrian space with shopping, dining, and market spaces centered on the open space and cathedral.*

Figure 7.37. Warm-up view toward the northeast. *This view highlights the connecting visual/pedestrian corridor connecting the western portion of the precinct to the northeast, intersecting the main commercial/ activity and visitor open space and market.*

Figure 7.38. Warm-up view to the southeast.

Endeavor (2): Paternoster Square

Design aspirations for Endeavor (2)

- A focused "square" from the northwest to St Paul's western steps.
- A possible spin-off of this orientation to and including the southeast redevelopment area.
- Strong visual corridors to both the dome and the northwest tower.
- A neighborhood environment.

In this endeavor (2), I applied a grid/square compositional structure oriented at a 60-degree angle to the cathedral (keeping in mind the redevelopment area to the southeast along Carter Lane). Key linear axes are again located within the block to connect key nearby contextual features: a view corridor to the cathedral from the intersection of Newgate Street and West Alexandria Lane to the southeast; and a cross compositional structure with an axis essentially east to west connecting the Amen Court area to the intersection of Newgate Street, New Change, and St Martin's Le Grande. This crossing structure provides further interior "block" pedestrian and service access corridors for blocks of office buildings.

I began playing with building massing, placing housing at the commercial market intersection, set back from the larger formal event spaces of the square and churchyard, surrounded by office buildings located along the axial structures. By using the paper cut-outs as symbolic buildings, I was able to manipulate and change shapes easily and quickly to adapt to various compositions. Use objects that you are comfortable using.

Many variations of building placement are possible within the overall compositional structure.

Major compositional structures and activators:

- axial/diagonality
- cross structure (intersection)
- grid/square
- angularity (60 degrees)
- repetition with variety.

Variations of a structure

Within every design concept and composition numerous variations can occur without disrupting or compromising the underlying compositional structure. The following examples illustrate how variations can occur due to phasing, development requirements, architectural considerations, etc. while the structure is maintained (always with minor adjustments). The lesson here is to begin with the compositional structure and investigate where it can lead regarding design generation.

Office building variations: the initial design composition consisted of office buildings that were larger masses, filling the development area allocated for each office complex. A variation consists of smaller building masses occupying the same space with additional relational features, such as interior semi-enclosed courtyards connecting and separating the individual buildings, and enhanced by a repetition with a variety pattern of heights.

Figure 7.39. Paternoster Square Endeavor (2) structural composition A. *This illustrates the use of the square and grid as compositional structure, augmented with connecting axes and intersections. The red structures represent the commercial market area facing the square and churchyard.*

Figure 7.40. Paternoster Square Endeavor (2) structural composition B. *This experiment uses two basic structures: the cross and the diagonal. The diagonal focuses on the cathedral from the major intersection and entry to the northwest; the cross provides visual and physical access into the square area from other key intersections and building complexes. The northwest corridor expands near the cathedral in a dimensional change, highlighting the church.*

Figure 7.41. Paternoster Square Endeavor (2) initial start-up view to the northwest. *I initially explored placement of housing and commercial center elements within the compositional structure, around the new Paternoster Square corridor. The two residential towers are lower than the cathedral and in direct association with the commercial center, oriented toward the cathedral.*

Figure 7.42. Paternoster Square Endeavor (2) initial start-up from the northwest. *The view, enhanced through graded dimensional change of the corridor, highlights and focuses on the cathedral and dome.*

Figure 7.43. Paternoster Square Endeavor (2) A. *The final composition incudes two residential buildings in direct relationship with the commercial center market area. Office buildings with retail commercial bases are located along the pedestrian view corridors and complete the structural plan. Car park is underground (as are most in the precinct), accessed via Newgate Street on the north and Alexandria Lane on the west. A smaller open space within the block serves as a passive space.*

Figure 7.44. Paternoster Square Endeavor (2) B.

Figure 7.45. Paternoster Square Endeavor (2) C.

Figure 7.46. Paternoster Square Endeavor (2) office variation A. *I show these images to underscore the flexibility of the compositional structure to accommodate different office building configurations.*

Figure 7.47. Paternoster Square Endeavor (2) housing variation. *The housing structures have been relocated, with one integrated into an office building on the site of the original interior square and the other remaining on its original site.*

Residential buildings variations: maintaining the housing location at the key interior intersection in close proximity to the commercial market area can facilitate mixed use, with office buildings and as free standing, maintaining the relationship of housing to the smaller interior open space square. Again, the variations are numerous and the underlying structure remains essentially intact.

Exercise 7.4 The Precincts of St Paul's Cathedral: Old Change, London

The Old Change area is south-southeast of the cathedral churchyard along the southern edge of St Paul's Churchyard Street (Carter Lane), and between the lane and Queen Victoria Street (alignment altered later)—another Second World War bomb-damaged site. The site is approximately 2 hectares (4 acres). This site reflects the precinct circa 1949–1950.

Exploration 2: Old Change

Design aspirations:

- Uses include office, financial and commercial retail.
- Direct physical response and relationship to cathedral and churchyard.
- Protect and enhance St Nicholas Church.
- Reflect design compositions and forms on Paternoster Square.
- Maximize the office/commercial space in the new development.

Where to begin? Be careful not to begin with detail or architecture before addressing the *urban* design determinants.

The churchyard is (was) immediately across old Carter Lane from Old Change with the cathedral dome unobstructed in view. As mentioned above, the churchyard was altered with an apparent realignment of Carter Lane/St Paul's Churchyard Street, but site we are using reflects the old alignment. Old Change is slightly to the southeast of the dome. Consequently, I reflected the orientation of Paternoster Square in the orientation of Old Change to the cathedral: a 60-degree angle grid.

In addition, St Nicholas Church (indicated on maps circa 1956 as still existing) is retained and protected in the design composition as an additional challenge for students. The 60-degree angle orientation (southeast to northwest) includes and encompasses St Nicholas with an open space feature emanating from old Carter Lane—connecting the cathedral to St Nicholas. The open space area to the northeast of the block reflects and responds to the open space (1956) on the north side of Old Carter Lane as part of the Gateway House complex.

Compositional structures and spatial activators:

- diagonality (60-degree angle orientation)
- grid plaza with gradation
- axis as connecting element (central to northeast)
- St Nicholas Church and Churchyard.

I intentionally reduced the scale in this example, focusing on a semi-enclosed market and festival area oriented toward the cathedral, augmented by office/financial buildings, residential uses incorporated into the market, and an open space protective area around St Nicholas Church.

The key issue here is the structure of the open space diagonal, which is oriented toward the cathedral dome. Many variations of associated uses are possible and the structure remains intact.

Figure 7.48. Old Change open space structure A. *Open space as plazas and concourses is utilized as the connecting structuring element for the Old Change area, focused on the cathedral dome and south façade, as well as St Nicholas Church to the southeast.*

Figure 7.49. Old Change open space structure B. *This larger view illustrates the relationship of Old Change to Paternoster Square, even if the two are not perceived on the ground plane together.*

Figure 7.50. Old Change view from the south. *The historic church structure is a key element in this composition, and is connected to the larger St Paul's spatial relationship while also composing a smaller-scale neighborhood intimacy of open space.*

Figure 7.51. Old Change view from the north.

Figure 7.52. Old Change overview. *The church is connected to the larger composition through a small cathedral-oriented open square and a semi-enclosed commercial arcade connecting to the south.*

The manner in which compositional structures can be utilized in design are numerous, and multiple structures can be incorporated into one composition, with one dominant. Combined with spatial activators (spatial verbs), the designer can address complex issues and still retain a fundamental order to the design.

Putting these previous experiments and explorations into perspective: they are learning exercises—ways in which to manipulate the elements and principles of design composition in ever increasing complex contexts. Each student can express his or herself in many ways—the more the merrier!

Further explorations in design composition

I am sure there are those who will disagree with this statement, but I offer that urban design has less influence on architecture and landscape architecture than many planners and designers assume. Urban design/planning regulations impact or influence location, size, setbacks, etc. and often get murky or troublesome when attempting to define and manage architectural styles and expressions.

In my professional and educational experiences, urban design has a critical role in educating the community regarding urban form relationships, the positive and negative impacts of design/development decisions. It also provides a design testing mechanism for urban form issues and challenges, something I refer to as the architectural (landscape architectural) test. By composing design probabilities to various degrees, the community is better able to assess design impacts and make adjustments to both policy and design compositions. Moreover, urban design provides probable design outcomes influenced and impacted by time—probability trajectories—and a structuring process for urban form that encompasses and relates to divergent expressions of architecture and landscape architecture, and forms the underlying order or structure over time to design policy.

In this section, I explore a number of additional compositional principles and elements that can contribute to the making of creative urban form:

- connectivity through design composition
- urban form testing (and community education)
- compositional structural catalysts
- edge energies: the dynamics of edge difference
- making spatial metaphors: meaning and functionality via the CST matrix.

Connectivity: the spaces that connect and relate one urban artifact to another—buildings, landscape features, natural features, roads and other infrastructure—are often the spaces wherein the dynamic interactions of the city's inhabitants, its people, take place.

Exercise 7.5 Connectivity exercises

Intent

Using the examples that follow as guidelines, explore the various types of connections that bring together, relate to and integrate the physical elements of the city. These connections can be direct or implicit, from a bridge to an arcade to a visual link. The connection is the human-scale element, wherein close contact is made with other people, from the elevator to the café to the market. Use your imagination and explore the myriad of spatial connections possible in urban areas, to enhance and energize those areas.

Principles

Connectivity is accomplished in many ways, beginning with the definitions of connect(ion): a link, an association, or a relationship between two or more entities and connect—to join or fashion together. In urban design, this form of connection is mostly but not always physical and spatial, defined by the coming together of two or more different elements. Key principles include:

- an association or relationship between two or more entities
- a spatial link or connection
- an implied connection (visual and through other senses)
- shared uses and activities and associated spaces
- places of human interactions
- dynamic edge-difference interfaces.

Tasks

Explore, in visual form, the various ways of making connections in an urban core area with sufficient density and intensity of development.

- Select a study area, either an existing dense district of mixed uses, ignoring or filtering out the existing ground-plane connections but leaving the buildings and major landscape elements; or, as I did for these examples, select an existing district and its street pattern and intensify the density and physical elements.
- Select a method or methods that are fast and effective for making three-dimensional compositions so that you explore and generate ideas rather than focus narrowly on "solving" a problem.
- Explore typologies that constitute connections: buildings, arcades, markets, open space elements, etc. and look for hybrids in your explorations.
- Explore compositional structures that are inherently connections.
- Explore edge conditions as dynamic interfaces between two or more different spatial elements.
- Explore implied connections.
- Explore connected incrementalism: the linking together over time of phases of development not necessarily related to or managed by one entity.

I use a fictitious urban area—Lake City (actually an old district in the Seattle area with alterations)— as the basis for these examples. Again, students should focus on the compositional structures and spatial activators rather than try to solve a specific design challenge. I call this section the Lake City Experiment.

Lake City: making connections and connected incrementalism

Making *connections through design composition* in the urban design process can contribute harmony and coherence to urban form—a key objective of urban design. It can be the difference between competent and creative, efficient and dynamic. Making connections involves establishing or enhancing relationships between and among elements and systems of urban form: buildings, open space (hard and soft), circulation elements, form patterns in neighborhoods and districts and more. Most development in cities occurs in increments, by different developers, property owners and jurisdictions with a myriad of different designers.

Connecting this incremental development is a key task and challenge of urban design, one I refer to as *connected incrementalism.* This connectivity is time-influenced and can be a part of an urban design strategy in community development processes. For example, as a project is designed and constructed, certain opportunities for *connection* can be integrated into the design for later development activity.

Let's play: I continue to use the paper-modeling process in design explorations as for me at least it is fast and loaded with discovery opportunities through the physical manipulation of the paper forms. Use whatever medium you are comfortable with but consider a plurality of media and methods, and certainly do not limit yourself to digital graphic programs in the generation phase.

Connections in design composition can be made with typology hybrids, physical elements and features in relationship, spatial connections such as visual points of view, and key art principles such as: interlocking; merging; diverse edge treatments; contrasts with dimensional change, intensity, value; and dominance or hierarchy. Let us play with some of these connections.

Lake City: compositional structures as connectivity vehicles

Compositional structures are by nature connecting entities. The structure itself brings together and connects elements (shapes—buildings, landscape features, circulation elements) into a defined order or composition. The connections can be implied or direct by articulating enough of the specific compositional structure, i.e. the square or circle. The structures can be combined in many different ways to articulate design compositions that can respond to complex urban form situations. In all the models below, red is commercial use, orange is medium-density housing, yellow is high-density housing, purple is office/work space, blue is water and green, of course, represents open space features of varying types.

The following examples apply to all compositional structures.

Figure 7.53. (A–C) Connectivity and the square. *Four office towers define a square compositional structure, defined by four corners equally separated—the connection is apparent and implied in the structure. Connections to adjacent sites and areas strengthen the relationships among urban blocks.*

A

B

C

Compositional structures are inherently connectivity forces in design. In addition, as in (B), elements within the structure can relate to and connect to offsite elements, furthering connectivity with an implied "interlocking action". Architects have a responsibility to meet clients'/users' program needs, budgets, structural and construction determinants, site factors, etc. but they can be expressive within those challenges. They also have a role in urban design to make the connections between and among those expressive architectural (and landscape) elements to form stronger overall design compositions and orders. This does not mean seeking compromise or copying related architectural elements or seeking a mean in design expression; rather, it asks for an integration or connectivity that celebrates and responds to expressive and even idiosyncratic designs.

In (C), a simple solid/void or "reflective" relationship can make a connection that can be perceived at the pedestrian scale.

Figure 7.54.
Connectivity: the square and typology connections (A). *In (A), office towers are connected by a retail/commercial pedestal.*

The pedestal typology containing retail shops and entertainment/dining facilities can be a solid base or an articulated base with interior arcades with strong directional movement, as in the diagonal structure in the model. It relates to and connects each office tower and relates to the adjacent blocks and street façades and uses.

Isolated or unrelated residential towers can be architecturally distinct and unrelated on or near the ground plane and pedestrian environment. In Figure 7.55, the lower-rise (two- to five-story), medium-density residential complex and associated open spaces provide a strong connection to the towers and contribute to a neighborhood scale.

Figure 7.55. Connectivity: the square and typology connections (B). *And in (B), three residential towers are connected by medium-density residential typologies (generalized) and open space elements.*

Figure 7.56. Connectivity: the square and the cross. *In (A), the two blocks (squares), separated by a major street, relate to a cross-structure open space that also structures and orders adjacent retail activities.*

Figure 7.57. Connectivity: the square and the cross. *In (B) the cross variation is composed of residential typologies connected by a market arcade, and related to the cross open space structure.*

Figure 7.58. (A–B) Connectivity and the circle. *Three office towers are set into an arc—a component of an urban center gateway—which connects them all by a single center point and radius, with the radius apparent and implied as the connecting entity. Gradation is used to provide repetition with variety in the tower masses. Major commercial centers are oriented to the south along the radii, forming part of the gateway. A central park with water and sculpture features provides a center focus, and an open market extends along the radius to the northwest.*

A

B

Figure 7.59. (A–B) Connectivity and the circle. *The same elements are now set in a radial burst as the connecting entity with a common center point and varying-length radii, providing variations in the development pattern surrounding the towers. The middle tower is pulled back from the intersection (arc), with a smaller foreground office building transitioning to the park. The main tower is also pulled back to expand the gateway park effect at the major intersection of arterials.*

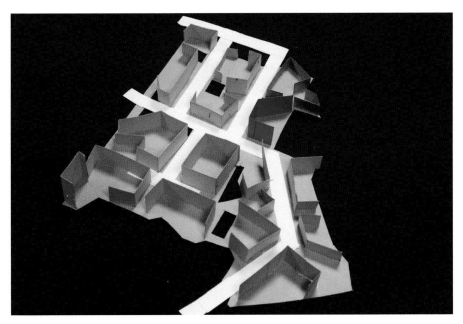

Figure 7.60. The "maze" as a connecting neighborhood component. *The maze is a dense, compact residential neighborhood typology with slow, narrow streets and pedestrian/bike paths with interior courtyards and local retail facilities (cafés, etc.) that connects and integrates with a number of high-rise residential structures. The concentrated building typologies are generalized into the maze form. The slow, narrow streets provide the basic structure for compact blocks.*

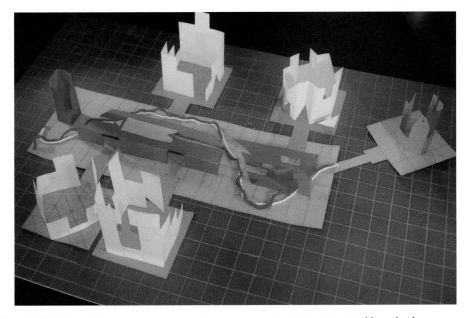

Figure 7.61. The axial structure as a connecting movement/activity spine. *Buildings, landscape features, and other activities are connected and structured by the axis, represented as a cohesive yet articulated structure—a linear retail commercial center and accompanying open space connect residential towers.*

Figure 7.62. Environmental art as connecting element. *In this example, used in the Villiers Island exercise, a housing complex/neighborhood component is connected to a larger body of water with a functioning art-sculpture project that moves surface runoff water through a natural filtering landscape into the body of water. The art sculpture contains both accessible and visual-only components, such as rain gardens, vegetable gardens, and water features for passive and active uses.*

Figure 7.63. Edge as connecting structure. *The edge of an open space area acts in consort with the open space as a connecting and space-activating structure with markets, cafes and outdoor displays.*

Figure 7.64. Triangle to triangle. *Three residential towers form a triangular structure with a retail center interlocked along a central axis.*

Figure 7.65. Axial landscape typologies as connecting elements. *Landscape typologies such as concourses, arcades, promenades, etc. provide strong connecting actions in the built environment. Multiple residential and office buildings are connected through a variety of landscape types of varying size and function.*

A

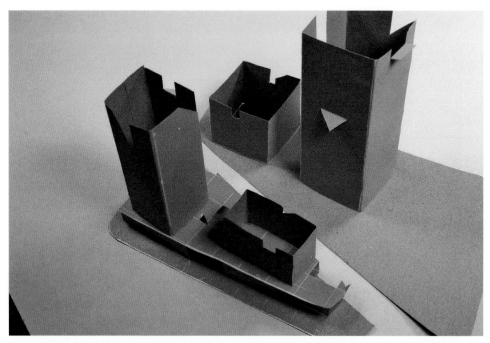

B

Figure 7.66. (A–E) Office cluster typology connectors. *In each of these five images, a typology is added as a connecting device or action, including retail pedestals, open space features such as plazas and promenades, and housing elements.*

C

D

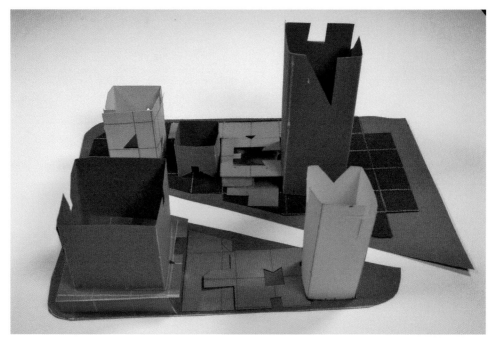

E

General overview and summary

As I reach the end of this endeavor, I certainly realize that students and others may not necessarily read this book from start to finish; instead, they will seek out parts of personal interest. Therefore, let me provide an overview of what I have attempted to cover in this work.

The intention is to make the critical connection, regarding urban design and physical planning, between the complex nature of human settlements—what we are designing for—and the act of design— the making of urban order . . . creating spatial structures for that complexity. My premise is that in order to address and contribute to a meaningful urban order or spatial structure, urban designers of all backgrounds require a working knowledge of the elements and principles of design composition. This is critical, as the complexity of human settlements is understood and engaged not from a "sea of words" (Hatton, 2017) but from the act of design—creating spatial metaphors that respond to human needs and desires.

Complexity

What is this complexity? When we view human settlements of all sizes and scales as living entities, living systems, we are confronted with the challenges of multiple and simultaneous interactions that define the dynamic (alive) forces and relationships within the human community. Thus, the discussion regarding creative or living systems emanating from contemporary physics and biology and their integral study—ecology. Part of this foundation in physics and biology is abstract, beyond transference to the design and planning domains; and a substantial number of principles contained in that foundation do and can apply to and refresh our approach to urban design based on the complexity of interactions in human settlements.

This complexity arises from the interaction of a trialectic of forces that comprise our settlements: culture, space and time—the CST matrix. As stated by Soja and others, settlements can only be viewed and understood in relation to all three of these components, not one or two. Thus, the idea of the *composition of complexity.*

Addressing complexity: the creative problem-solving process

Dealing with these complex interactions in the meaning and functionality of settlements is not sufficiently addressed with normative or linear problem-solving processes. They may be comprehensive and competent but they are not creative (possibly leading to discovery, novelty and innovation). They are different and opposite processes. Thus, the discussion regarding creative problem-solving (CPS) which lies at the heart of the design process—an evolving, non-linear process with initial uncertainties, ambiguities, openness, and a tolerance for diversity and differences. The CPS process is the foundation of design.

Engaging the CPS process: play

Play: a free activity with little or no fear and no failure; a non-competitive activity where the initial rules change and adapt as the play progresses; an activity with an uncertain outcome, open, creative.

I refer the reader to *Play in Creative Problem-solving for Planners and Architects* (Kasprisin, 2016) for a detailed discussion of play. Play is an open, creative process well suited for the design domains in that the use of symbolic objects of all types, crafted or digital, are utilized in the exploration of design compositions. This exploration can lead to the discovery of new directions, patterns, and ideas that then lead to novel solutions and possibly innovation. This discovery process is essential to creative processes. Experimenting, exploring, "failing" (not really), learning from what doesn't work, etc. can lead to the discovery of new patterns, directions, etc. that did not exist before the play.

Play and gaming are both effective tools in design but they are different: *play* is a free activity with changing rules and directions whereas *gaming* is a structured activity with set rules and usually a winner/ loser—competitive. Therefore, "playing a game" is an oxymoron. Play is useful in the generation of ideas whereas gaming is useful in the processing and evaluation of ideas and information—one is divergent (on the edge, away from the center) while the other is convergent (coming together, assessing). Both are necessary in the design process.

How you play varies across different domains. Friedrich Froebel invented kindergarten in the early 1800s. He developed "gifts" for young children to use in play that were symbolic objects rather than set toys with prescribed themes or identities. These objects ranged from wood blocks (cube, sphere and cylinder) to yarn to wood slats (16 in all, with more added later by colleagues, totaling 21 gifts). As mentioned earlier in the book, people influenced by Froebel's kindergarten process and gifts included Klee, Kadinsky, Gropius, Buckminster Fuller and Frank Lloyd Wright, among others.

This is all connected—from creative systems theory to making a paper model . . .

And, in the words of artist Chuck Close,

The advice I like to give young artists or really anybody who'll listen to me, is not to wait around for inspiration, inspiration is for amateurs; the rest of us just show up and get to work. If you wait around for the clouds to part and a bolt of lightning to strike you in the brain, you are not going to make an awful lot of work. All the best ideas come out of the process. They come out of the work.

(Close and Drake, 2012)

Thanks for engaging with these ideas.

Professor Emeritus Ron Kasprisin

Bibliography

Allison, Ken and Thornton, Victoria, 2014: *London's Contemporary Architecture*: Routledge, London, UK/ New York.

Close, Chuck and Drake, Ascha, 2012: *Chuck Close: Face Book*: Harry N. Abrams, New York.

Froebel, Friedrich, 1898: *The Education of Man*. Translation. Reprint: Dover Publications, New York, 2005.

Hatton, Brian, 2017: "Repositioning: This Think Called Crit . . .". In Stoppani, Teresa, Ponzo, Giorgio and Themistokleous, George (eds), *This Thing Called Theory*: Routledge, Abingdon, Oxfordshire.

Holden, C.H. and Holford, W.G., 1951: *The City of London: A Record of Destruction and Survival*: Architectural Press, London.

Holford, William, 1956: *Report to the Court of Common Council of the Corporation of the City of London on the Precincts of St. Paul's*: University College London, London.

Kasprisin, Ron, 2016: *Play in Creative Problem-solving for Planners and Architects*: Routledge, New York.

APPENDIX I
DRAWING TYPES FOR URBAN DESIGN

Principles at work

Urban design representations range from identification and analysis of context to idea generation to community education/involvement to specific and detailed formal design outcomes. The subject is spatial so the manner of representation requires a spatial language that is diverse and pluralistic in its use. One size does not fit all.

Most designers and planners have preferred representation methods and techniques ranging from digital graphics to hand-crafted graphics. Part of it is comfort, part is educational background and influences. I use crafted graphics because of the ease and speed of the process. I also integrate many crafted graphics with digital tools, as we shall explore in this appendix. Each has an appropriate application; again, one size does not fit all.

Drawing is a method of transcribing and conveying (as in writing, speaking, playing music, etc.) the language of design. Drawing consists of symbols (alphabet) and meaningful expressions or relationships of space in graphic constructs (sentences and paragraphs, etc.). I refer to the drawing/representation process as visual thinking. You do not need to be an architect or artist to "talk visually and spatially" if experienced in some very basic methodologies. And like any learned language, understanding the principles of the language and practicing related methods and techniques are critical to your success of representation.

For non-designers, as a starting point, there are basic types of visual constructs or communication that enable them to engage in the act of design, assembling spatial metaphors of relationships within community. These include but are not limited to the following:

- Orthographic drawing (plans, elevations, sections, etc. as two-dimensional representations).
- Diagrams (semi-abstract drawings with symbols that express principles and relationships of a larger whole).
- Axonometric drawings (paraline drawings that represent more than one dimension—x, y, z—where lines that are parallel in plan, elevation and section remain parallel in the axonometric representation).
- Three-dimensional physical constructs or models (from discovery models to process models to presentation models).
- Perspective drawings.

There are a number of basic methods in applying these types of visual constructs:

- crafting (making drawings and models by hand with specific tools and equipment—a direct approach)

- digital graphic methods (making drawings and three-dimensional constructs with digital applications or software—an indirect approach)
- model-making (hand-constructed three-dimensional constructs using various materials and equipment for discovery, process and presentation model formats).

Over the years I have evolved from perspective drawing to the use of axonometric drawings and discovery models. Perspectives are effective and composed of vanishing lines that can distort relationships in a visual scene. For example, the decision to view a place from one point of view versus another immediately enhances and diminishes features within the perspective, a possible value judgement. Axonometric drawings are essentially areal views and present a larger scale, often reducing the pedestrian scale. Each has its appropriate applications.

Let's review some of these basic types.

Drawing types

Diagrams (two- and three-dimensional)

Diagrams are semi-real/abstract visual constructs that portray essential principles and relationships between and among design elements in a composition. Related to urban design, diagrams can represent site influences, space program elements and relationships, and structural relationships from urban district to building complex, among others. They are conventionally represented by various types of drawings (and models), including plans, elevations, sections, axonometric drawings, perspectives (areal oblique relationships for example, down the scale ladder). Information and principles pertinent to the specific scale are portrayed with graphic symbols and irrelevant information (relative to scale) is filtered out. Diagrams are well served with reference and orientation information (scale and direction) and significant background information.

I use diagrams as a means to summarize and distill the big patterns and relationships in urban design analysis; or identify and relate key factors in contextual analysis. They provide an excellent format for the presentation and discussion with key stakeholders of analysis and ideas in workshops or charrettes. They also provide the designer with an assessment tool: as data are analyzed and synthesized, the diagram itself (the act of making it) can unveil additional directions, questions and ideas.

Key principles and methods

- A diagram identifies, assembles and relates the key elements and principles of design composition into a spatially referenced and oriented base context—organizational, structural within context.
- Conventional, unique and hybrid symbols are used to define elements and relationships—semiotics.
- A diagram can be represented within the wide array of drawing types and three-dimensional models.

Key characteristics

- Spatially referenced and oriented orthographic base information at standard or conventional scales. Can also apply to axonometric drawings. Perspective diagrams provide sufficient non-scale reference and orientation.

- The use of a clear and consistent symbol alphabet that is category-consistent and scale-relevant.
- The symbol alphabet has conventions as well as ample opportunity for innovation. Conventions include:
  - line weights for black-and-white representations including value shapes and patterns to indicate use and hierarchy of information—a language of emphasis (a curb edge receives less emphasis (fine line) than a building outline (darker/thicker line))
  - color for the same reasons—use, priority (warm colors make shapes appear closer; cool colors make shapes recede), local color
  - north compass orientation
  - graphic scales where possible
  - incorporation of key place-identity features (historic building, land features, etc.) that can orient and reference the observer.
- Consistency principles include:
  - same symbol per element or category
  - establish a dimensional hierarchy for symbols according to importance within the category (for example, an asterisk can be used for commercial center and each asterisk is sized according to the class and type of center, or color-coded appropriately)
  - symbol consistency: make certain that the symbols are consistent in size and reproduction whether digital or crafted, as any variation can be interpreted as different information
  - for non-conventional symbols, provide clarity in their design; avoid decorative symbols that can be distractions in the larger composition; assess how they appear in a larger and complex composition.

Orthographic drawings

Orthographic drawings are representations of objects, spaces etc. viewed at right angles, straight on: from above (plan—usually 1,000 feet above); straight on at eye level (elevation, section); and as a "cut" where an object is cut and viewed as a sectional plane (vertical or horizontal—a house plan is a horizontal cut or section taken about 4 feet (1.5 meters) above the floor plane).

These types of drawings are basic to the engineer, architect, landscape architect, planner and urban designer as they can be set to various scales (metric, standard and imperial). All drawings are accompanied with numerical and graphic scales and orientation (north arrow). In sectional drawings, the vertical and horizontal planes that are "cut" are always highlighted by additional line weight or a value (dark infill). Imagine running a skill saw through a table along its horizontal surface. Viewing the table straight on at 90 degrees toward the cut reveals the horizontal and vertical planes that have been cut through and the objects behind that cut that were not affected (lighter-value drawing).

Sectional, elevation and plan drawings

Elevation and plan drawings are common and familiar drawing types for students. Sectional drawings on the other hand can cause confusion and concern. Therefore, they are highlighted in this section.

Sections often confuse students new to drawing methods. Here are some guidelines for approaching sectional drawings.

1   *Always view the cut plane (vertical or horizontal) as a sheet of glass* that separates everything in the foreground (between the observer and the cut) and what remains behind the glass (cut). Discard the foreground.

2   *Reference plans and elevations and photos if appropriate*: choose where you want to cut through the object(s) to display a particular viewpoint, level of detail, vertical or horizontal relationships. If using crafting methods, begin with tracing paper, no eraser, and set your cut line on a plan; raise up in elevation all features, lines, cuts, walls etc. that are on that cut and establish a vertical sectional plane where cut features are highlighted in importance (line weight or value).

3   *Establish a cut/reference line*: on a plan or elevation or both, establish the cut line and indicate in what direction the cut is viewed (there are standards and conventions in the design professions for these symbols). The cut line can be altered: that is, changing directions if the line indicating the altered course is perpendicular to the observer (thus, not seen).

4   *Cut all vertical and horizontal planes* along a section line. Why? The cut expresses the visual relationships of horizontal and vertical spaces—along the cut.

5   *No depth*: there is no depth regarding perspective; there is depth regarding the planes seen beyond the cut and they can be visually highlighted for emphasis or de-emphasis based on line or shape value.

6   *Context information*: sections can benefit from contextual information in the background planes (mountains, key features, buildings, etc.); they are less important in the hierarchy of the section and are thus drawn or represented in lighter values or weights.

Remember:

• sections can show elevations within them and other features in the distance (away from the cut line)
• sections always have a directional view
• view and the "buzz saw" are always noted on plan for reference of the observer
• site sections (larger scale) are better with background elevated planes context as part of section
• line quality, whether hand crafted or digital, is critical to emphasize the hierarchy of elements within section: important—heavier weight; less important or background context—lighter weight
• *shadows and depth*: as in plan and elevation, shadows in section can be effective ways to indicate the depth of vertical features, cast at 45 degrees; used to indicate setbacks in buildings and other detail.

Axonometric drawings

• The axonometric drawing is a form of paraline drawing where all lines that are parallel in plan, elevation and section remain parallel in the axonometric. Thus, it is a valuable and easy type of drawing to learn and utilize in design studies.
• There is distortion in most axonometric drawings but in most design applications (not construction) this distortion is tolerable.

- An axonometric drawing is effective when three major planes are revealed in the graphic, necessitating the use of an angle other than 0–180 for orientation, such as 45/45, 36/60 or 60/30.

For those students and professionals who enjoy the ease and joy of the crafting process, below I offer some guidelines through a simple exercise.

Exercise A.1 cube and pyramid

Intent

Construct a cube and a pyramid, each approximately 4 × 4in or 10 × 10cm.

Tools

- preferably an adjustable triangle or a 45 or a 30/60
- a straight edge to establish and maintain the 0–180-degree base line
- pens and pencils
- tracing paper, tape etc.
- vellum grid paper for finals
- (no erasers).

Tasks

- Work from a plan with elevation drawings and/or photographs or appropriate sourced information at desired scale.
- Once the plan is established, orient it to a conventional angle using the 0–180-degree line as a base reference line: orientation can be 45/45, 30/60 or 60/30 (I prefer the 30/60 and its reverse as these are excellent angles to illustrate three major planes of the subject space). Since 30 degrees is closer to the 0–180 base, planes oriented to the 30 degree will display more length (see examples).
- For students, show all of your construction lines on your first tracing paper effort or draft.
- Using reference material, elevate all vertical corners, points etc. from the angled plan base (the plan always remains the same—parallel lines) to their appropriate scaled dimensions.
- Connect the upper plane lines from upper corner to upper corner if they are all perpendicular to the plan.
- If not, measure each vertical from the base (they can be at different heights) and connect the top points. For the cube, it is a simple matter of finding one vertical height and connecting all four other corners as they are the same height and all perpendicular to all verticals.
- Without tracing but using your tracing paper, trace in freehand or with straight edge the final image.
- For the pyramid, find the four corners of the base and the center-point height and connect the dots.
- Now play with them as if they are buildings by adding and subtracting shapes.

APPENDIX I

Quick sketching: contour drawing

Contour drawing does not utilize perspective principals such as estimated vantage points, horizon lines, station points, etc., but rather requires the student to be aware of the edges and contours of every object or scene he or she is drawing—observing and drawing what is seen, not what is estimated or from memory. This is a fun and easy drawing technique to teach students and provides them with a quick and effective way of drawing in perspective.

The basic principle to remember is that the object or scene is described by edges or contours of shapes—from strong shadow edges to soft transition edges. The shadow defines the shape upon which it falls.

This technique requires practice so that the student breaks the tendency to look and memorize rather than look and draw what he or she sees. Anyone with basic instruction can learn how to contour draw, opening up another world of communication. It requires focus and observation skills (developed, not inherited) to be aware of the contour features of an object and all shapes within that object. If you find yourself drifting, eyes glued to the drawing not the object, then you have drifted from observation to memorization.

Drawing on the Right Side of the Brain (Edwards, 1979) is an excellent guide for key techniques in contour drawing. Your personal library collection will thank you. Practice both the pure and modified contour drawing techniques to improve observation and drawing skills.

Principles and tasks

- Use drawing tools that have less friction with the drawing surface such as soft pencils (HB to 4B), felt-tip pens, Conte pencils, etc.; avoid any tool that will scratch or drag on or into the paper such as technical pens, as these will slow your movement (ballpoint and metal-tip pens are not recommended as they drag and gouge).

- Once you have placed your drawing tool on the paper, do not raise it up . . . if you want to go back to a point, keep the tool on the paper and move back. This is hard for some students, but you must keep the tool on the paper as it helps to maintain your focus on the image contours; if the contour lines are smooth, you are probably going too fast and not observing the subject.

- In modified contour drawing, establish a frame of view—a view finder—not unlike the lens of a camera. Some instructors have students establish a grid around and/or within the view window, as an excellent place to begin is at a point on the corner of the frame interior—a place where a major shape ends in the composition, for example.

- Begin to draw what you see from or of that edge (curving line, straight, intermittent, etc.) and what its characteristics are that you can transfer to the sketch (up/down, angle, curve, etc.).

- I often draw in the major shapes at first—the overall outside edge or contour—for compositional fit on the page, then begin entering the interior of the object with interior contours.

- At times, I may like a drawing that has gone beyond the frame boundaries, so I change the frame boundaries.

- Think values and value edges (soft—dotted; hard—complete line), patterns, edges, all contours.

- I suggest beginning with one- to three-minute quick exercises to learn how to go from what you see in the object to transferring that to the paper.

- Look out for:
  - smooth lines usually indicate a lack of concentration or observation
  - cartoon-like images are an indicator of memory reliance not adequate observation
  - not looking up from the sketch indicates memory takeover and no observation.

The advantage of practicing pure contour drawing is the lesson of observing the actual contour characteristics of the shape or object, regardless of how the initial drawing appears.

Model-making

Let's clarify the term "model" as we begin: a model is a two- or three-dimensional physical construct composed of various materials used to represent a design composition. Three-dimensional crafted models, made by hand, are key tools in exploring and evaluating spatial relationships/designs not observed as effectively in orthographic representations. Study models, like diagrams, can begin with semi-abstract/realistic shapes and symbol shapes representing larger patterns of composition with minimal detail. Models increase in complexity as the design process evolves. With the use of digital graphics in design, the model is an excellent accompaniment as it provides the designer with a process model to assist in evaluating design progress. Models can be scanned, digitized and further processed or manipulated with digital graphic applications.

I classify *models* into three types: discovery; process; and presentation/representational.

Discovery models are semi-abstract constructions of basic compositional principles that are the initial stages of idea generation; they are without style or other details that can be distracting. Many of the models in this book may be considered discovery models—looking for innovation in and during the construction/manipulation phase, focusing on the elements and principles of a composition.

Process models also have a discovery aspect to them. They are essentially study models that explore design relationships with more and more detail added as the design progresses.

The *presentation or representational models* is an expression of a finished design product, suitable for public and/or client use, marketing/financing and other purposes. It is a detailed representation of a completed design in most cases.

I am spending a bit more time on models in this section because they are excellent tools that work well with both digital and crafted graphic processes.

Models that I advocate for student and professional use include the following:

- Corrugated cardboard models for larger site contexts, including model cut-outs for building types and arrangements.
- Compressed cardboard/chipboard models for the construction of buildings and topography in particular.
- Tagboard, railroad board and others, usually in white, which are used to contrast with contextual massing (usually in gray chipboard), designating new design elements.
- Color construction paper or card stock.
- Wood and plastic blocks, including interlocking types.

Foamboard, wood, plastic and other materials may also be used but these require special tools to cut and manipulate.

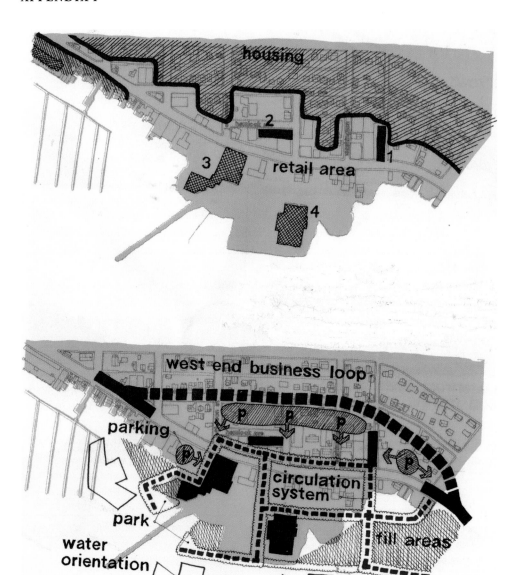

a

Figure AI.1. (a–e) Plan diagrams 1. *The plan drawing, an orthographic view to the ground plane from above, is referred to as a base map when the plan contains basic reference and orientation visual information. Additional information, such as proposed massing ideas, is then added to the base for assessment and analysis. Plan drawings can range from conceptual or schematic, as in example (a) to neighborhood districts (b) to larger-scale key element plan diagrams (d) to specific site plan (e) drawings. The student will notice that I have kept the plan diagrams loose and schematic, as the focus is on conceptual design methods.*

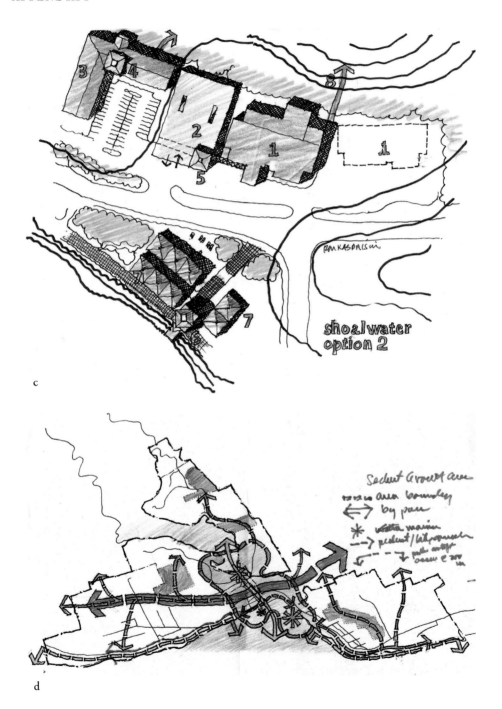

shoalwater
option 2

c

d

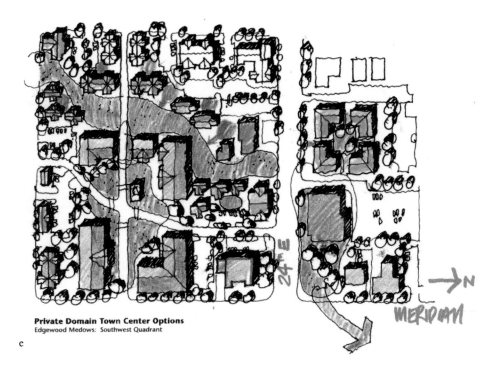

Private Domain Town Center Options
Edgewood Medows: Southwest Quadrant

e

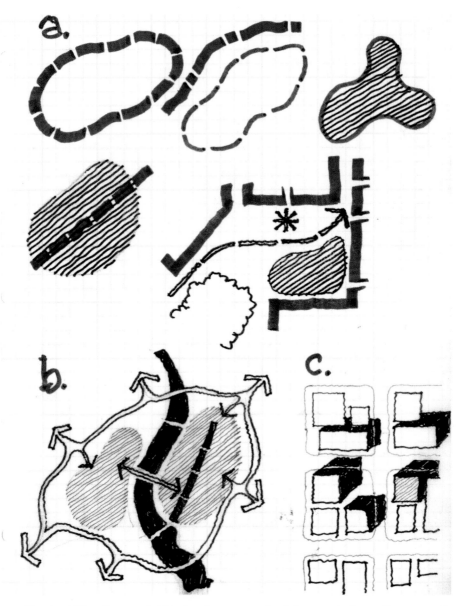

Figure AI.2. (a–o) Plan diagrams 2. *This plan diagram series (a–o) depicts semi-abstract illustrations of key principles, constraints and opportunities that are summarized by filtering out other data that are not relevant at that particular stage or scale. They are meant to convey useful symbols in the construction of semi-abstract plan diagrams. There are situations where color is not useful while line type, texture and value are critical to the visual communication.*

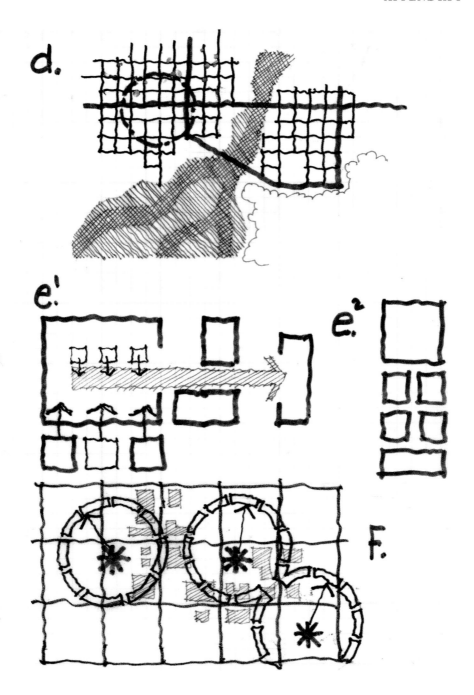

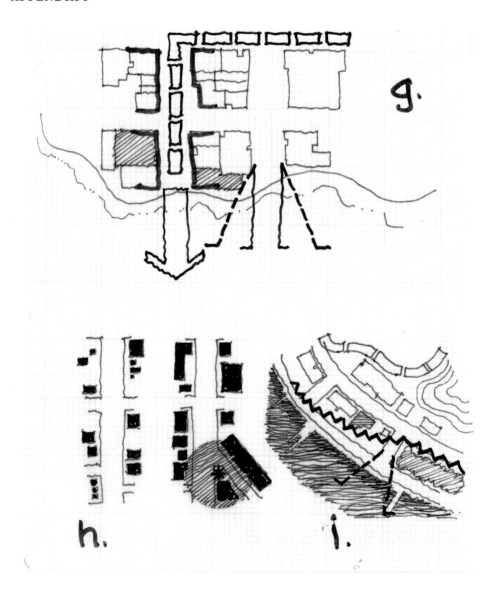

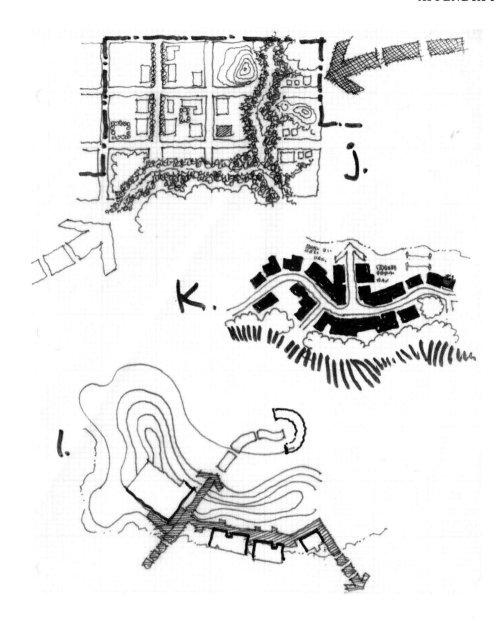

j.

K.

l.

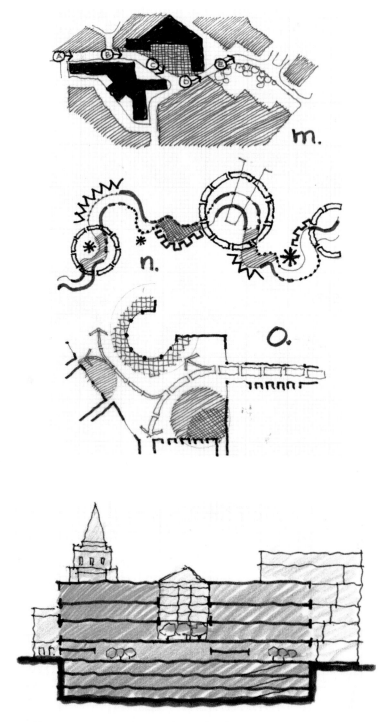

Figure AI.3. Building section. *Line value is used to graphically portray a hierarchy of horizontal and vertical elements. Elements that are "cut" in section are darker in value while non-cut elements are lighter in value or line weight. Features below, at, and above grade are included in the sectional cut, with the ground plane highlighted.*

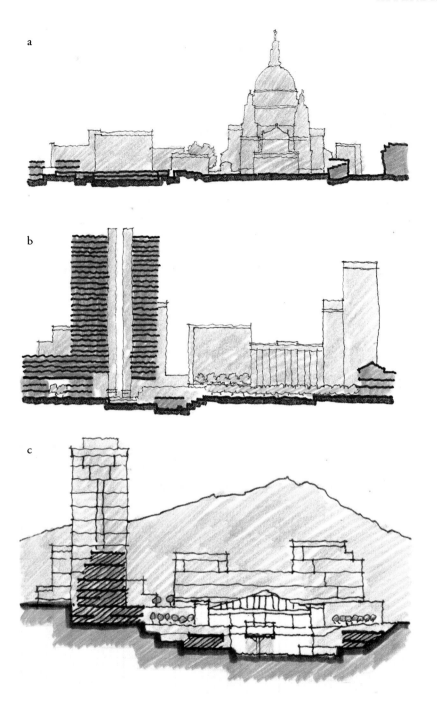

Figure AI.4. (a–c) Site sections. *The site section utilizes the same principles as the building section. Based on the cut-line decision through the site and the direction of view, the section illustrates the cut ground plane and sub-grade features (underground parking, sunken plazas, utilities, etc.) and above-grade natural and building features. The lighter-value lines are maintained for all features in elevation while the darker and bolder lines are used for vertical and horizontal planes that are cut through (ground, walls, floors, ceilings, parking lots, streets, water features, etc.) only along the cut line.*

a

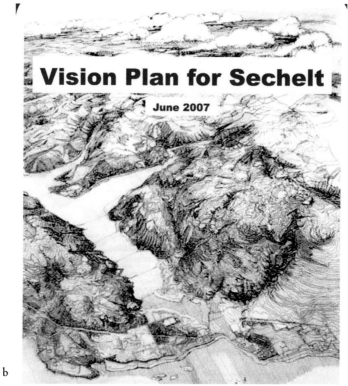

b

Figure AI.5. (a–b) Areal perspective diagrams. *The areal perspective can be used in place of plan diagrams where contextual images can strengthen the message. Unlike an axonometric drawing, these diagrams cannot be measured to scale. Example (a) portrays the City of Seattle City Hall site and complex (blue) with sufficient context in the surrounding area. The detail is limited to massing with the exception of the City Hall site and adjacent parkland. Example (b), by Professor Emeritus James Pettinari (University of Oregon), presents a larger view of Sechelt, BC.*

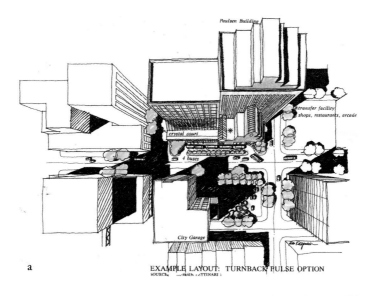

a

EXAMPLE LAYOUT: TURNBACK PULSE OPTION

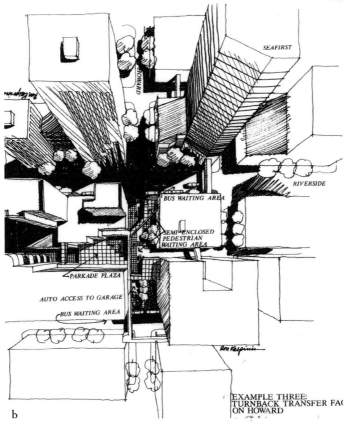

b

Figure AI.6. (a–b) One-point areal perspectives. *This type of perspective is essentially a plan and perspective combination, where the plan can be to scale to illustrate key elements (in this case a transit transfer facility in downtown Spokane, WA) and highlight the verticality of contextual high-rise buildings for context. Depicted here are two options for the facility used in public information meetings and with Transit Board members.*

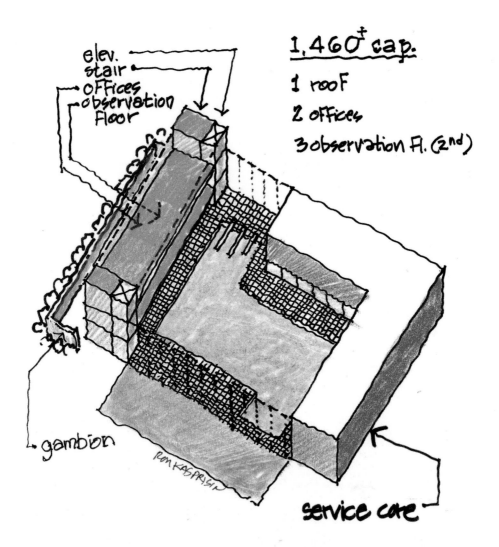

elev.
stair
offices
observation
floor

1,460⁺ cap.

1 roof
2 offices
3 observation fl. (2nd)

gambion

Ron Kasprisin

service core

SAFE HAVEN POOL
BUILDING COMPONENT

Figure AI.7. Axonometric diagram. *The axonometric view provides an areal-like image that is useful as a diagram that combines a plan view and a three-dimensional element, as in this diagram for a tsunami shelter within a proposed community swimming pool. The reader will note the extent to which I use axonometric drawings, so I have limited the examples in this section.*

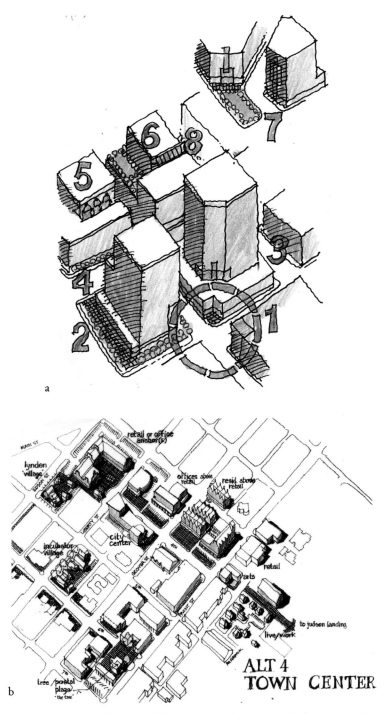

Figure AI.8. (a–b) Axonometric drawings. *The axonometric drawing is useful for portraying the overall design intent by design district with design guidelines. The orientation of this base plan is 30/60, left/right and the basic requirement is that all vertical lines are perpendicular to the 0–180 line (no slanted verticals, please). In (b) the axonometric drawing is useful for portraying the larger downtown view with key connections to city center uses.*

a

b

c

Figure AI.9. (a–c) One-point eye-level perspective. *This perspective provides an eye-level human view into space. It is helpful for evaluating and visualizing the human dimension. I use it less now than in previous years, as I tend to focus on the axonometric diagram for structure and order.*

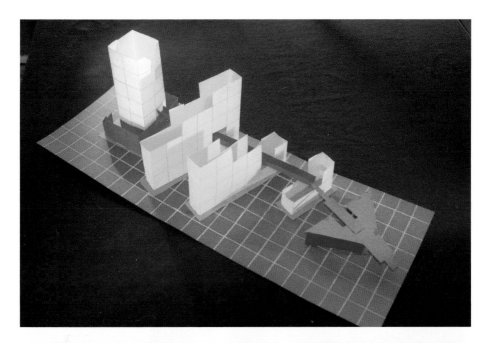

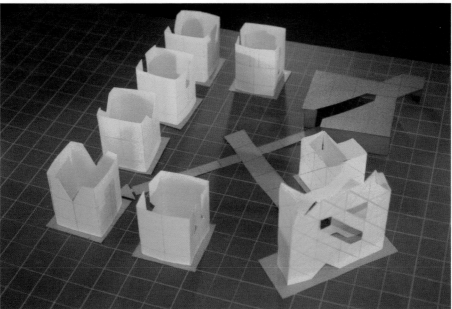

Figure AI.10. Construction paper model. *Construction paper provides a fast and effective way of generating ideas in composition. Using scissors and/or paper-cutting knives, the process is fun and constructive as many idea variations can be done quickly. The color coding is an additional benefit for identifying uses and other activities. These models are used extensively in this work for their flexibility in conceptual design work.*

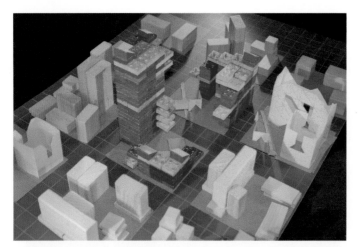

a

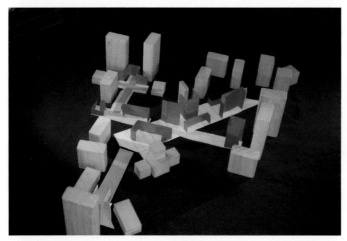

b

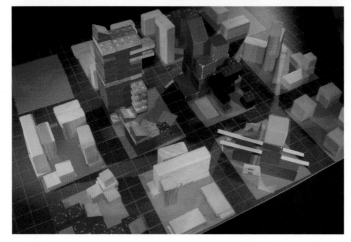

c

**Figure AI.11. (a–c)
Model with wood blocks.**
*This model of a downtown
district uses several types of
wood blocks, ranging from
interlocking to colored to
plane elements. This was
more of an experiment in
the use of blocks and in
later stages I reduced the
variety of blocks to minimize
distractions. I include it here
to demonstrate their variety.*

Bibliography

Edwards, Betty, 1979: *Drawing on the Right Side of the Brain*: Houghton Mifflin Co., Los Angeles, CA.

Kenmore, City of, 2010: *City of Kenmore Open Space Opportunities: Making Connections*: Kasprisin Pettinari Design, Langley, WA.

Kitsap County/Kasprisin Pettinari Design, 2006: *Downtown Design Handbook*: Kitsap County Department of Community Development, Silverdale, WA, and Kasprisin Pettinari Design, Langley, WA.

Sechelt, BC, District of, 2007: *Visions for Sechelt*: John Talbot & Associates, Burnaby, BC, and Kasprisin Pettinari Design, Langley, WA.

APPENDIX II
EXPERIMENTS IN BASIC COMPOSITION
The basis for place-making

*T*hese experiments and exercises represent assignments given to my graduate urban planning and design students over the years in Urban Design Composition. They accepted the challenge with gusto and over-came fears and reticence regarding the crafting process—working with their senses, with manual manipulation of physical materials and tools. For many students, computers and digital technologies were the only tools they had worked with in problem-solving, including urban planning. This presented a significant challenge as they were guided in other options for design exploration. This is not about crafting versus digital processes. It deals with a plurality of approaches to (urban) design, using crafting and digital where appropriate.

I appreciate the students' energy, diligence and feedback during the conduct of these many exercises as I know they were challenging and at times perplexing. My hearty thanks to all who participated in those classes and exercises.

The urban design process is often referred to as "place-making"—a form-based interpretation of urban meaning and function into spatial metaphors; sensory and sensual built environments that are considered special in the eyes and experience of the observer. The more aspects of *urban meaning and functionality* are incorporated into the process, the more complex becomes the challenge of place-making—beyond package or franchised applications. Integrating the rich stories of community with the compositional principles of art is a necessity and critical challenge for contemporary designers, and often overshadowed by the demands of economic and functional program requirements. Some designers resist the connection to and foundation provided by art as the basis of design. This connection that needs to be reinstated to provide a clear basis for design principles, not merely trends and clichés.

Fashioning spatial compositions that respond to and structure this *urban meaning*, maintaining a compositional integrity within the complex urban design process, begins the *art of urban design*. This is the place for playful exploration of design using crafting methods as a base method that can in many applications be transferred to digital processing methodologies.

Exploration leads to discovery; and discovery leads to creativity expressed in novel solutions that can lead to innovation. Using methods and tools that enable this discovery process is critical to the overall design process as a creative problem-solving process. Exploration is a process of generating ideas, beginning with uncertain outcomes, following leads and learning from "failures". It is not a linear process. Crafting methods (drawing, model-making, cut-outs and *play* in general) all require the physical manipulation of materials into design compositions—a journey into the unknown on a path that emerges only after each step is taken. This physical manipulation can be frightening for students and professionals alike, but that fear or reticence can be muted with engagement and practice. Manipulation is critical to discovery as the process entails experimentation and exploration with both structured and known principles, such as conventional typologies, and unstructured and unknown or uncertain explorations where new principles emerge.

Remember, *play* is a free activity with the absence of fear where initial rules change and are replaced by new rules as the play progresses to an uncertain outcome. It is also non-competitive, with no winners or losers (as opposed to gaming). Therefore, "playing a video game" is an oxymoron.

Digital tools and techniques can supplement and complement this process, but I encourage students and practitioners not to rely exclusively on them as they can reduce and distract, in my experience as an educator, from the discovery process through pre-set structures and formats; and, most importantly, can be a disconnect from key crafting senses. I realize there is a great deal of opinion, pressure and debate surrounding digital versus crafting methodologies in the urban design process. But it is not one versus the other. I argue for a plurality of techniques within the larger process; and I leave the final decision to instructors and students. I can only urge students to engage their fears surrounding this physical sensory engagement and learn the joy of *play* in design.

This appendix describes exercises I use in my "Urban Design Composition" coursework to prepare urban planning students for advanced urban design studios. If some appear to be class assignments, that is because they are! Those students with previous design backgrounds also benefit from revisiting compositional principles. Sadly, in my experience as an educator, some design students are never introduced to them beyond examples, journals and conventions. As I stated in the Introduction, intelligence and motivation are not sufficient in themselves to engage in design, the making of place. Making *place* requires an understanding and a practiced experience with the elements and principles of composition as the foundation for crafting spatial metaphors for human settlements.

My planning students enjoy these exercises, realizing the learning curve as they go through them sequentially, and I hope readers will as well. They are offered as a base for educators, designers, and laypeople as hands-on experiments in composition. They are guides, not absolutes, which in themselves are open to experimentation. I encourage instructors and students to challenge and change them to fit their needs and contexts while maintaining their underlying intent.

Design requires the immersion of the person (and his/her personality) into the process. Design is not antiseptic, devoid of feeling and opinion, personal values and passions; and it requires dedication to the needs and passions of communities and their environs—a very complex journey. Being able to identify and appreciate urban form, through history and case studies, is a starting point; and understanding historic morphology is not sufficient as a base for design. The CST matrix defines the context and requires best practices in planning and design investigations. And learning how to play with form is the other side of the equation.

Sequence of experiments and exercises

The exercises are designed to be a sequential learning process, from simple shape manipulation to advanced urban design sketch problems. They are designed to build confidence, skill, and an evolving understanding of the elements and principles of design composition through practice. The sequence generally includes the following.

* Simple and abstract manipulation of primary shapes and volumes, beginning with two-dimensional formats and advancing to three dimensions.
* Applying basic principles of composition to various shapes.
* Introducing space program needs and typologies as play pieces.
* Experimenting with urban design sketch problems with basic context and environs included.

Skill requirements

As emphasized in *Play in Creative Problem-solving for Planners and Architects* (Kasprisin, 2016), skill development is critical to engaging any design challenge and requires some form of hands-on manipulation of tools, objects, shapes, etc. in addition to digital tools and technologies. This is play as in crafting (seeing, touching, feeling, turning, folding, gluing, messing up and getting dirty). Many of my planning students have minimal, if any, drawing and model-building experience and begin with some trepidation at using their hands as opposed to a mouse or stylus. Consequently, many of the exercises use construction paper, tape, glue, and scissors as beginning tools (remember kindergarten if you were fortunate). This makes the play accessible and fun for most participants. I also introduce axonometric drawing skills as a way of communicating and studying three dimensions of objects and compositions. This is complemented by more human-scale, ground-level perspectives, albeit limited. Plan diagrams, semiotic images, round out the toolbox for most students at this stage.

Remember, fear is a necessary ingredient of creativity (Webb, 1990). We all have some reticence to various degrees regarding art and design as accomplished through the senses—a direct connection between mind and body. We need to recognize and work through fear's manifestations. Here is a key hint: when in doubt, when "circling the wagons" in reticence or uncertainty (as where to start), sit down and begin to play—anywhere, at any point in the process—cut, tape, glue *anything* to get started. Then the rest of the process begins to flow, making connections and evolving. Have fun!

I do limit examples of work in order not to influence students' efforts. One effort is not a solution, it is a starting point, so embrace your initial frustrations and enjoy. The suggested exercises can be modified in many different ways to suit individual and cultural needs. I provide a sampling of students' work at the end of this appendix and the variations are numerous. They are not to be judged; rather, they are to be celebrated as learning efforts—engagement in design-making.

Primary shapes

Primary shapes are the building blocks of basic design composition. They are the parent shapes from which all other shapes are derived. They represent a pure mathematics of shape (four equal sides forming four right angles; a single radius defining a circumference). And they are flexible, dynamic, and capable of creative manipulations in complex situations.

Primary: first or highest shape in rank and importance; pure—the square, circle, line.

The flexibility and dynamics of primary shapes (remember: shapes are physical elements—the "nouns" of spatial language)

Principles at work

The following exercises ask the participant to explore the many different ways of expressing the primary shapes without losing their integrity and original identities and characteristics. In other words, take them to the point of breaking in complex manifestations to explore the many ways of adjusting their main components (centers, radii, angles, perimeters, corners, edges, etc.). This is similar to working with the primary colors of various palettes: red, blue and yellow. They are not the same and exhibit ranges of difference, particularly in value and intensity.

Exercise 1a Observation of primary shapes

Intent

Increase your awareness and observation skills of manufactured components in the urban environment, from building components to landscape features; understand the complexity of the geometry of the built environment. Many new students take this geometry for granted and this exercise helps them learn the components of the spatial language.

Tools

- three-ring binder
- camera
- sketchbook.

Tasks

1   In your daily travels, take along your tools and begin observing the various geometrical patterns (and fractals) in the built environment. Begin assembling photographic representations of the three primary shapes and volumes (cube, sphere, axis) and their derivatives (triangle to the square, pie to the circle, dash to the line) in nature and the built or manufactured environment. The peak of a building is a triangle, the windows are rectangles etc. Sound simple? Begin to appreciate them as elements and subsequently as elements in relationship. "A circle in nature?" you ask. Besides the sun and moon and planets, there is the tree: a circle with a single center with consistent radii and modified circumference by contextual environment, but a circle none the less.

2   Collect the samples in a physical binder so that they can be referred to, displayed and annotated. Label each image. Look for the small within the large and continue to observe the geometry of the natural and manufactured worlds.

Exercise 1b Observation of primary shapes

Intent

Repeat the first component of Exercise 1 with the following addition: ask students to identify and record derivatives and partial aspects or components of the primary shapes in both the natural and manufactured worlds.

Exercise 2 Manipulating the primary shapes

Intent

Experiment and understand the primary shapes and how to positively manipulate them into complex shapes that are able to fit into real contexts while retaining their shape integrity or key characteristics. You will find that using crafting methods is less time-consuming than doing this exercise digitally. The more you practice and experiment, the more variations and manipulations you will discover.

Tools

- construction paper
- scissors
- glue and/or tape
- protractor and/or compass
- cutting board.

Tasks

Within an area of 4–6in/10–15cm in size, construct the following.

1 For each shape (circle, square and line), represent it as a solid and, on a separate area, a void (be playful).
2 Now focus on key physical characteristics of each shape and represent each shape using some of those characteristics—enough to maintain the shape integrity and identification. For example, when playing with the circle, focus on a radius, then an arc (which represents and identifies two or more radii by its very curvature), then a circumference or part thereof, etc. In other words, a circle can be represented by a center point, a radius and a partial arc. The square is similar: play with the right-angle corners, the diagonals, the equal and parallel sides, etc. For the line, it can be dashed, curved, a vector, a flowing river, etc.
3 Cut out each primary shape from paper, 4–6in/10–15cm across (use construction paper or an easy-to-cut type of cardboard). Manipulate each shape at least three different ways to alter the conventional or parent shape.
4 Suggestion: use scissors or a sharp knife to cut into the shapes. For example, a square can be represented by four corner pieces, a triangle and the remaining corner, two equal lines at right angles and the remaining corner; a circle by an arrow and a center point. Do as many of these as you can. This is a basic but valuable exercise.

Exercise 3a Making two-dimensional compositions using primary shapes—the circle

Intent

The next step in understanding the positive manipulation and flexibility of primary shapes is to fashion compositions from each. Begin with the circle and use its main characteristics in the formation of a composition that comprises of numerous circle components.

Tools

- scissors
- construction paper

- glue
- protractor and/or compass (bottle caps and coffee-jar lids also work well)
- cutting board
- cutting knife (optional)
- safety awareness.

Tasks

1   Assess the main characteristics of the circle (circumference, diameter, radius, center, arc, etc.) and select and arrange them in various compositions. Cut out pieces and glue down to another sheet of construction paper.
2   Make each effort (minimum three) approximately 4–6in/10–15cm.
3   Utilize various spatial transformational actions and principles to derive various compositions, e.g. repetition with variety, gradation, superimposition, etc.

Exercise 3b Making two-dimensional compositions using primary shapes—the square

Intent and tasks

Repeat Exercise 3a using the characteristics of the square (four right-angle corners, two sets of parallel lines, diagonality, four corners, etc.).

Exercise 3c Making two-dimensional compositions using primary shapes—the line

Intent

To repeat, some may not consider the line as a primary "shape". However, I do, as it constitutes a key element in the making of shapes and as an axis. It ranges in nature from a vector to the boundary of another shape.

The line has many characteristics for use in compositions: linearity, movement, direction, continuous, broken, delicate, bold, etc.

Tools

Same as Exercise 3a.

Tasks

The variations for the line exercises are almost unlimited, and the more variations you construct, the more appreciation you will develop for the power of the line in compositions.

Exercise 4a Making two-dimensional compositions using the square and circle

Intent

This series of exercises challenges the participant to combine into compositions the characteristics of the square and the circle. It begins a series of more complex compositions. Review and familiarize yourself with the principles of composition and the transformational actions discussed in previous chapters to assist you in these exercises, at least as a starting point.

Tools

- scissors
- construction paper
- glue
- protractor and/or compass (bottle caps and coffee-jar lids also work well)
- cutting board
- cutting knife (optional)
- safety awareness.

Tasks

1   Select a number of key characteristics or components of the square and the circle for experimentation. (Do not try to mentally solve or generate a composition before actually physically playing with the material and components.)
2   Keep the size of exercise reasonable—4–6in/10–15cm in area.
3   Begin by cutting out shape components and move around on a flat surface to find starting point(s). Then begin assembling a composition knowing that it is a start and can lead to more advanced compositions—the more experiments, the more possibilities.
4   Examples: a hollow circle with a solid square is a good starting point; or cut them in half and play with the halves as they still represent the primary shapes.
5   Experiment with the basic principles: repetition, gradation, repetition with variety, etc.
6   Students usually find it easiest to start the exercise on a grid pattern (both horizontally and vertically) and learn how to manipulate the grid.

Exercise 4b Making two-dimensional compositions using the square, circle and line (axis)

Intent

Use the same approach as in Exercise 4a but add a line shape. Experiment with angles (30/60, 45, 90), with the line as a connecting device.

Exercise 5 Adding the vertical dimension

Intent

As an introduction to volumetric experiments, add vertical planes to your two-dimensional compositions. As above, I encourage students to begin by placing a grid with a light color pencil onto construction paper and playing with the vertical planes.

Tools

Same as previous exercises. You can include vertically inclined objects such as straws, toothpicks, etc.

Tasks

1   You can start this exercise using one or all of the two-dimensional efforts in Exercises 4a and 4b; or you can use them as inspiration and begin with a new horizontal composition.

2   Another approach: start with the vertical planes as components of circle, square and line and construct vertical compositions that in turn define horizontal patterns; then assess and think with both dimensions, seeking further complexity.

3   Review the various types of vertical planes: perpendicular to ground plane, curved, folded, tilted, continuous, broken, etc.

4   Do as many as time and energy permit as you progress from a nebulous starting point to compositions that exhibit key principles of composition.

What to look for

•   Do your shapes relate to one another or do they simply float on the base?

•   Are they scrambled? Is there *connectivity* among them?

•   Is there a sense of focal point or center of interest?

•   Are your primary shapes still recognizable through their components?

•   Can you identify an overall compositional structure within the compositions? If not, how can you tinker with or reinforce the existing composition to further the structural strength?

•   Is there any drama resulting from the combinations of vertical and horizontal planes? From differences in values (light to dark) of the papers?

Exercises 6a and 6b Using different exercise materials for horizontal and vertical compositions

Intent

As I discuss in Kasprisin (2016), using a plurality of approaches and tools can expand the design discovery process and lead to new directions. This is because each tool type has its own physical characteristics that affect the compositional outcome. For example, a wood block can be square or rectangular; a cylinder is circular; a line can be a curvilinear string or a straw or a wood slat. These shapes and objects are essentially fractals and effect and are reflected in the final outcomes.

Tools

•   For this exercise, I use two different types of objects: classic wood blocks with dowels for connectivity, as square block and rectangular block; and a variety of wood block shapes, including cylinders.

•   I also add string, paper strips, and wood slats to add to the mix of elements.

Tasks

1 Again, keep the size of the exercise reasonable—not too small and not large to become cumbersome and "busy work". For these exercises, I prefer to work at a base size of 18 × 24in/40 × 60cm.
2 I start with a grid base, in this case on illustration or poster board (with some rigidity), with pencil.
3 Let the vertical plane play define the underlying "plan" or horizontal composition.
4 Be aware of how the new shape elements affect the horizontal and vertical characteristics of the composition.
5 I then select a horizontal composition from previous experiments and use that as a base for the vertical planes as a starting point before making the changes to the horizontal composition that emanate from the vertical experiments.

Exercise 7 Constructing and manipulating the basic volumes—the cube

Principles

Using the primary shapes in volumetric form, construct complex shapes without losing the "parent" form. This is similar to the first two-dimensional exercise as you learn how flexible the primary shapes are and how to develop complex forms using their essential and basic characteristics. For example, the cube (square) has a center, eight equal corners, two main diagonals and can be broken down into smaller grids, cubes, triangles, rectangles, pyramids etc.

Intent

Familiarize yourself with the cube by manipulating it into varying complex arrangements without losing the "parent" characteristics.

Tools

Use crafting methods and tools for this and other exercises as a starting point as this puts the participant in direct connection with the shapes.

* construction paper or tag/poster board; avoid thick, hard-to-cut papers and cardboard
* scissors
* mat knives/X-Acto-type knives
* paper glue or tape
* soft pencil
* triangle
* straight edge for cutting
* cutting surface.

Tasks

1 Construct a cube approximately 6in/15cm per side.
2 Construct a second cube with an inverted pyramid inside.

3   Construct a third cube with a circle or cylinder extracted from it or penetrating the cube.

4   Use your imagination and play with various other versions without destroying the cube "parent" characteristics.

Exercise 8 Cube transformations

Intent

Planning students love this exercise, as it brings them closer to making something real. Use additive, subtractive and dimensional transformational actions to manipulate the cube into a building form—house, office building, etc.

Tools

*   various forms of cardboard that are easy to manipulate and cut with some rigidity
*   cutting tools
*   glue
*   chipboard
*   poster board
*   frosted tape.

Tasks

1   A 4–6in/10–15cm base is advised.

2   Review the additive/subtractive/transformational actions and begin to manipulate the cube form by taking out sections, corners, etc.

3   Using axonometric drawings can be easier than constructing the cube in that, with a series of overlays, a number of variations can be done quickly.

Exercise 9 Sphere transformations

Intent

The intent with the sphere is the same as for the cube and the line: understanding characteristics and components and constructing forms that are complex without losing the "parent" shape.

Tools

*   Various paper products can be fashioned into diameters and circumference slices to construct the sphere.
*   Construction paper and tag or poster board are suitable for most constructions.
*   Straws and wood skewers are also useful for center support structures.

Tasks

1   As a starting point, construct two variations of a sphere with paper.
2   Based on those constructions, use additive and subtractive transformations to manipulate the starting.
3   Use portions of the sphere in constructing compositions, as the retention of key components maintains the parent identity.
4   Some students may find it easier to work with axonometric drawings and construct manipulations with overlay drawings.

Exercise 10 Line/axis transformations—as volumes

Intent

The line can be dynamic in its varied physical constructions, from narrow line to broad strip, straight or curved with movement and direction, continuous or broken or intermittent. Play with the many variations of the line and increase the complexity of the constructs as you progress through the exercises. The axis in urban design is a powerful organizing structure in most compositions. This exercise can assist the student in appreciating the line's variability.

Tools

•   construction paper, tag or poster board, illustration board
•   paper glue
•   scissors and X-Acto-type or mat knives
•   colored pencils.

Tasks

1   Experiment with various forms and shapes of "line", expanding your understanding of what a line is and the broad interpretation of what it can become.
2   Add vertical planes to increase a sense of depth and height.
3   Expand the idea of line with movement and directional patterns.

Exercise 11 Combining volumes in composition

Intent

To increase the complexity in the compositions, combine the three primary volumes—sphere, cube and axis—in at least three different ways. Again, refer back to the principles and transformational actions of design composition. The more experiments you construct, the more in-depth your understanding of volume manipulation in compositions will become.

Tools

I use a variety of tools for this series of experiments, including construction paper, wood slats, yarn, and wood blocks. Feel free to experiment with a variety of tools, conventional and otherwise.

Tasks

1 The first experiment used construction paper. Overlay or superimpose one primary volume onto another to get a third and distinct form. You can use vertical and horizontal planes or complete volumes. Remember: placing nouns—objects as shapes on a spatially referenced base map, for example—merely locates those objects in space. This is a language of relationships so demonstrate and visualize the relational interactions between and among those objects and the underlying physical context—this is the real communication!

2 The second experiment uses wood blocks as the base tool, with additive tools such as paper and yarn.

3 Keep on experimenting, using these examples as a starting point.

4 Also use derivatives of the primary volumes in your compositions, such as the pyramid and the cylinder.

5 Remember the key principles of composition at work:

    a) Gradation—variations in light, color, texture, sound and smell.

    b) Repetition—a recurring shape or pattern of shapes.

    c) Repetition with variety—a recurring shape or pattern of shapes that can change size, value, texture etc. in alternating sequences.

    d) Variety—one composition that has varied shapes.

    e) Alternation—a recurring shape or pattern of shapes that has a specific rhythm to their repetition, such as ababab/b, aabbaa, b/ababbabababab.

    f) Dominance—decide and highlight or emphasize or dramatize—the largest, brightest, the alpha, the maximum contrast etc.

    g) Patterning—an arrangement in form with at least two repetitions, possibly indicating change or emergent pattern.

Compositional structures

The experiments in this section expand the construction of forms into significant compositions using the compositional structures described and defined earlier. The student may benefit from repeating basic principles and structures as a prelude to these experiments.

Principles

From the circle, square, and line come a variety of compositional assembling forces, frameworks and structures that emerge as structuring devices, referred to as *compositional structures*. These are hybrids of the circle, square, sphere and cube that bring together, construct, relate to and assemble various organizational parts, elements, and relationships into spatial constructs or compositions. Remember that *organizations* are relationships of use, activities, social interactions, etc., not assembled into a specific form or spatial composition.

Form results from a connection among relationships of the organizations, and the crafting process. This pre-dates and provides currently popular form-based design and zoning applications.

Goldstein (1989) offers a solid base for these explorations and includes 16 compositional structures. Other variations and hybrids are possible, of course. This experimentation series is an important step in understanding and playing with rational means of making form. As situations and physical contexts become more and more complex, these hybrids can serve the designer well in fashioning meaningful order in complex human settlements.

Compositional structures

- axial
- bridge
- cantilever
- centrally placed object
- circle
- curvilinear dominant
- diagonal
- diamond
- even spread
- grid
- horizontal
- L-shape
- radial burst
- square
- triangle
- two centers
- vertical.

Obviously, these are derivatives of the main or primary shapes and volumes. This section experiments with a number of these structures to demonstrate their ability to assemble a composition and make it cohesive.

In most of these exercises, I utilize more than one compositional structure, making one dominant.

Tasks

- Limit the work area or paper size to 8 × 10in–11 × 17in/20 × 25cm–28 × 43cm approx. for ease of work effort.
- Use easy-to-manipulate materials such as construction paper or card stock.
- Work fast and construct as many experiments as possible, using scissors and glue or tape. Do not try to be fancy.

Exercise 12 Compositional structures—repetition with variety

Exercise 13 Compositional structures—axial

Exercise 14 Compositional structures—square and grid

Exercise 15 Compositional structures—diagonality

Exercise 16 Compositional structures—L-shape

Exercise 17 Compositional structures—radial burst

Spatial reference systems

Before moving to context-oriented exercises, let's discuss the use of spatial reference systems as starting points for design composition and as guides during the longer process. They are meant to be flexible, not rigid, and can be manipulated in the same manner as the primary shapes. In many cases the primary shapes make up the base for these reference systems.

Principles

Spatial reference systems are compositional structures that are used to provide a reference and orientation base for more complex compositions. I also call them *ghost* or *transparent structures* because in many cases they are not visible to the naked eye in the final outcome; rather, they are hidden in the larger spatial construct. They are an important foundation especially for beginning design students in that they enable more complex assemblies to occur in a clear order.

In urban design, spatial patterns are often adopted as policy implemented by others over an extended time-frame. Change comes with the many hands that implement the design framework. Given a firm reference structure or framework, the original, underlying, and organizing urban design principles can withstand and adapt to incremental changes over time.

For beginning designers, the circle, square, and axis provide the starting points, expanded by the sphere, cube, and channel/ribbon/axis. Remember the early exercises of manipulating the primary shapes: circle, square, and line. Using a grid, for example, the designer can provide a horizontal matrix for reference and order both as orthographic composition and organic, "free-flowing" compositions with a ghost underlay.

Here are starting structures for spatial reference systems:

- Grid hybrids
    - square
    - rectangular
    - circle
    - triangular (diamond)
    - broken
    - radial.
- axial hybrids.

Tasks

- Drawing or paper constructions are suitable for this exercise in grid variations.
- I suggest keeping the grid variations as a base guide or template for future work in the studio.
- Also try combinations of the various grids to increase flexibility and variety or complexity in underlying grids (depending upon context).
- Graph paper is an option.

Exercise 18 Transparent square grid, triangular grid and circle grid

Intent

Playfully craft an organic, free-flowing vertical plane(s) onto the grids (separately, of course).

Tasks

- Use the grids to provide reference points at key cross points and by varying the size of the grids within the larger base grid as this provides additional reference points and intersections that are useful in making tighter curved lines.
- When the base plan is crafted, rotate the drawing to either 30/60 or 60/30 degrees and elevate the vertical plane(s) in axonometric drawing format.
- Eliminate the underlying grid by tracing over; or, if in construction paper, relocate to a clean sheet of paper without the grid. You now have a "free-form" composition that is in fact based on a grid.

Exercise 19 Transparent broken grid

Intent

Essentially the same intent as Exercise 18. By constructing a broken grid as the base, you can experiment with a situation where the underlying context has landscape or built form features that require the grid to be broken or modified to accommodate the context. This allows the grid and grid variations to be used as a base guide and still respond to and respect underlying contextual features and situations.

Tasks

- Prepare a diagram of the key and critical contextual features that are to remain and be included in the larger composition.
- Experiment with a number of grid variations that allow an initial flexibility in composition options. These variations can be accomplished by constructing smaller grids at key locations within the larger grids and/or changing the angles of parts of the grid to 30/60 or 60/30, for example.

Exercise 20 Radial burst system

Exercise 21 Axial reference systems

Examples of student work with compositional elements and principles (followed by more complex experiments)

a   b

   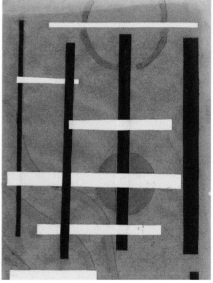

c   d

Figure AII.1 (a–j). Student examples. *The following examples are from composition exercises by graduate students in urban design, most of whom had no previous design background. They are meant to suggest materials, methods of experimentation and assembly. Instructors can assign a variety of tools and methods to accomplish the intent of the exercises. Students whose work is illustrated include: Eddie Hill, Kevin Teng, C. Padilla, Jeff Arango, Jessie Stein and Zhi Wen Tan (all University of Washington). Additional students who contributed to the urban campus and St Paul's projects include: Max Baker, Mike Brestel, Ian Crozier, Peter Huie, Joanna Kairserman, Anders Martinucci, Elizabeth, Moll, Rebecca Perkins, Luke Camerota, Irving Chu, Kyle Cotchett, Kaylie Duffy, Eric Guida, Chase Killebrew, Jennifer Meulenberg, Dat Cao Nguyen, Hallie O'brien, Diana Settlemeyer, Manette Stamm, and Nathan Stueve. Thank you all.*

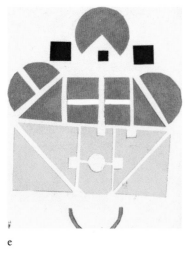

e

f

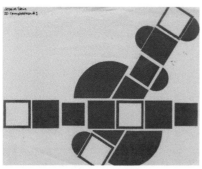

g

h

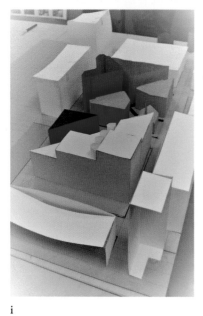

i

j

Exercise 22 Urban campus

Intent

At the three-quarter point of the composition course, students are assigned more complex composition exercises that require them to apply the elements and principles they have practiced in earlier exercises. This exercise consists of a two-block downtown urban campus program. Nearby and adjacent context was provided, and students are asked to construct a composition that meets certain program and contextual requirements.

Tasks

- Using the elements and principles in the semi-abstract exercises, compose a design that meets the general program requirements and responds to the contextual features and issues described in the class handout.
- Clearly demonstrate and articulate the elements and principles that were used in your design decisions.
- Identify the design proposals in white poster board within the base model.
- Focus on overall composition principles rather than architectural forms or styles.

Tools

This exercise utilizes hand-crafted paper and cardboard models. Other tools may be employed, depending on the experience and skill level of students.

a

Figure AII.2. (a–b) Urban campus. *This exercise caps a series of urban block compositions that essentially are set in North American grid contexts. Students are asked to respond to a basic space program (use and floor area), and surrounding context (buildings and other features that are specified).*

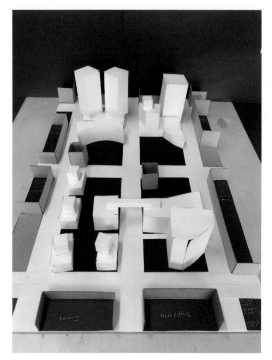

b

Exercise 23 St Paul's Precinct, London

Intent

St Paul's Precinct was selected for a number of reasons: heritage/historic site and structures; non-orthographic context; non-North American context. The site conditions reflect London in 1949, following the Second World War bombardment damage to and around the cathedral site. Project areas were selected from those bombardment areas and students were asked not to reference the construction infill since the war. Students were asked to apply the elements and principles of design composition to selected sites with two major objectives: 1) maximize the economic value of the sites in relation to surrounding areas, regarding massing and heights; and 2) respond to and enhance St Paul's Cathedral and church grounds.

Tasks

- I provided the base map of cardboard and historic base map to reduce the time that students were involved in project preparation.
- Students were asked to prepare several design composition studies for critique over a two-week period, essentially engaging in a sketch problem.
- Students prepared design composition proposals in white poster board for insertion into the base model.

Tools

- chipboard, cardboard and poster board
- scissors, cutting knives
- paper glue,

Keep it simple!

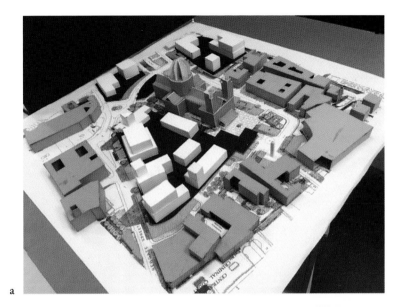

a

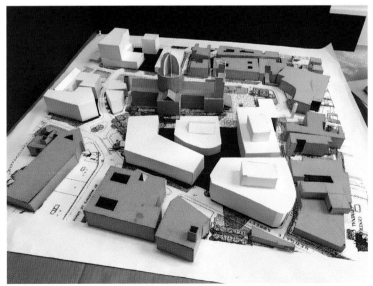

b

Figure AII.3 (a–b). St Paul's Precinct. *The final exercise of the quarter challenged the students with a non-orthographic context, historic precincts and buildings, and a different cultural context. These are two of the class models prepared as a part of their last urban design composition course.*

APPENDIX II

Bibliography

Goldstein, Nathan, 1989: *Design and Composition*: Prentice-Hall, Inc. Englewood, NJ.

Kasprisin, Ron, 2016: *Play in Creative Problem-solving for Planners and Architects*: Routledge, New York.

Webb, Frank, 1990: *Webb on Watercolor*: North Light Books, Cincinnati, OH.

APPENDIX III

WORKING WITH PEOPLE

The politics of urban design

Introduction

I include this section to highlight a vital part of the urban design process—working with people and genuinely interacting with the CST matrix and community forces. We are designing for people, not simply producing techno-smart cities that are efficient and well monitored for operational functions. Working with people is an art that requires preparation, openness, genuine interaction and personality. Too often the design and planning professions put up barriers to healthy interaction with communities because it can be stressful—the process puts the professional on the spot and takes the planning/design process out of the office/studio and onto the streets. It can be messy, but it is critical to the success of creative urbanism.

As design professionals, our core mission is to plan and design with and for people, the community. But at times we forget that mission as we become immersed in policy, quantitative analysis, computer simulations, and, of course, form-making. Most of us recognize people as key ingredients (beyond marketing objects) in what we do, yet many of us continually find ways and means to minimize our engagement with the good folk of cities, towns and villages when designing for "quality of life", applying "context-sensitive" design verbiage, designing "people-friendly" places and environments, and, of course, planning and designing for sustainability. All slang phrases, professional jargon—and we have all engaged in this type of discourse somewhere within our experience. So, note the sarcasm and let us try to engage in meaningful community interactions. Recognize the fear and move on. Most professionals are somewhat traumatized by the very thought of working with people, experiencing fear or reticence at the very thought of "presenting" or "facilitating" at public meetings. We spend more time laying down paper trails and going through the motions with hand-holding/feel-good exercises and techniques than really engaging with community. Harsh? No! After 50 years of working in the urban design field, I can attest to its accuracy. And yes, people can be a real pain . . .

Nevertheless, working with people is an inherent and necessary action for all aspects of community planning and urban design. Best intentions are often short-circuited because of fears, tight budgets, shortened timeframes, arrogance, ignorance or politics. Design is a function of culture, and culture represents the patterns and forces of human behavior over time that are integral to the workings of a city, town or village. They change and are dynamic. More often than not, public input is lacking or poorly engaged and the degree of compromise to design resolutions increases dramatically. Therein lies a critical issue for design: reducing or eliminating compromise.

Principles for working with people and reducing compromise

- Begin with aspirations not predetermined outcomes (requires planning without goal-driven process).
- Use a creative problem-solving process (open, uncertain, embraces ambiguity, divergent).

- Structure for consistent, coherent, interactive and evolving public participation.
- This is the community's process, not the consultant's, so make sure they own it!
- Referee with compromise-awareness techniques.
- Use broad scale to detail scale ladder.
- Process is uncertain and the dynamics of the process evolve to resolution (not necessarily linear).
- Establish polarities within the participant groups to define the initial scope of the dialogue, expanding boundaries as dialogue increases in complexity.
- There are no "bad ideas"; the process filters out unworkable ideas and proposals.
- Engage people with accessible visual information as part of community dialogue; avoid PowerPoint and other "presentation" media formats where participants are "lectured to", not included.
- Visual aids should be referenced, oriented and context-related for easier assimilation by participants.
- Do not over-rely on digital graphics as they can be perceived as "formal", "complete", cartoonish, or detached from context.
- Interdisciplinary collaboration.
- Extend time durations where possible.
- If you are a facilitator, be one; do not try to be the "star".

Let's discuss some examples and experiences relating to these principles.

A personal awakening: the urban renewal experience

As a young architect–urban planner fresh from graduate school in the late 1960s, the architecture–engineering–planning firm where I was employed sent me to a small town approximately 20 miles from Boston as the project urban designer for a downtown urban redevelopment project, funded through urban renewal. And, in the 1960s and 1970s, urban renewal had money, autonomous boards and police power (eminent domain)—powerful ingredients.

An important note: I pursued an advanced degree in urban planning in order to become a more community-oriented architect. I went into that project thinking that *I* was there to improve the community—via the design project. I discovered the hard way that my dedication to architecture, my fascination with design, and my dedication to planning were problems waiting to surface in relation to the community's interests.

I lived with a family politically connected to both the local redevelopment board and state legislature. I reveled in the layers of politics within the community: Democratic against Republican, Democrat against Democrat, ethnic rivalries (French, Italian, Irish, Greek, and others)—a real and rich "salmagundi". And all uniting for national politics. At the local watering hole, the mayor's table was always reserved and set for "pols" and other guests, including consultants such as our design team. For young designers, the atmosphere was heady and politically charged—exciting to say the least. I was convinced that the community's downtown plan was in good hands—ours.

The bottom line here is that our dedication to the community was more of an infatuation with the project, but we could not see that at the time.

Of particular concern to me years later was the realization that I and my colleagues walked the streets doing "building condition assessments", among other surveys, and made decisions based on future design potential for design's sake (and economics), rather than on the value of the existing context and community values. The predetermined rush to design too early in the process eventually created a confrontation between key elements of the community and the larger redevelopment process. Playing with space as an economic engine was playing with power.

And, of course, when the design proposal, complete with elaborate drawings, a 10ft × 4ft (3m x 1.5m) model, etc. was approved by the redevelopment board, the team took the final design to the public for approval, thinking that we had really helped this community grow. But the sweat ran down my back as I listened to the concerns and consternations of a community about to be significantly disrupted. It took me a while to understand why we had failed; why the design was not accepted. The base answer was that the design really was not about community but more about our rapture with the design process. The community eventually won, with a significant reduction in the scope of the design and a major retention of existing physical context. Lessons learned.

A side-story tells a lot about the underlying politics of design from a different boardroom perspective—the bank. Soon after the design team's grand scheme was unveiled to the public, including a proposal to remove the existing 1800s bank building and replace it with a new office building, I joined the local politicians at the mayor's table for lunch to be followed by a presentation to the bank's board in the boardroom. Of course, drinks were ordered and everyone had a great discussion about the new plan. What I did not know was that everyone else was drinking water (not martinis), while I was being totally set up.

I arrived at the boardroom a bit foggy, proceeded to make the presentation with a tongue that felt about 4 inches wide, and made a complete fool out of myself, and the board was in on the "joke". So, they had set the new kid on the block up for a major lesson—engage with the larger community more, not less. The occupants of high-backed chairs laughed and clapped at my dilemma and the politics of design spoke: the plans were changed after more input and the bank building remained (as a part of a full street façade of culturally significant buildings).

The project was eventually modified for the better with a major realignment of the street pattern, improved parking, retention of the historic context, and removal of the new super-block scheme we young designers had thought would improve the community. There were compromises met, concessions, and lessons learned because of late changes in an established and "hard" plan. There were design opportunities and principles lost in the early stages of the process because we assumed ownership of that process.

There are many similar stories of well-intentioned design processes that through ignorance or arrogance missed an opportunity due to a lack of interactive public engagement—essentially addressing the CST matrix with best practices. Experienced designers understand that engaging the public can be fraught with tension and conflict, from the attendees with special interests and agendas, to the dedicated activist or advocate who is unable to see the larger perspective, to the attendee seeking "stage-time" in order to run for elected office, and so on. Then there are the real users, concerned citizens, people with a genuine interest in the future of their community. You need to work with all of them, understand the creative differences among them, and provide ideas, experience, an "ear", and assist them in being authors of their own futures.

Working with people becomes a multi-task complex process:

- co-informing and co-educating
- co-authors and co-owners of the process
- co-participants in the path of creative uncertainty, discovering the emergent design, not imposing it
- co-evaluators of built form: the designer from outside and the public participant from within.

Key principles and approaches

Before proceeding with case studies on interactive approaches to working with people, I want to connect applied public participation practice to a theory base: *creative systems*, discussed in more detail in Chapter 2.

Theory and practice exist as a polarity; each requires the other to function and evolve. They are not separate endeavors. Theoretical considerations often originate from reflections on unusual relational patterns observed and experienced in the field. They are considered or assessed with regard to the wider philosophical, cultural, and scientific perspectives of the larger community and its time-frame. Emergent theory must be tested and experimented with in the field or it has little value. This does not always produce clear results but it is still valuable in the testing process, regardless of success or "failure". There are few short-cuts, no magic techniques or applications; conditions are continually changing, necessitating changes or hybrids in established approaches and typologies. And so it is when working with people. People are the basis for "smart cities", not technology.

There are public involvement practices that continue to work, and these are the basis for most inter-actions between designers and the community. The designer has a responsibility to continually tinker and experiment with new hybrids.

- Principle 1: Begin a design process with an uncertain outcome (versus a goal-driven process) as "visions" and goals can be based on clichés, fantasy, conventions and packaged plans.
- Principle 2: With an uncertain outcome approach, the process must be dynamic as a creative problem-solving process that may lead to the discovery of novel ideas and innovations.

Connections of theory to practice

In practice, I came across three key sources of applied creative systems/problem-solving that are useful in design and public involvement processes. The first is from psychiatry, dealing with human relationships involving both individuals and group settings (Johnston, 1984/1986 and 1991). The second is found in school design programming processes (Verger, 1994) that employ an evolving visual matrix for problem-solving. And the third is an excellent exploration of creative problem-solving applicable to design, planning and public involvement issues (Cropley and Cropley, 2009). I used the Cropleys' *Fostering Creativity* exten-sively in *Play in Creative Problem-solving for Planners and Architects* (Kasprisin, 2016).

Johnston explores and experiments with ways to engage the interactions in human relationships, dealing in part with the recognition of creative differences among people (couples, groups, neighborhoods, staffs, etc.) and how those differences affect various levels of relationship and the larger problem-solving process. His Institute for Creative Development (Seattle) explores ways to identify the polarities separating differences in individuals and within groups, and develops means and methods to "bridge" those differences without compromise, expanding in turn the dialogue container(s)—the evolving scope of discussion. This work may be transferred directly from small-group human relations to community interactions regarding design and planning.

Verger explains the means to systemically manage and expand dialogue on complex design issues, including uses, budgets, management etc., seeking resolution in progressive group discussions. He uses a scale-descendent visual matrix process that progresses toward a thirdspace reality—a third and distinct outcome—avoiding compromise as much as possible. This process is also an excellent example of beginning with an uncertain outcome and allowing the dynamics of the process to enable potential creative outcomes to occur.

I have experimented with Verger's techniques in practice as a means to shift initial participant foci or agendas to another level of discussion, without asking for compromise. This also brings in principles discussed in *Thirdspace* (Soja, 1996) where the dialogue is intended to seek a level different from the beginning positions, retaining key principles of participants and arriving at new and innovative outcomes. These principles are key components in understanding culture's role in the design of space. They can be based on clichés and rigid or fixed packaged public involvement methods, or they can be open, creative and most definitely *uncertain in outcome*. This is where the work of the Cropleys contributes significantly to the larger public interaction process through their exploration of creative problem-solving that is non-linear, evolving, initially ambiguous, open and uncertain, where the process itself is the dynamic that can lead to discovery, novelty and innovation.

Key principles for interactive public involvement processes: working with people

Working with people is an interactive process; there is no such thing as an interactive product without an interactive process

Many public involvement processes use techniques labelled "interactive" when in fact they consist of filler/ public relations jargon. *Interact* means to act on and between or among one another. The design and facilitation of public involvement activities has an interactive core that structures the discussion of information and ideas. The urban designer is a co-participant and guide working with citizens and stakeholders. This is not an easy or perfect process so be prepared to hybridize the process as it engages real situations. Various ways and means of interactive formats are discussed in the case studies.

Each participant brings ideas deserving of a place in the dialogue no matter how initially "outrageous"

At the outset of every meeting, workshop, intensive or gathering of people, ideas are brought to the table for discussion that can be contradictory, infuriating, off-base, out of context, and so on. They are considered options for inclusion in the dialogue. There are ways for the process and nature of the dialogue to render many initial ideas as dead-ends, with no future value, based on the process. Let the process accomplish this task, not contentious "debate".

The interactive process is guided by a principle of uncertainty: a journey without goals

The result of every gathering is achieved through the dynamics of the process; it is not a prescribed or predetermined outcome that is "discussed" or vetted through debate. This requires more, not less, preparation by the designers—and, yes, there is a time in the process when concrete ideas or products are discussed, and these are the result of the process. This principle will have detractors regarding the "journey without goals", particularly planners who are accustomed to taking input from stakeholders then returning with alternatives—and goal-driven. A goal is defined as an end one strives to attain. There are places for goals, as in games and structured events with strong rules of conduct. However, I argue that goals as ends to attain have no place in the phase of the design when public authorship is desired. As scale levels become mature and more specific, as in budget and timing, space programming etc., goals can emerge as benchmarks. I use words like "aspirations", "notions", and "emergent patterns" in place of "goals" to remove as much of the stigma of "predetermined outcome" as possible.

There are writers who engage the writing process by crafting sentence to paragraph, discovering characters and situations along the way through crafting, allowing the story to emerge (with aspirations and notions, of course), but without a formula or goal. And there are writers who work from a set structure or formula, filling in characters and plot sequences essentially knowing the outcome in advance. When I paint a watercolor I have a choice: try to wrestle the painting into an exact preconceived image that I began with, exactly like the study; or let it go, begin with that study idea as an affirmation and follow the dynamics of the actual painting process, working with fluidity, wetness, atmosphere, flow, drying, and serendipity as the painting emerges. Sounds like design to me.

As there is no goal, the aspiration is to maintain the integrity of the creative energy of
the process in order for the process to generate creative results

Being uncertain as to outcome from the outset places more responsibility on the energy and integrity of the overall process. This requires preparation. Having a structure of interactive activities for a workshop also means that change and alteration are critical if the workshop progress changes, as many do. Designing exercises that elicit ideas and interactive dialogue among people is very different from keeping people busy for two hours with feel-good, time-consuming games that are not interactive but simply entertainment.

An interactive process is culturally specific

Community is not an abstract concept. The patterns of human behavior as expressed in cultural patterns, traditions, and actions are space- and time-based as well. Every public involvement format and process addresses cultures and their differences as a basic requirement. A number of years ago, working with the architectural firm of Tonkin Hoyne in Seattle on HUD VI (Housing and Urban Development Agency) projects, at any given meeting there may have been a half-dozen to a dozen different ethnic groups requiring multiple translators and approaches. Many people were reticent to speak openly because of their history with "government" in their native lands. Asking simple questions such as "How do you and your family use a front yard?" became in-depth indicators of cultural differences with myriad responses, requiring the design team to reassess the concept of "front yard".

The process is scale-descendent

So much information and so many ideas are possible that the structure of the dialogue requires a series of "containers" that are scale-relevant and scale-descendent (from the big picture to the specific detail) in order to work through the complexities of a given issue. All the components (economics, transportation, downtown design) are all interrelated and within each is at least one set of polarities. In 1993, I was asked to design and facilitate a "Vision Process" as a prelude to a comprehensive plan for the City of Bellingham, WA. The process was formatted as a sequence of five all-day conferences with a committed group of diverse citizens for consistency (250-plus), three weeks apart. The key point is that the process was scale-descendent in space and topic. The first conference began with historians, geologists, and others who provided the local audience with the "big picture"—from the formation of Bellingham's land form and salmonid streams to small fishing and logging towns around Bellingham Bay to the formation of the larger city itself. This big picture then led to a second session that described and discussed what urban design is and what it means to the community. Session three covered district-level scales regarding issues and potentials. Sessions four and five then focused on consensus resolution of issues and problems, working from city scale to district to specific areas (waterfront, downtown, historic areas, etc.).

The process is spatially oriented, occurring in the context of specific places with representational media that describe and assess layers of spatiality

Herein lies the value and importance of visual communication throughout the process, to distill information and its meaning, to portray context in ways that the layperson can understand and perceive, and to assist the community in envisioning and generating ideas—undergoing architectural tests and assessments of ideas in understandable, visual ways. As Professor James Pettinari and I explained in *Visual Thinking for Architects and Designers* (Kasprisin and Pettinari, 1995), understanding any dialogue in the context within which it occurs is crucial to the process. How that context is understood, presented, and placed into the dialogue is critical to enabling a quality discussion of issues and ideas. This process is also scale-descendent, as Pettinari's "scale ladder" diagrams indicate, descending from a planetary view down to room scale, with each level containing pertinent information and filtering out non-relevant information—a decision-making process in itself.

Rudolph Arnheim's (1969) description of the comprehension of reality revolves around sensory experience and the media of its representation. This is critical to all community dialogue processes especially those that deal with spatial issues. Visual media are more perceptual and verbal media more intellectual—both are ways of processing information and both are critical to the process. The visual media form the foundation for increasing public awareness by placing ideas and concepts in spatial contexts. The use of non-objective art, graphic ornamentation, detailed augmentation, or excessive narrative accounts, and an over-reliance on (antiseptic and cartoonish) digital graphics can risk losing the relevance of what people see and understand. Spatially referenced plans, diagrams, axonometric drawings, and site sections are among the most effective visual formats for public involvement processes—especially when crafted and digital methods are both utilized in the process.

The process is time-dependent

Sounds obvious! Yet the time period allocated for public involvement is critical to the success or failure of the process for the following reasons.

- Too short a time-frame can make people suspicious of the process as rapid methods lack depth and can lead to long-term problems. An example is the classic show-and-tell PowerPoint presentation over three sessions. This is totally inadequate.
- A short time-frame does not provide the time required to work through public issues beyond the initial agendas and conflicts.
- Too long a time-frame can lead to a loss of participant attention and consistency. People often attend workshops and intensives after work or during a busy day with families, so they are tired and less focused. Stretching out the process can lead to a loss of consistency and disrupt the learning curve that is necessary when laypeople encounter design issues and strategies.
- If consistency is lost, the information learning curve is broken, requiring a constant reiteration of basic information that can stall or delay the process unnecessarily.

History is relevant but cannot drive the process; the present is highly focused but often charged with emotion and reactions to current events; the future is uncertain. The designer's challenge includes identifying historic aspects that are still connected to the present and/or have transferable lessons. In some cases, remnants from the past can be used as bridging devices between historic patterns and current issues on forge new design strategies, or at least an increased understanding of the effects of past actions on present form.

In the New Westminster, BC, case study, I discuss the challenge of the New Westminster Downtown Development Association's request for a one-day charrette/intensive. One day it was, but with months of preparation. In "Visions for Bellingham", a five-conference time-frame (all-day Saturdays interspersed with three-week preparation/reflection breaks) proved successful. In American Institute of Architects (AIA) Rural/Urban Design Assistant Teams (R/UDAT) design charrettes, a five-day onsite intensive is required to complete an in-depth process with a definable product at the closure of the charrette. This is followed up one year later by team leaders to review progress and make adjustments to strategy if necessary.

The process is both quantitative and qualitative, and convergent and divergent

Working with people is an art; in addition to generating ideas, it requires specific and accurate background information and evaluation. "Winging it" may have short-term emergency success based on the designer's charm level, but it will ultimately fail, as will drowning the public with data, charts, and "knowledge". The designer needs to understand the roles of convergent and divergent thinking during this process: convergent thinking involves the processing (bringing together) of information and ideas for testing and evaluation; divergent thinking involves the generation of ideas, usually away from the stable "center" of the process. I discuss this extensively in *Play in Creative Problem-solving for Planners and Architects* (Kasprisin, 2016).

Conflicts and differences are inherent to the process

Given the complexity of society, there is no assumed consensus at any gathering that focuses on future probabilities. The door needs to be left open. Significant differences occur between seemingly strong allies. Serious conflicts often emerge as the scale of issues increase in complexity. In "Visions for Bellingham", among the 250 people who attended the five conferences, developers and property owners often clashed with environmentalists and "slow-growth" proponents. "We have plenty of land so let's spread development out" and "Stop filling the wetlands and cutting forest recharge areas" were common comments. Being prepared for conflict is critical, can lower the fear factor for planners and can be assisted by:

- Smaller discussion groups followed by information sharing with the larger group.
- Scale-descendent structure of issue discussion.
- *Thirdspace* techniques (see the "Community of Learners" case study, below).
- Treating all initial ideas as viable options.
- Structuring the discussion with compromise referees to intercept and deflect compromise patterns in the dialogue (see Johnston, 1991, for a discussion on compromise patterns and resolutions).
- Letting the process absorb much of the conflict. This does not always work but with sufficient time can lessen or mute key conflicts without confrontation; confrontation can only increase conflict, inviting compromise in order to lessen anger or placate participants; and compromise sets the foundation for future conflicts rather than resolving them.

Each scale level has a cluster of polarities that define the limits of that level's initial dialogue

Conflicts and polarities do not have to be earth-shaking or between implacable enemies to disrupt the process. There are limits and differences in every discussion, no matter how civil or friendly, and can actually be the source of idea generation. They also define the "container" for initial discussion. I like to use the color wheel as an example of the "polarity cluster" idea. A color wheel is generally composed of 12 colors, including the primaries red, yellow and blue, which break down further in to secondary combinations (red-orange, orange, yellow-orange, for example). Within the color wheel are opposites that are used together in complementary forms, or, as in some sports uniforms, to create attention through vibration (high key conflict). The opposite of any primary is the sum of the two remaining primaries, and conversely the opposite of a secondary color (orange for example) is the remaining primary (blue). Like the color wheel, the polarities define the extent of the basic color spectrum; they define the initial container.

When looking at the color wheel, there is much complexity represented by the circle and the potential mixtures that are possible. There are multiple "opposites" or polarities evident, including lesser opposites for the red-orange to the green-blue. And if we start compromising and mixing everything together (starting with all three primaries), we get gray.

In design and planning, these "color opposites" are readily apparent in most meetings where conflicts over budgets, priorities, facilities, approaches, etc. differ significantly and in subtle ways as well as among supposedly cohesive groups. There are methods and techniques for uncovering and identifying the many levels of opposites or polarities around a meeting table or in a workshop. An interview process or survey can be utilized to identify the positions and agendas of various individuals in a group—not typing them but seeking different patterns, seeking levels of polarity. During the process, polarities can be encompassed in a new and distinctly different and workable dialogue.

Each scale level strives to generate an emergent reality or pattern that is carried to
and helps define the next scale level container

Attempting a quality dialogue with a room full of people is not advisable and does not lead to significant progress. As in "Visions for Bellingham", the scale can begin with a historic cultural/geological overview perspective in a large group setting. Once that information sharing is accomplished, however, small group interactions are a better option for detailed discussions, clarifications, etc. that can then be shared with the overall assembly. Too many issues discussed in a large group can delay and dilute the process.

The scale-level concept is integral to the uncertainty principle. In small groups, working with compromise referees, a discussion can lead to new ideas and concepts that were not anticipated at the outset. These ideas are emergent realities or patterns that emanate from the dynamics of the process, not the facilitator or individual participants. They form a bridge between one scale and the next, providing the "next step" for expansion of the dialogue container and the topics of discussion.

The larger the moral dimension, the smaller the permitted compromise; and,
conversely, the smaller the moral dimension, the more compromise is acceptable

Significant material is available on the value of compromise (and associated problems). I use Johnston's compromise fallacy descriptions when preparing a referee for a workshop. They consist of the following:

- unity fallacy (searching for one answer through dialogue)
- separatist fallacy (dividing and separating issues into separate dialogues and formats)
- 50/50 fallacy (asking each polarity to give up 50 percent in order to resolve an issue).

The process seeks thirdspace as a separate and distinct outcome that embraces the creative differences of participants without compromising those differences; it also encompasses key principles of creative differences

In the "Community of Learners" case study that follows, as well as others that utilize the emergent reality matrix, the process is designed as follows.

- Elicit dialogue from all participants without negative feedback (small groups).
- Stimulate discussions with a background referee to maintain the positive energy and direction of dialogue, identifying compromise tendencies as they arise.
- Document key components distilled from group discussions visually, on large note cards. Begin forming a matrix on a wall for all groups to see and refer to—the emerging matrix.
- Continue to create scale-descendent discussions that result in additions to the matrix, being aware of any new emergent patterns.
- Shift the focus of individuals from personal issues and discussions to the emerging patterns on the wall matrix.
- While not always successful, this process can result in ideas and resolutions that depart from personal agendas and positions to a new emergent outcome.
- Identify and articulate new sets of relationships rather than components emerging from the gestalt matrix.

Simply put, these interactive involvement processes require both an intellectual thought process and a cognitive perceptive approach using the senses. In most cases, graphic illustrations such as diagrams, perspective drawings, axonometric drawings, three-dimensional models (and gaming models), etc. are valuable in spatial orientation and referencing ideas and issues for participants. Great care must be taken in this "representation of place", which should be targeted for the participants and the context (and not merely public relations). Movement exercises, music, play-acting and storytelling can all be effective in given situations to engage participants as long as they do not drift into entertainment without interaction. Video games, computer games, etc. are less effective as they are less interactive for small to medium-size group discussions.

Every outcome is an emergent reality or pattern, immediately altered and changing as it is identified

Each level of dialogue, including an event's conclusion or resolution(s), constitutes an emergent reality or pattern that is space- and scale-specific in a real context (with multiple dimensions). Assume this outcome will change again and is not static. The emergent pattern provides a new base for further (design) actions and dialogues. Designers "make things" and are required to translate/interpret through design these emergent steps. As Johnston points out in *Necessary Wisdom* (1991), the second half of the creative process consists of observing what we design as it is placed in context, reflecting and learning as the process begins anew.

This process is not formless and requires constant design involvement in the transitions from level to level.

CASE STUDIES: NEW WESTMINSTER, BC, AND "A COMMUNITY OF LEARNERS", REDMOND, WA

Two case studies that include design charrettes or intensives help conclude this section with descriptions of (imperfect) interactive processes that improved the final design recommendations.

New Westminster, BC: downtown design guidelines and neighborhood design guidelines charrettes for four neighborhoods

Client aspirations

Nettie Tam, Director of the New Westminster Business Improvement Association (BIA) (New Westminster, 1996), requested a one-day design charrette process for the downtown to develop design guideline strategies. New Westminster is a dense urban area on the Frasier River, east of Vancouver, BC.

I was contacted by John Talbot & Associates of Burnaby, BC, to join the design/planning team for the charrette process. John is a community development specialist experienced in community facilitation. My first reaction to John's request was "sorry . . . there is no such thing as a one-day charrette". However, the client persisted and the team prepared a strategy for the charrette process, which proved successful in numerous ways, including:

- key interactive participation by 40 local stakeholders (consistency and diversity) for downtown
- set of consensus design guidelines produced at the charrette that were adapted and implemented by the city
- transference of the same process to four other neighborhoods in the city, all with the same successful production (one day) and adoption of the design guidelines.

Of course, this process took more than one day: here's how.

Stakeholders

The director secured participation from 40 key stakeholders representing downtown property owners, merchants, residents, elected officials, city staff, and others. To ensure effective interaction between the city and the BIA, co-chairs were nominated from each organization to provide leadership for the process and the Downtown Action Team stakeholders.

- *Principle*: consistency in participant attendance throughout the process.
- *Principle*: diversity in stakeholder composition.
- *Principle*: commitment by and coordination of key agencies and organizations.

Issue sessions

City planning staff organized and conducted six stakeholder issue sessions or visioning committees prior to the charrette to obtain and document ideas, concerns, potentials, and constraints from stakeholders and the general public at evening meetings organized by the Talbot group. These sessions occurred between February and March 1995 to lay the foundations for the focus area or areas of concern from all affected groups, public and private. Each committee consisted of between 10 and 20 business, community and municipal members. A public meeting was held in June 1995 to review the first draft of the "Downtown Action Plan" and a revised draft was distributed in September 1995. The design charrette then occurred in November 1995.

This "one-day charrette" was loaded with information.

Areas of focus included: downtown vision, social vision, transportation, downtown and waterfront development, arts/culture/heritage, and economic development.

Time-frames

A short time-frame, three months, aided in maintaining interest, freshness, and participant consistency in developing issues and vision documents. Including public review and comment periods, the final issues documents took ten months from beginning to the design charrette event.

A one-year action plan resulted from the process, encouraging a strategy for near-term success in order to promote a longer-term implementation strategy.

Design charrette planning

Planning for the one-day charrette included a number of key tasks, as follows.

Assess background materials: background visual information was collected from numerous sources including three-dimensional models of the downtown, photographs, field surveys and site visits, drawings, maps, and other graphic materials supplied by the BIA and the city.

Prepare charrette base drawings: I enlisted four graduate students from the University of Washington to assist in the preparation of materials for use during the charrette. The students prepared areal oblique and eye-level perspective sketches, plan diagrams, and base maps of existing conditions for areas of concern or interest identified in the vision sessions. This step proved extremely valuable in that the design team members were immediately able to access these base drawings and begin their design translation work.

Assemble design team: the BIA and city identified a number of area architects, all of whom designed projects for the New Westminster area, providing a level of commitment and familiarity with the area. They were recruited to donate their skills and experience for the design event.[1]

Design team training session: I accepted a challenge from John Talbot and the BIA/city to design and facilitate a training session for the architects, knowing that, as one architect appearing to lecture to others, there may be resistance to the idea of "training" among such a talented and experienced group. Following some good-natured jabs and shared humor at one another, the training session was well accepted. "Sensitizing" is probably a better term than "training", and, the session included the following.

* Role and task of the designers: translation and interpretation of what the stakeholders were offering as well as the issues and visions put forth by the six vision committees.

- Awareness of the role of the listener: as architects, we all love to design and draw expressively, sometimes with so much energy and enthusiasm that we allow our own ideas to dominate the conversation; after all, we are designers. A quality discussion occurred with the design team as to the real authors of the process: the stakeholders and the communities they represented in New Westminster. The designers brought the following to the process:
  - experience in local context
  - experience in building typologies suitable for the local context
  - abilities to interpret and express ideas and notions from the stakeholders into concrete design solutions
  - a reasonable response with creative energy to the ideas and notions expressed
  - graphic visualization experience and skills.

There was one last task for me during the session. Many of the architects were distanced from the crafting methods necessary for an effective charrette session due to their experiences with production-based digital graphics, so they needed to revisit drawing by hand quickly and effectively. With some encouragement, initial fears and reticence were confronted and all did a masterful job in visual communication.

Charrette process

The charrette began at 9 a.m. and ended at 5 p.m.—on time! The process concluded with a presentation and discussion among the design team, charrette leaders, and stakeholders with consensus reached. City staff produced the final report for distribution and adoption within three weeks of the charrette.

The charrette occurred in an event/conference-type space with room for small-group tables and a separate alcove area for the design team that was separated but still visible and accessible to the larger group area. Graphics and photographs were displayed around the room for orientation and reference and not limited to digital projections.

Sequence of events:

- Introduction and descriptions of day's planned activities.
- Review of vision committee work.
- Small-group discussions with designers present at every small-group table as listeners.
- Group sharing of morning sessions.
- Stakeholders embarked on a field trip and "treasure hunt".
- Stakeholders toured the project area by bus with facilitators from BIA/city/charrette team representatives also on board.
- In the treasure hunt, stakeholders were given cameras and asked to find areas and features that they liked and disliked, as well as selected features identified by the charrette team in order to further enhance their observations and understanding of contextual issues.
- The design team gathered in the alcove or "design studio" during the treasure hunt and began interpreting and exploring ideas from the vision committees and the morning's input from group discussions, recorded by facilitators and student recorders.

- The discussions allowed stakeholders to revisit the published results of the vision committees and add to that resource with new ideas. The design team worked for about 3-plus hours, intensively, before rejoining the stakeholders when they returned from their field trip. (As a side note, the limited time the design team actually had to engage design ideas emphasizes the importance of critical crafting skills to accomplish this phase in such a short period.)

- Designers presented the ideas, interpretations, and translations to stakeholders and listened to a stakeholder critique of the design team's work—all recorded and documented.

- The visualizations presented by far, with base drawings provided by the graduate students, greatly increased the quality of the stakeholder response.

- Designers returned to the studio area and incorporated the comments and suggestions from stakeholders into the next iteration of design translations.

- Stakeholders proceeded to discuss further refinements and were then encouraged to visit and observe (but not interrupt) the design team at work.

- Around 4:30 p.m. the design team pinned up all work, over 35 drawings, on walls for a large-group presentation, discussion and final comments.

Needless to say, the energy level was high and a creative and interactive atmosphere prevailed, with a consensus achieved by the stakeholders. The process was uplifting for all participants, including the designers. Many commented to me that participating in a creative intensive with such close interaction with the community was an extremely rewarding experience.

The success of the "Downtown Action Plan" encouraged the city to conduct four further one-day charrettes, one for each of four near-downtown urban neighborhoods. The same process was used with some adjustments made for topic and stakeholder makeup. Each charrette process concluded with the adoption of design guidelines.

New Westminster summary

- divergent groups
- city staff leadership
- staff (and other professional) and peer facilitation
- local design community participation and sensitivity training
- selection of stakeholder group for diversity
- preliminary issues workshops
- technical database assembly
- technical context visualization preparation
- charrette process
- visual-based product outcomes.

A final note on graphic preparation: designers sketched over the pre-prepared images; the new components were copied then scanned into the areal perspectives, for example, so that the designer did not have to redraw the entire image—an effective tool in charrette time-frames.

Figure AIII.1. Design charrette sketch example. *The sketch illustrates the free and fast hand-crafted drawings constructed during the short design window.*

"A Community of Learners": opportunities for the Redmond Elementary School site, Redmond, WA

Prepared by the University of Washington Center for Architecture and Education, College of Built Environments, April 1996.

Background

In 1995, the Lake Washington School District within the City of Redmond, WA, voted to lease the historic elementary school and site for future civic uses. The University of Washington Center for Architecture and Education proposed a public involvement process to envision new opportunities for the building, the site, and the surrounding area as a "community of learners". A multi-disciplinary team was assembled using faculty and graduate students from the College of Education and the College of Architecture and Urban Planning (now the College of Built Environment) to identify site opportunities, space programming options, and viable design options. The team was led by Professor Ron Kasprisin, Department of Urban Design and Planning.

The project process began in February 1996.

APPENDIX III

Public involvement process

The Redmond Elementary School process was designed in three parts:

1   A community workshop with educators, residents, parents, and city officials to be held on site in an all-day workshop format.
2   A design charrette or intensive held at Gould Hall, University of Washington, three weeks following the community workshop.
3   A follow-up design intensive onsite.
4   A report preparation phase resulting in a brochure product for public distribution.

The design charrette phase of the Redmond project consisted of two one-day events—one at the UW and one onsite. The architects and urban designers translated and interpreted the outcome of the community workshop into the final strategy for "A Community of Learners". Participants at the two events could observe, input resources, and make evaluations.

Of particular value in this case study is the design and facilitation of the community workshop, using a process called "delography"—the focus of this section.

Workshop design

The workshop was designed in a scale-descendent manner:

•   discussion of the area and offsite activities and surrounding context
•   discussion of potential onsite activities
•   discussion of building activities.

Each scale level used the following user types as baseline evaluation criteria, with each type assigned one of three priority levels: (1) high, (2) medium, (3) low.

•   children
•   adults
•   seniors
•   community
•   organization
•   other.

These criteria were identified at the beginning of the community workshop. The workshop outline was as follows:

•   Team site walk.
•   Introduction by facilitator to larger group.
•   Background presentations by city/school board staff.

- Small-group discussions using multiple round-table sessions followed by a summary and idea download by each small group, followed by large-group sharing using emergent reality matrix, then repeated through all scale levels.
- Compromise fallacy guidance provided by facilitator at each table with separate recorder (staff) taking notes.
- Each participant asked to "idea download" after each session by printing in large letters on 5×7in note cards three to five points from each scale-level discussion.

Emergent reality matrix

Following each discussion, the note cards were given to two graduate students who assembled them on a large wall surface in matrix form. Ambiguous at first, the matrix began to expand and develop discernible patterns. Three such matrices were constructed during the day, one for each scale level (offsite, onsite, and building).

As the discussion evolved during the course of the day, the matrices began to emerge on the wall with the following impacts.

- Topics and areas of focus were identified and prioritized (number of cards).
- Patterns of use began to emerge (and move away from personal agendas).
- New patterns were identified and highlighted.

More importantly, as the matrices became more complex and visually more pronounced regarding topics, patterns, and group preferences, the initial individual agendas and positions that had been brought to the table were absorbed into the larger whole. Round-table discussions became more focused on the emergent reality matrix than on previously stated positions. In effect, the wall matrices shifted the attention from person-on-person to the emerging (wall) patterns. The visualization of the matrix became a new focus for the larger discussion.

The matrices were photographed in place, then disassembled for later cataloguing and quantification. This resulted in a list of prioritized activities by user type and priority for each type for each scale. Thus, there was an emergent consensus with minimal compromise that did not require a final vote by the group because the vote was inherent in the discussion process.

Offsite activities:

- transportation
- shuttle
- green belt walkways
- linkage, river trail
- visual connections
- center for community events
- traffic
- general business
- electronic information
- community sharing sources.

Onsite activities:

- outdoor events
- passive recreation
- active sports
- amphitheater
- interpretive trail
- parks/gardens
- flexibility for future.

Building activities:

- performing arts/theater
- sports/informal recreation
- cultural, arts, and crafts
- emergency shelter
- library/media center
- meeting space
- adult/evening classes
- extended school activity/day care
- administration space.

Conclusions and Applications in Practice

Why is this public process, *working with people*, important for the design profession?

- *It provides quality interactive connection with user-client as well as administrative-client.*

Working with people is difficult due to personality characteristics, diversity, differences, agendas etc. Designing and facilitating well-structured yet meta-determinant (uncertain-outcome) processes increases the education of the public and results in both quality engagement and quality outcomes.

- *It reduces unnecessary conflict, misinformation, and misunderstandings, allowing more effort and energy to be devoted to positive design issues and relationships as opposed to piecemeal arguments.*

Many well-intentioned professionals in design and engineering are reticent regarding public participation due to various fears of working directly with people. This can result in the use of methodologies that are entertaining (but with little value), temporarily stimulating (as practiced by many public relations firms), hand-holding, and time-eaters. Not much gets accomplished. Meetings, workshops, and charrettes (if poorly conceived and implemented) can be disrupted by participants who lack key information or feel as if they are being talked down to, ignored or marginalized. A poorly prepared graphic display, lacking in key orientation and reference, can disrupt a meeting and discussion just as poorly structured discussion sessions can drift in and out of compromise "solutions" and arguments, moving further away from the real issues. Interactive workshops with structure, flexibility, and visual aids can reduce unnecessary conflict.

- *It identifies an in-depth space program that directly relates to time/historic and cultural aspects (CST) of the community or urban meaning.*

The results of a well-structured interactive session can reap rewards in the space program that describes the needs, desires, and potentials of the *urban meaning/functionality matrix.* The more quality information on "what and how much" for each level and cell of the matrix, the richer the design outcome. The more designers can respond to the complexity of the urban meaning matrix, while not perfect, the richer the composition of the built environment—creative.

Key components of quality interactive public involvement for designers

- Designing for and with people (and their environments).
- Utilizing cooperative learning processes:
  - positive interdependence
  - face-to-face interactions
  - individual accountability
  - interpersonal and small-group skills
  - sufficient processing time
  - sufficient visualization skills beyond digital graphics.
- Sound preparation and visualization of data and information in lay terms.
- Context-responsive.
- Visualizations of context: sensory perception of reality using visual language.
- Identification of and respect for creative differences.
- Scale- and spatial-descendent levels and containers for dialogue.
- Meta-determinant process—the uncertainty principle:
  - aspirations are necessary beginnings
  - predetermined outcomes are potential disasters leading to compromise.
- Awareness of compromise fallacies:
  - unity fallacy
  - separatist fallacy
  - 50–50 or blending fallacy.
- Design for urban meaning, not simply technology: culture, space, and time/history as well as urban functionality.
- People are the co-authors of and in the built environment.
- "Smart cities" are only as smart as the people who live within them.

Conflict resolution

Finally, let's review some key aspects of conflict resolution in planning and design. Conflict is a natural and recurring ingredient in interactive public involvement. Here are some guides that can assist in managing conflict, deflecting it and even using it as a positive force in dialogue.

Three aspirations:

1   To have aspirations not goals (goals tend to become rigid, set, determined).
2   To maintain the creative energy of the process (enables openness, appreciation of change and diversity).
3   To invoke the meta-determinacy principle (let go of the rigid, be open to what evolves through the process).

Know the type of conflict

- zero sum (pure win or lose)
- mixed-motive or trading (leads to compromises)
- pure cooperative or unification (one answer fits all).

Face conflict rather than avoid it

- avoid denial
- resist circling the wagons (indecision, lack of commitment)
- avoid suppression (openness)
- disallow postponement
- respect yourself, your interests, and the interests of others
- accept cultural and creative differences
- distinguish between interests and positions
- identify common and comparable interests
- identify any need for third parties, such as:
    - facilitators
    - mediators
    - counselors
    - referees
    - recorders
    - visualization skills.

Polarity analysis: define conflicting interests and the limits or boundaries they initially set for the dialogue

- listen
- be alert to natural tendencies for bias, judgements, and compromises
- move dialogue whenever possible (emergent reality matrix) away from compromise
- use different skills for different conflicts
- know yourself and your personal perspectives
- be critical of ideas, not people
- focus on the best decision or direction, not competitive winning
- encourage everyone to participate using oral and/or written methods as options, as not everyone is outgoing and verbally expressive

- restate if not clear and avoid jargon
- facts on both sides are requirements for quality dialogue and issue exploration
- use a referee process to diffuse or deflect emotion-dominated dialogue.

Note

1 New Westminster Downtown Design Charrette Team: Nettie Tam, Executive Director BIA, John Talbot (John Talbot & Associates), Ron Kasprisin (Kasprisin Pettinari Design, Architects and Urban Planners), Ken Falk (Creekside Architects), Doug Massie (Doug Massie Architects), Graham McGarva (Gaker/McGarva/Hart Architects), Eric Pattison (Decosse Pattison Architects), City of New Westminster Planning Department: Mary Pynenburg, Lisa Spitale, Stephen Scheving, Leslie Gilbert, Brian Coates, Lilian Arishenkoff, University of Washington graduate students: Augustine Wong, Michael Kimelberg.

Bibliography

American Institute of Architects, 1992: *R/UDAT: Regional & Urban Design Assistance Teams:* American Institute of Architects, Washington, DC.

Arnheim, Rudolph, 1969: *Visual Thinking:* University of California Press, Berkeley, CA.

Bellingham, City of, 1993: "Visions for Bellingham": City of Bellingham Community Development Department, Bellingham, WA.

Capra, Fritjof, 1982: *The Turning Point:* Simon & Schuster, New York.

Cropley, Arthur and Cropley, David, 2009: *Fostering Creativity:* Hampton Press, Cresskill, NJ.

Johnston, Charles, MD, 1984/1986: *The Creative Imperative:* Celestial Arts, Berkeley, CA.

Johnston, Charles, MD, 1991: *Necessary Wisdom:* Celestial Arts, Berkeley, CA.

Kasprisin, Ron, 2016: *Play in Creative Problem-solving for Planners and Architects:* Routledge, New York.

Kasprisin, Ron and Pettinari, James, 1995: *Visual Thinking for Architects and Designers:* John Wiley & Sons, Inc., New York.

New Westminster, City of, 1996: "New Westminster Downtown Action Plan": City of New Westminster, BC, Canada.

Redmond, City of, 1996: "A Community of Learners": College of Built Environments, University of Washington, Seattle, WA.

Soja, Edward W., 1996: *Thirdspace:* Blackwell Publishers, Cambridge, MA.

Verger, Morris, 1994: *Connective Planning:* McGraw-Hill, New York.

Webster's New World Dictionary Second Concise Edition, 1975: William Collins & World Publishing Co., Inc., New York.

INDEX

INDEX